The Seedtime, the Work, and the Harvest

Southern Dissent

UNIVERSITY PRESS OF FLORIDA

Florida A&M University, Tallahassee
Florida Atlantic University, Boca Raton
Florida Gulf Coast University, Ft. Myers
Florida International University, Miami
Florida State University, Tallahassee
New College of Florida, Sarasota
University of Central Florida, Orlando
University of Florida, Gainesville
University of North Florida, Jacksonville
University of South Florida, Tampa
University of West Florida, Pensacola

THE SEEDTIME, THE WORK, AND THE HARVEST

New Perspectives on
the Black Freedom Struggle in America

EDITED BY JEFFREY L. LITTLEJOHN,
REGINALD K. ELLIS, AND PETER B. LEVY

Foreword by Stanley Harrold and Randall M. Miller

University Press of Florida
Gainesville · Tallahassee · Tampa · Boca Raton
Pensacola · Orlando · Miami · Jacksonville · Ft. Myers · Sarasota

Copyright 2018 by Jeffrey L. Littlejohn, Reginald K. Ellis, and Peter B. Levy
All rights reserved
Published in the United States of America

This book may be available in an electronic edition.

First cloth printing, 2018
First paperback printing, 2019

24 23 22 21 20 19   6 5 4 3 2 1

Library of Congress Cataloging-in-Publication Data
Names: Littlejohn, Jeffrey L., 1973– editor. | Ellis, Reginald K., editor. |
   Levy, Peter B., editor.
Title: The seedtime, the work, and the harvest : new perspectives on the
   black freedom struggle in America / edited by Jeffrey L. Littlejohn,
   Reginald K. Ellis, and Peter B. Levy.
Other titles: Southern dissent.
Description: Gainesville : University Press of Florida, 2018. | Series:
   Southern dissent | Includes index.
Identifiers: LCCN 2017032193 | ISBN 9780813056678 (cloth : alk. paper)
ISBN 9780813064383 (pbk.)
Subjects: LCSH: African Americans—Civil rights—History—20th century. |
   Civil rights movements—United States—History—20th century. | United
   States—Race relations.
Classification: LCC E185.615 .S376 2018 | DDC 323.1196/0730904—dc23
LC record available at https://lccn.loc.gov/2017032193

The University Press of Florida is the scholarly publishing agency for the State University System of Florida, comprising Florida A&M University, Florida Atlantic University, Florida Gulf Coast University, Florida International University, Florida State University, New College of Florida, University of Central Florida, University of Florida, University of North Florida, University of South Florida, and University of West Florida.

University Press of Florida
2046 NE Waldo Road
Suite 2100
Gainesville, FL 32609
http://upress.ufl.edu

Contents

List of Figures vii

Foreword ix

Introduction 1
Jeffrey L. Littlejohn, Reginald K. Ellis, and Peter B. Levy

1. Florida State Normal and Industrial School for Coloreds: Thomas DeSaille Tucker and His Radical Approach to Black Higher Education 10
   Reginald K. Ellis

2. African American Women and Community Medicine: Civil Rights Workers in the Age of "Self-Help" 28
   Teresa Blue Holden

3. Southern Discomfort: The Rise and Fall of Civil Rights Attorney James F. Gay, 1942–2008 53
   Jeffrey L. Littlejohn and Charles H. Ford

4. Revisiting the Urban Revolts of the 1960s: York, Pennsylvania— A Case Study 84
   Peter B. Levy

5. "What We Eat Is Politics": SNCC, Hunger, and Voting Rights in Mississippi 115
   Mary Potorti

6. Riot, Revolution, or Rebellion? Civil Rights and the Politics of Memory 154
   Rosie Jayde Uyola

7. Ferguson, USA: A Scholar's Unforeseen Connection and Collision with History 183
   Stefan M. Bradley

8. Religion and the Black Freedom Struggle for Sandra Bland 197
Phillip Luke Sinitiere

Afterword: Bearing Witness; How the Movement Changed My World 227
Waldo Martin

List of Contributors 231
Index 233

Figures

3.1. Virginia State NAACP Youth Council   57
3.2. Norfolk sit-in   62
3.3. Executive committee of the Virginia State Youth Conference   69
3.4. Central YMCA integration demonstration, 1965   71
3.5. James Gay, president of the Young Democrats   73
3.6. Photo of James Gay from the *Journal and Guide*   77
4.1. York, Pennsylvania, census tracts by race, 1960   90
4.2. York, Pennsylvania, population, 1930 to 2010   91
6.1. Baltimore '68: Riots and Rebirth Mosaic Monument   163
6.2. Individual story tiles created by mosaic participants   166
6.3. Nearly a year after the fortieth anniversary of the Newark riots, Newark mayor Cory Booker unveiled a commemorative plaque   174
8.1. Good Hope AME Church   199
8.2. Protestors from the Unitarian Universalist congregations of Houston   203
8.3. Houston activist and Nation of Islam member Deric Muhammad   204
8.4. Sandra Bland Parkway sign   209
8.5. Ebenezer behind Waller County Jail   213
8.6. The author, Karisha Shaw, Carie Cauley, and the Reverend Hannah Bonner   215
8.7. "She Speaks" event emcee Kayenne Nebula   219
8.8. Sandra Bland arrest site memorial   220

Foreword

The common view of the civil rights movement is that it began after World War II and moved along a progressive arc toward the passage of civil rights legislation and new respect for African Americans and other minorities. The assumption is that the movement ended much discrimination and opened opportunities in education, housing, business, entertainment, and other areas from which minority groups had been excluded. The common narrative acknowledges the stiff and often violent resistance to civil rights activists and the continued racial discrimination in many areas of American life, but its basic thrust is a story of triumph over the nation's past wrongs and injustices.

Such a view of the civil rights movement no longer holds sway among those historians who have read and listened to the accounts of a variety of civil rights activists, researched public and private records, and expanded the scope of inquiry beyond the South. In the process, they have discovered new interests, people, and priorities that the common narrative ignores or leaves in the margins. The new investigations of the civil rights movement reveal a more complicated, contested, and incomplete civil rights story than many textbooks suggest. The new understandings of the civil rights movement also take a longer perspective on the movement, dating it back to the American Revolution and earlier. They also expand investigation into many civil rights efforts that did not initially receive national media attention.

The new studies also cover the struggles over means and ends within reform movements dating from the early republic to today. Since the eighteenth century, campaigns for racial justice have been especially marked by divergent views and forces. There has been tension between moral appeals to conscience and direct political engagement, gradualism and immediatism, and peaceful and violent means. Advocacy of racial integration has contrasted with black nationalism. Such divergence among forces within the movements has continued to fascinate historians and to challenge any neat portrait of supposed reform unity.

One important shift in writing about organized efforts on behalf of racial justice has been toward greater recognition of the central roles African Americans, both men and women, played in defining and directing such efforts. For example, during the antebellum antislavery movement, which also sought equal rights for black people, Frederick Douglass, a former slave, emerged as the leading black advocate of emancipation. Black women, such as Sojourner Truth, also pointed the way to freedom. Some black and white abolitionists advocated peaceful means to end slavery and promote racial justice and integration in the United States. Others countenanced violence. Some black abolitionists emphasized a separate black identity and suggested that black aspirations required racial separation.

The essays collected in *The Seedtime, the Work, and the Harvest: New Perspectives on the Black Freedom Struggle in America* analyze similar tendencies within the twentieth-century civil rights movement. They delve into complicating factors in order to better understand the movement's beginnings, breadth, and objectives. They investigate the movement's leaders' diverging perspectives and emphases. They expand the range of civil rights concerns to include health care and food. They introduce leaders who have received little attention in general histories. They show the varieties of leadership and the importance of local organizing in many places. They enlarge understanding of the breadth of civil rights activism by including northern places, noting that the "race problem" was never a southern one alone and that seeing the issues broadly redefines and reinforces the importance of place. Taken together, they emphasize multifaceted activities, the role of women in the movement, antiblack violence, and black-nationalist ideology and activism. They link current issues with long histories. These are broad concerns. The essays especially note that in the struggles for civil rights, racial justice, and people's power, dissent took many forms, used various methods, and extended deep into a national consciousness. By addressing so many facets, *The Seedtime, the Work, and the Harvest* is a welcome addition to the Southern Dissent series.

Stanley Harrold and Randall M. Miller
Series Editors

Introduction

JEFFREY L. LITTLEJOHN, REGINALD K. ELLIS, AND PETER B. LEVY

> Today is the seed time, now are the hours of work, and tomorrow comes the harvest and the playtime.
>
> W.E.B. DuBois

Moving beyond what some have termed the "master narrative," embodied by the first six episodes of the television documentary *Eyes on the Prize*, the essays in this collection complicate and ultimately enhance our understanding of the modern struggle for racial equality. When the Public Broadcasting System (PBS) released *Eyes on the Prize* in 1987, it was met with virtually universal acclaim. One national magazine called *Eyes* "required watching" and another declared that the film presented "not only a splendid accounting of what happened during the most active years of the movement, but also why it was so important."[1] Building on nearly a generation of studies of the civil rights movement, written by journalists, veteran activists, and historians, as well as the advice of over a dozen scholars, the documentary traced the rise and development of the movement. Opening with coverage of *Brown v. Board of Education* (1954), Emmett Till's murder in 1955, and Rosa Parks's refusal to relinquish her seat on a Montgomery bus, the documentary moved through the 1950s to the triumphant march from Selma to Montgomery, Alabama, a decade later, which culminated with President Johnson's signing of the Voting Rights Act of 1965. As the editors of this book can attest, the film has the ability to capture the attention of students like few others ever made and leaves viewers with a firm sense of the courage and sacrifices of thousands of ordinary men and women, from the freedom riders who braved firebombs and white mobs to schoolchildren who risked their lives in face-offs with snarling German shepherd dogs and baton-wielding state troopers.

Yet as even the producers of *Eyes* recognized, this "master narrative" had its shortcomings. Especially when coupled with "remembrances presented during Black History Month and Martin Luther King, Jr. birthday celebrations," as well as "heritage tours, museums, public rituals, textbooks, and various artifacts of mass culture," these works "distorted and suppressed as much as they . . . revealed about the civil rights movement," to borrow Jacquelyn Dowd Hall's words. Put somewhat differently, the master narrative de-radicalized figures like Martin Luther King Jr. and Rosa Parks, truncated the timeline and geography of the movement, and exaggerated the achievements of the black freedom struggle in order to fit with the dominant progressive storyline of American history. It also tended to overemphasize the role played by men and national organizations while underestimating the significance of women and community-based institutions.[2]

Even before *Eyes* was aired, a handful of scholars had begun to publish case studies that suggested an alternative or revisionist approach to understanding the civil rights movement. Somewhat along the same lines, the producers of *Eyes* developed eight additional episodes that tracked the rise of Black Power in the years following the march across the Edmund Pettus Bridge.[3] At the forefront of this effort to complicate the master narrative stood Patricia Sullivan and Waldo Martin, who, in addition to publishing their own works on what became known as the "long civil rights movement," began in the mid-1990s to codirect a succession of summer institutes on the civil rights movement at Harvard University's W.E.B. DuBois Center in Cambridge, Massachusetts.[4] Indeed, *The Seedtime, the Work, and the Harvest: New Perspectives on the Black Freedom Struggle in America* grew out of one of these institutes, or seminars. For four (hot) weeks the seminar's participants immersed themselves in the literature of the centuries-long fight for racial equality. Along the way, they interacted with numerous scholars, from Leon Litwack, the elder statesman of the revisionist school of race relations in America, to Peniel Joseph, the driving force behind the emerging field of Black Power studies. They were also blessed by visits from a handful of veteran activists, including Esther Cooper and Dorothy Burnham, whose efforts to tear down Jim Crow while members of the Southern Negro Youth Council in the 1930s and 1940s helped plant the seeds for the rise of the modern civil rights movement. Coming from a wide array of institutions, from HBCUs, such as Florida

A&M, to small liberal arts schools like Wheaton College, the participants brought with them a diversity of life experiences and perspectives that immeasurably enriched their discussions. Both during the seminar's official meetings and in bars, restaurants, and dorm rooms (as well as poetry slams) they discussed their own research on subjects ranging from youth in the movement to urban rebellions and shared thoughts on ways to enhance their work as teachers. As they met, the Trayvon Martin case, which involved the shooting of an unarmed black youth by George Zimmerman, a self-appointed neighborhood watchman, came to a conclusion when a jury acquitted Zimmerman of all charges, reminding the seminar's participants (if they needed reminding) of the ongoing nature of the struggle for racial equality and of the urgency of their work as educators. While not all of the seminar's participants have essays in this volume (some because they had previous publication requirements), all contributed to the final product either directly, by reading all or some of the works, by sharing their thoughts during the seminar itself, or through some combination thereof.

Since the release of *Eyes on the Prize* scholars have pushed the boundaries of the movement back in time, expanded the field of subjects well beyond national figures and organizations, incorporated women into their narratives, produced a startling array of community studies, explored the intersection of the black freedom struggle and the Cold War, and forged a reconsideration of the history of the Black Panther Party. Included in this outpouring of research and writing are a number of outstanding anthologies, several of which themselves helped spur innovative approaches to our understanding of the movement.[5] At the same time, the proliferation of college courses and public discussions of the civil rights years suggests that the demand for more works has not abated. In the past couple of years alone, a half dozen works on the civil rights movement have been highlighted in the *New York Times Sunday Book Review*, including Peniel Joseph's biography of Stokely Carmichael and Waldo Martin's examination of the Black Panther Party. The fact that works such as Danielle McGuire's *At the Dark End of the Street: Black Women, Rape, and Resistance* and Michelle Alexander's *The New Jim Crow* have generated so much buzz both inside and outside academia confirms that the appetite for fresh examinations of the black freedom struggle remains high. Needless to say, the ongoing struggles for racial equality from Ferguson and Baltimore to

Charleston and Fruitvale Station demand that we continue to interrogate the past so that we can arrive at a more informed understanding of our own times.

The essays in this collection both confirm some of the findings of this recent outpouring of scholarship and suggest new avenues of investigation. First, several of the essays demonstrate the value of the revisionist impulse to place the modern struggle for civil rights within the context of the longer black struggle for equality and to focus on places and times that often lie outside the master narrative. For instance, Reginald Ellis's study of Thomas DeSaille Tucker, who served as the first president of Florida A&M, one of the oldest and largest historically black colleges in the nation, disrupts one of the most firmly held assumptions about the black freedom struggle, namely that Booker T. Washington dominated the debate over the role that black colleges should play in the South until W.E.B. DuBois challenged him. On the contrary, Ellis shows that Tucker promoted a vision of education in the Deep South that paralleled DuBois's vision—namely one that was equal to that provided to the most talented white students—before DuBois issued his sharp critique of Washington early in the twentieth century. Similarly, by focusing on Norfolk, Virginia, Jeffrey L. Littlejohn and Charles H. Ford contest one of the fundamental premises of the master narrative, namely that the NAACP was a voice of moderation that focused primarily on attaining racial equality by pursuing legal suits and backroom lobbying. On the contrary, James Gay and his brother Milton employed a wide array of strategies, from voter registration drives and marches to sit-ins and boycotts. And they continued to press for equality even after the federal government enacted sweeping civil rights legislation, by opening black businesses, running for political office, and filing suits in the courts that demanded that the city and state comply with the law. Likewise, in his examination of the urban revolt in York, Pennsylvania, Peter Levy reminds readers that urban rebellions took place in hundreds of cities, including small and midsize communities, rather than just large metropolises with majority- or near-majority-black populations, like Detroit and Newark. He also shows that the claim that the racial uprisings of the 1960s differed from those earlier in the century, that they were "commodity" rather than "communal" riots, meaning that they largely involved attacks on property as opposed to interracial violence between blacks and whites, demands reevaluation.

Furthermore, several of the essays in this collection suggest that we are only beginning to adequately answer the question, what did the black freedom movement want? This question did not originate in the mid-1950s and early 1960s. On the contrary, the stirrings of black activism during the early decades of the twentieth century prodded various individuals and organizations with vastly different viewpoints to pose it. For instance, the NAACP issued a pamphlet titled "What Does the Negro Want?" in 1918, during the First World War. Its author, Professor John Hawkins, listed fourteen "articles" or goals—including an end to lynching, better housing, and equal job opportunities—to parallel the fourteen points laid out by President Wilson in his famous "Fourteen Points" declaration. About a dozen years later, the Commission on Interracial Cooperation published a similar declaration with the same title. This version highlighted nine goals, most notably the eradication of legal discrimination based on skin color, equal educational opportunities, better housing, sanitation, and police protection, better job opportunities, and the vote. The demand was for "in short[,] . . . no special privileges, but simply even-handed justice and a fair chance in the struggle for existence."[6] As the southern-based civil rights movement personified by Martin Luther King Jr. and the demand for desegregation and the vote was eclipsed by the Black Power movement, personified by Malcolm X and his successors, Robert Penn Warren, the famed southern author, reiterated this question in a book entitled *Who Speaks for the Negro?* Likewise, in their jointly written work, *Black Power*, Stokely Carmichael and Charles Hamilton sought to clarify the presumably new demands posed by the more radicalized movement. In different ways, these works revealed that more than just a desire to end legal discrimination lay at the core of the civil rights movement—that a quest for political power (not just the vote), economic independence, and cultural pride underlay the movement.[7] To this list of goals, the articles by Teresa Holden and Mary Potorti add the demands for food and health care. Indeed, as both of these pieces suggest, in the absence of these fundamental needs, the rest of the demands appeared somewhat superfluous. Yet at the same time, movement activists learned to weave the fight for food and health care together with the struggles for the vote, economic independence, and self-worth, in part by demonstrating the degree to which the foes of racial equality used their political and economic power to keep blacks hungry and in ill health.

In addition, several of the essays in this volume illustrate the impact of the "cultural turn," on the historical scholarship of the black freedom struggle. At about the same time as Jacqueline Dowd Hall began to call for a revision of the master narrative of the struggle for racial equality, a variety of scholars and social critics began to push for a reorientation of focus of historical scholarship in general.[8] And two of the pieces illustrate the ways that the "cultural turn," which has reenergized the study of history in the recent past, can and does enhance our understanding of the struggle for racial equality. More particularly, Rosie Jayde Uyola's interrogation of the public's uses (and abuses) of the memory of the urban rebellions in Newark and Baltimore in 1967 and 1968 exemplifies the influence of the cultural turn. Written by a scholar comfortable with and adept at interpreting cultural sources, this essay reminds us that to understand the nature and impact of the movement we must move beyond the master narrative that focused on the fight for civil and legal rights and political power, narrowly defined. Indeed, as more than a handful of scholars and veteran activists have contended, the most lasting legacy of the surge of the black freedom struggle of the 1950s and 1960s may have been on culture. Or, as Komozi Woodard has written, "the Black Cultural Revolution was so unprecedented that important historians such as Vincent Harding and Manning Marable have reached for such terms as watershed and zenith to calibrate its sustained impact during the Second Reconstruction in the United States."[9]

Finally, since W.E.B. DuBois's legacy loomed large throughout the 2013 NEH Seminar, we felt it was imperative to include in this volume writings by scholars who, like DuBois, have coupled their research expertise with their commitment to battling racial injustice. In August 2014, Stefan Bradley, a professor at St. Louis University, joined his students to protest the killing of Michael Brown in Ferguson, Missouri, and then in a series of blogs, one of which is reproduced here, to explicate and give voice to his and his students' actions. Similarly, Phil Sinitiere reacted to the death of Sandra Bland by crafting a blog that sought to provide historical perspective on the decades-long local struggle against racial injustice in Waller County, Texas—where he lived and where Bland, a former student returning for work at Prairie View A&M, had been arrested for failing to use her turn signal and later died in police custody. In addition to exemplifying DuBois's legacy as a scholar-activist, these two pieces also demonstrate that the black struggle for freedom is not simply something that took place in the past but, rather, is a vital part of the world in which we live.

Put somewhat differently, by expanding the chronology and geography of the movement, beyond the "old South" from roughly 1955 to 1965, by analyzing individuals who stood outside the oversimplified molds of accommodationist or radical, by moving beyond the call for legal and civil rights to the broader demand for basic human rights, and by considering the impact and intersection of politics and culture, past and present, the essays in this volume both reflect the new directions that the study of the black freedom struggle have taken and expand our understanding of it. Indeed, by reconceptualizing the black freedom struggle and encouraging readers to view the South as more than a narrowly defined, geographic and time-bound region, this collection reflects the claims of revisionist scholars who argue that race was never just a "southern problem." On the contrary, as Matthew D. Lassiter and Joseph Crespino have argued, "the notion of the exceptional South has served as a myth, one that has persistently distorted our understanding of American history," one that allows those who reside outside of the South (defined geographically) to maintain a belief in "white racial innocence" and their faith in "an essentially liberal national project (if only the red states would stop preventing the blue states from resurrecting the Great Society.)"[10] In other words, this book fits into the Southern Dissent series because, not in spite of, its investigation of the "race problem" all across the nation.

Notes

1. "Reviews," *Eyes on the Prize* website, accessed June 30, 2015, https://web.archive.org/web/20150502220302/http://www.pbs.org/wgbh/amex/eyesontheprize/about/press.html.

2. Jacquelyn Dowd Hall, "The Long Civil Rights Movement and the Political Uses of the Past," *Journal of American History* 91 (Mar. 2005): 1233–63. For good reviews of the scholarly literature on the eve of Dowd Hall's review essay, see Steven F. Lawson, "Freedom Then, Freedom Now: The Historiography of the Civil Rights Movement," *American Historical Review* 96 (Apr. 1991): 456; Adam Fairclough, "Historians and the Civil Rights Movement," *Journal of American Studies* 24 (Dec. 1990): 387–98; Charles W. Eagles, "Toward New Histories of the Civil Rights Era," *Journal of Southern History* 66 (Nov. 2000): 815–48; and Kevin Gaines, "The Historiography of the Struggle for Black Equality since 1945," in *A Companion to Post-1945 America*, ed. Jean-Christophe Agnew and Roy Rosenzweig (Malden, MA: Wiley-Blackwell, 2002), 211–34. For critiques of Hall's "long civil rights movement" framework see Eric Arnesen, "Reconsidering the 'Long Civil Rights Movement,'" *Historically Speaking* 10 (Apr. 2009): 31–34; and Sundiata

Keita Cha-Jua and Clarence Lang, "The 'Long Movement' as Vampire: Temporal and Spatial Fallacies in Recent Black Freedom Studies," *Journal of African American History* 92 (Spring 2007): 265.

3. See for example William H. Chafe, *Civilities and Civil Rights: Greensboro, North Carolina, and the Black Struggle for Freedom* (New York: Oxford University Press, 1980); Robert J. Norrell, *Reaping the Whirlwind: The Civil Rights Movement in Tuskegee* (Chapel Hill: University of North Carolina Press, 1998); David Chalmers, *And the Crooked Places Made Straight: The Struggle for Social Change in the 1960s* (Baltimore: Johns Hopkins University Press, 1991); and Shawn Leigh Alexander, *An Army of Lions: The Civil Rights Struggle before the NAACP* (Philadelphia: University of Pennsylvania Press, 2012). The later episodes of *Eyes on the Prize* rectified some of the misgivings about the original series. Yet, at the same time, they tended to replicate the progressive narrative that Dowd Hall critiqued and did not address her call to push the story of the fight for racial equality back in time.

4. Sullivan's work includes *Lift Every Voice: The NAACP and the Making of the Civil Rights Movement* (New York: New Press, 2009), and *Days of Hope: Race and Democracy in the New Deal Era* (Chapel Hill: University of North Carolina Press, 1996); and Sullivan and Armstead L. Robinson, eds., *New Directions in Civil Rights Studies* (Charlottesville: University of Virginia Press, 1991). Martin's work includes Waldo E. Martin and Joshua Bloom, *Black against Empire: The History and Politics of the Black Panther Party* (Berkeley: University of California Press, 2013), *No Coward Soldiers: Black Cultural Politics in Postwar America* (Cambridge, MA: Harvard University Press, 2005), and *Brown v. Board of Education: A Brief History with Documents* (New York: Bedford, 1998). Sullivan and Martin also coedit the University of North Carolina Press's John Hope Franklin Series in African American History and Culture, which in the past fifteen-plus years has published some of the most highly regarded works in African American history and the long civil rights movement, including a number written by veterans of the DuBois Center's Summer Institutes. For example, in the 2013 seminar, participants met Blair Kelly, an institute veteran, and read her excellent study, *Right to Ride: Streetcar Boycotts and African American Citizenship in the Era of Plessy v. Ferguson* (Chapel Hill: University of North Carolina Press, 2010).

5. See particularly Armstead Robinson and Patricia Sullivan, eds., *New Directions in Civil Rights Studies* (Charlottesville: University of Virginia Press, 1991); Emilye Crosby, ed., *Civil Rights From the Ground Up: Local Struggles, a National Movement* (Athens: University of Georgia Press, 2011); and a series of collections edited by Komozi Woodard and Jeanne Theoharis: *Want to Start a Revolution? Radical Women in the Black Freedom Struggle* (New York: New York University Press, 2009); Jeanne Theoharis, Komozi Woodard, and Charles Payne, eds., *Groundwork: Local Black Freedom Movements in America* (New York: New York University Press, 2005); and Jeanne Theoharis and Komozi Woodard, eds., *Freedom North: Black Freedom Struggles outside the South, 1940–1980* (New York: Palgrave, 2003); Peniel E. Joseph, ed., *Neighborhood Rebels: Black Power at the Local Level* (New York: Palgrave, 2009); Laura Warren Hill and Julia Rabig, eds., *The Business of Black Power: Community Development, Capitalism, and Corporate Responsibility in Postwar America* (Rochester, NY: University of Rochester Press, 2012);

Judson L. Jeffries and Charles Jones, eds., *The Black Panther Party [Reconsidered]* (Baltimore: Black Classic Press, 1998); and Brian Ward, ed., *Media, Culture, and the Modern African American Freedom Struggle* (Gainesville: University Press of Florida, 2001).

6. W. N. de Berry, "What the Negro Wants," *American Missionary* 68, no. 12 (1914): 543–47; John R. Hawkins, "What Does the Negro Want: Fourteen Articles Setting Forth What the American Negro Expects after Helping to Win the War for Democracy" (New York: National Association for the Advancement of Colored People, 1918), accessed July 8, 2015, http://herb.ashp.cuny.edu/archive/files/what-does-the-negro-want_b051bb3363.pdf; R. R. Wright Jr., "What Does the Negro Want in Our Democracy?" in *Proceedings of the National Conference of Social Work, June 1–8, 1919* (Chicago: Rogers & Hall, 1920); Commission on Interracial Cooperation, "What Does the Negro Want?" (Atlanta: Commission on Interracial Cooperation, 1906), accessed July 8, 2015, http://digitalexhibits.auctr.edu/files/original/5b59338aa39c43ee052636abb0cf72f2.jpg.

7. Robert Penn Warren, *Who Speaks for the Negro?* (New York: Random House, 1965); Stokely Carmichael and Charles Hamilton, *Black Power: The Politics of Liberation* (New York: Vintage Books, 1967).

8. For a sense of the cultural turn, see James W. Cook, Lawrence B. Glickman, and Michael O'Malley, eds., *The Cultural Turn in U.S. History: Past, Present, and Future* (Chicago: University of Chicago Press, 2008). The volume includes Waldo E. Martin's "'Be Real for Me': Representation, Authenticity, and the Cultural Politics of Black Power" and Roy Rosenzweig, "The State of Cultural History: A Conference in Honor of Lawrence Levine," *Journal of American History* 93, no. 3 (2006): 755–804.

9. Komozi Woodard, "It's Nation Time in NewArk: Amiri Baraka and the Black Power Experiment in Newark, New Jersey," in *Freedom North*, 288.

10. Matthew D. Lassiter and Joseph Crespino, eds., *The Myth of Southern Exceptionalism* (New York: Oxford University Press, 2010), 7.

1

Florida State Normal and Industrial School for Coloreds

Thomas DeSaille Tucker and His Radical Approach to Black Higher Education

REGINALD K. ELLIS

On the eve of postwar Reconstruction in the South, prominent African Americans longed for an institution that would lead to the advancement of the entire race. Focusing their attention on politics, and understanding the need for an intelligent voting mass, these leaders emphasized the crucial role that education would play in transforming black life throughout the country. Importantly, in the late nineteenth century, the debate over the proper education for African Americans emerged as a central issue in the black experience. Historian and sociologist W.E.B. DuBois led the charge, declaring that African Americans were capable of being trained in the liberal arts, which would ultimately achieve Bishop Henry L. Morehouse's goal of creating a "talented tenth" within the black community. Once properly trained, this group of educated leaders could instruct the masses of African Americans in democratic, protestant values. On the other hand, using Samuel C. Armstrong's model of vocational education for African Americans, Booker T. Washington argued for the acceptance of agricultural and industrial education for the masses of the black population that was only a few decades removed from slavery. Importantly, many white philanthropists of the late nineteenth and early twentieth century sided with Washington's approach of industrial education for African Americans and therefore supported educational institutions that used this approach.[1]

With Washington and the Tuskegee Institute hailed as the models for black education in the South, white political leaders began to support the idea of establishing institutions of higher education that would create a "better Negro." This new "industrialized negro"—trained to be punctual, diligent, and obedient—would be better able to serve the white business community at the dawn of the second industrial revolution. Despite the popularity of the Tuskegee model with whites, however, many African American leaders had their own ideas about the proper education of their people, which included forms of liberal arts as well as industrial education. Moreover, as historian Amilcar Shabazz demonstrates in his work *Advancing Democracy*, black leaders who fought for the creation of educational institutions had no interest in an integrated school system. Their ultimate desire was to obtain sufficient funding for the creation and maintenance of their own black institutions. Furthermore, while many of the early black colleges faced de facto segregation, schools that were created following the Supreme Court's decision of *Plessy v. Ferguson* (1896) confronted a more overt system of de jure segregation. Whether segregated by custom or law, these institutions had to appear nonthreatening to their white benefactors by revealing themselves as schools that promoted the training of "better" Negroes, not smarter ones. This chapter will therefore examine the creation of the Florida State Normal and Industrial School for Coloreds (FSNIS), predecessor to Florida Agricultural and Mechanical University (FAMU), while also detailing the role of its first president, Thomas DeSaille Tucker. Acting through his institution, Tucker played a crucial role in American history, as he created a black state-supported college with a liberal arts curriculum in the era of Booker T. Washington. Furthermore, this work will analyze the role of the black middle class in shaping the ideas of black colleges and universities at the turn of the twentieth century.[2]

To gain a better appreciation of the early years of FSNIS, it is important to understand the man who was chosen to lead the institution in its infancy. Thomas Tucker was born in Victoria, in Sherbro, Sierra Leone, on July 21, 1844. His mother was the hereditary princess of Sherbro, which made him an African prince. The name Tucker came from an Englishman on his paternal side; de Saliers traced its origin to an ancient noble family of Marseilles of eastern France. At the age of twelve, young Tucker traveled to the United States with a missionary of the American Missionary

Association (AMA), George Thompson, to complete his education, which led the young scholar to Ohio's Oberlin College. The chief objective of the AMA prior to the end of slavery was to promote the belief in Christianity while training the freedmen in the basic forms of education.[3]

On July 7, 1863, Simeon Jocelyn and George Whipple, two of the AMA's leading figures, received a letter from A. N. Beecher of Oberlin College about young Thomas Tucker. Beecher wrote Jocelyn and Whipple explaining the financial struggles that the young man faced. The Oberlin official began his letter by giving a brief introduction of his young student, describing him as "one of the Monroe boys brought over by George Thompson from Africa a few years ago." Explaining Tucker's character and scholarship, Beecher recalled that the young student was "a first rate scholar, diligent in personality and in his studies, also a young man of good character principles." With the overall purpose of this letter attempting to raise the awareness of the AMA officials of Tucker's need for financial aid, Beecher informed the administrators that he had paid Tucker an allowance of one dollar per week for work that the student performed around the Beechers' house and garden. Sadly, Beecher explained that he also charged Tucker one dollar per week, besides furnishing him room and board. In an attempt not to demonize himself, Beecher recalled that Tucker was charged his earnings for performing domestic duties, because his family had nine children and they needed the funds for survival. The Oberlin official closed this note by asking the AMA administrators to help support Tucker's matriculation with financial assistance. Explaining the ultimate need for the support, Beecher ended by stating, "Thomas Tucker will have to leave school if there is not some way [financially] before long."[4]

Tucker received other letters of support from members of the Oberlin staff—such letters of recommendation as the one transcribed to Whipple from Oberlin professor E. H. Fairchild. Professor Fairchild explained that the young scholar's financial aid would not become available until the summer, and that Tucker was therefore in great need of financial assistance. Moreover, Fairchild recalled that Tucker was "indebted twenty-five dollars for his tuition, and still has a liability of ten dollars for his board." Further explaining the debts the student had collected, the professor revealed that Tucker had been sick and accrued a three-dollar doctor bill, bringing his debt to a total of thirty-eight dollars for the academic year. In closing his note, Professor Fairchild encouraged the AMA administrators to allow Tucker to teach at the Mendi Mission, in Fort Monroe, in Hampton, Virginia, so that the student could earn the financial support that he desperately needed.[5]

To certify that Tucker was in good standing with Oberlin College, George Whipple requested further information from the school. C. H. Churchill, professor of math and natural philosophy at the college, wrote in support of one of his favorite students at the liberal arts college. Professor Churchill recalled that the young scholar had progressed through the preparatory classes and ascended to his junior year of college. The professor also noted, "Tucker has proven himself a diligent, faithful and very successful student, and by his excellent deportment and high moral character has endeared himself to his classmates and teachers." In closing his letter of recommendation, Churchill stated, "I can most cordially commend him as a capable and trustworthy young man."[6]

Tucker believed that he could help his own cause by sending a note to Whipple himself. In his correspondence with the AMA, the student informed the administrators that he was aware of their need to obtain teachers for the freedmen in the South. He proclaimed, "I herewith take the [opportunity] . . . of tendering you my services as a teacher for four or three months as you may deem [necessary]." Knowing the role that religion played in the AMA, however, Tucker informed the administrators that he would be unable to perform any ministerial duties. He concluded his letter with the request, "Should my offer meet with your acceptance, you will be pleased to inform me at your earliest convenience of the same that I may make arrangements accordingly."[7]

After this strong show of support for Tucker, the administrators of the AMA accepted the request of the Oberlin officials and allowed him an opportunity to teach in their organization. The 1863 *American Missionary Association Annual Report* reveals the young scholar as the only teacher of African descent at Fortress Monroe. Fairchild wrote of Tucker's situation in his new occupation as a teacher at Fortress Monroe, explaining that Tucker was satisfied with his arrangements in Hampton and looked forward to the task at hand. In addition, Fairchild explained that, given Tucker's poor financial situation, the student would be better off if he taught two years at the fort so that he could complete his course of study at Oberlin.[8]

At the time Tucker served as teacher for the AMA, there were more than fifty missionaries in the Hampton Roads area. Although most of the missionaries were white, at least three black AMA workers served in this area between 1862 through 1865. Most of them were young and from New England, New York, and Ohio. According to some scholars, Hampton was the first and one of the most important centers of the AMA work during the civil war. Therefore, successes and failures of missionary work with Hampton's freedmen were almost solely the product of AMA efforts.[9]

Inside the fort, a school was opened in John Tyler's Villa Margaret. Conducted in a front room on the first floor of the teacher's small house and initially consisting of only about half a dozen black students, the classes nevertheless represented the beginning of an educational program that would soon encompass seventeen states and the District of Columbia. Unfortunately, there was a terrible typhoid fever epidemic going on at the school during Tucker's years there. According to Joe Richardson, there were only five or six people living at the Tyler House in November 1863. Many of the workers were so ill from the fever that the school had been suspended during that year. This cancelation occurred because many of the teachers at the fort lost their lives due to this epidemic. While this deadly disease claimed the lives of many of the AMA teachers, the association's belief in a supreme being maintained them, as they viewed their agents as "Christians soldiers waging a battle against illiteracy, ignorance and sin in the South."[10]

As Tucker's work as an educator continued at Fort Monroe, his financial situation remained poor. Many of his friends and professors were worried about his condition and requested that the AMA provide some clarification on his salary and status. One of his professors, E. H. Fairchild penned a note on behalf of Tucker's friends, stating, "The misunderstanding of some is that he receives . . . ten dollars per month and pays his own expenses to and from his field of labor." The correspondence's tone moved from mild to aggressive, as Fairchild recalled that "Tucker is a worthy young man . . . and his service in this state would be worth more than truancy. Perhaps the association is not aloud [sic] to pay him more, if not, is there any reason why our auxiliary association may . . . make an appropriation for him!"[11]

In response to this letter, Tucker wrote to assure his friends and faculty that he was being well treated in Virginia. In this note, Tucker showed his amazement at the way the ex-slaves reacted to the prospect of freedom and education, while also describing his journey from Ohio to Virginia.

Here I am at last, in a slave state. How strange are the workings. . . . Who could have thought three years ago that such mighty and important changes would so soon take place? How dark and gloomy then were the prospect of liberty to the many who are now free; since God moves in a mystical way, why should we ever doubt any of his perfections. . . . Our journey was on the whole arguable. We arrived in bad [conditions] . . . about four in the morning and waited until five in the evening for the departure. If I give to the works a faithful picture of my life and experience in the United States as I intended to do so it is necessary to know and meet these peculiarities of society.[12]

As Tucker's synopsis of his situation reached his friends and professors in Ohio, the principal at Fort Monroe, Lewis Lockwood, stepped down to focus on other problems that the AMA faced. With the desire to replace the mild-mannered Lockwood with more of a disciplinarian, the association appointed Charles P. Day as the school's new principal. Explaining Day's approach to discipline, letters in the AMA archives reveal that the new principal was a firm believer in corporal punishment. Warning Day that such forms of punishment might have psychological effects on Tucker, the association encouraged the new principal to use his new forms of punishment discreetly. This warning amused Day, for Tucker had whipped a pupil his first day in the classroom. After this emotional and physical outburst, Tucker remarked, "I in all seriousness repeated the reply of Christian to Apollyon, Rejoice not over me O mine enemy for when I fall I shall rise again." After the young educator gave a philosophical defense of the punishment that he inflicted, he recalled his regret for his actions, explaining that, "I did whip the first day but I was extremely sorry." Tucker later reflected on his punishment of the student and the situation by saying it "was attributed to the downfall to his ignorance of the 'vices' in which the children had been raised." Furthermore, he supposed, "in governing children as well as adults much of our success depends on our ability to read human nature." In the area of disciplining the students, he believed that Day was "decidedly superior." The young educator recalled that, "with Day's experience, he ought to know more of human nature than an African who had been engaged in mere theoretical pursuits for the last six years." Tucker argued that he had a "decent stock on his hand . . . of mere book knowledge . . . and could any amount of intellectual acquirement suffice to make any practical at the same time, perhaps I might say without egotism that a direct transition from the [students'] room to practical life in the common walks of men would insure me success." Obviously, the young scholar did not feel comfortable performing forms of physical abuse on individuals who had suffered from this type of punishment on a daily basis under the institution of slavery. Moreover, it was hard for the student to remove his emotions from seeing the anguish in the faces of the individuals whom he physically punished. Surely these individuals hailed Tucker as a hero, for he shared the similarity of being a person of African descent. Notwithstanding his self-proclaimed lack of a knowledge of "human nature," many of the ideas that Tucker had about education and the preservation of the black community were planted during his time as an instructor at Fort Monroe.[13]

As Tucker's time at Fort Monroe drew to a close so too did his education at Oberlin. Although he had initially hoped to return to his beloved Africa after graduation in order to help train the people of Sherbro, the young scholar ultimately decided that he was no longer useful in his home country due to his family's dealing in rum and slaves. This point hints that the Tucker family were active participants in the transatlantic slave trade, which demoralized the young man after he was removed from that situation. Moreover, he was saddened to report that Charles Jones, a fellow Mendi student in America, had joined the U.S. Army, thus losing sight of their objective in coming to the United States. Judging from Tucker's sentiments, the two likely traveled to America in order to prepare themselves educationally to return as workers in their "benighted country." In Tucker's last letter in the AMA archives, he wrote of his colleague, while revealing his personal desire to remain in the United States:

> Far from any desire to forget and forsake Africa; I still yet as I have in the past cherished the deepest sympathy for my native land. . . . My family influences in Sherbro, as you well know, are very extensive. Returning there I would be subjected to trials and temptations, which you perhaps cannot well conceive of in this country. As your Sherbro mission is the only one you have in Africa, and as I could not return and labor there without great disadvantages, I preferred to be where I could be most efficient. I could willingly go to such a

place as Shengay, Sierra Leone[,] anywhere where I can be farthest from my relatives.[14]

The years at Fortress Monroe for Tucker were productive and profitable. These years gave him an opportunity to uplift and educate the newly freed African Americans. Tucker later graduated from Oberlin College in 1865, the same year that America emerged from its civil war. Following graduation, he moved to Kentucky and opened a day and night school for the education of the newly freed race. After living in Kentucky for a while, he moved to Louisiana, where he focused on elevating his race. His tastes and inclinations led him to study law at Straight University (present-day Dillard University), where he eventually received his law degree in 1882. A few years after opening a successful law practice with partner R. B. Elliot in New Orleans, Tucker decided to take his talents to the booming black town of Pensacola, Florida, where he met his law partner, J. D. Thompson, and gained a large clientele.[15]

Tucker's new home in Pensacola proved influential in his future appointment as the first president of the FSNIS. Upon his arrival to the Florida Panhandle in 1884, Pensacola's black community was "about as prosperous as any of their race in the South." Therefore, this move proved not only a great business venture but also a timely positioning that would allow for Tucker's future leadership in Florida.[16]

During the same year that Tucker moved to Florida, the black middle class of that state began to assert themselves as the leaders of their race. For example, over two hundred of the most prominent black leaders met in Gainesville, Florida, for the State Conference of the Colored Men of Florida. This meeting was scheduled to create a plan for African Americans in Florida a few years removed from the false promises of post–civil war Reconstruction. Well aware of the political unrest within the state of Florida and on the national level, this meeting addressed issues of local and national civil rights. One issue that the leaders of this convention discussed was the Danville Massacre. The event that took place in Danville, Virginia, in 1883 focused on the new racial etiquettes in that area. As African Americans began to step out of their "place," racial tension escalated, eventually leading to a massacre. As racial roles continued to change in Virginia, white traditionalists desired to redeem their positions in Danville. On that basis, "white democrats took control of the city and spread rumors of black insurrection throughout the state." According to historian Jane Dailey, this event muffled any attempt that the black community had made in gaining any political capital in Virginia during the election of 1883. Furthermore, the role of violence in politics spread from state to state, and this successful display of intimidation discouraged the black community from participating in the political process.[17]

With the Danville incident serving as the backdrop for the convention, leaders urged its members to devise a plan that would create a more intelligent voting mass. At this convention, over two hundred prominent black leaders of the state met to discuss pertinent issues concerning the future of the African American community. Local mainstream media outlets covered the convention with varying views of the total outcome. For example, the *Florida Times-Union* gave a synopsis of the convention two days following the proceedings. The editor of the paper recalled the voice of one of the most prominent spokesmen for education at the convention, John Willis Menard. Menard responded to questions of separation of the races prior to the *Plessy v. Ferguson* decision by stating, "If we must have separate schools and separate cars, let them have the same conveniences and advantages as those provided for the whites." Moreover, Menard and other leading members of the convention argued that proper education would ensure an intelligent voting mass throughout the state and the nation. Therefore, this group decided to use its last bit of political capital on black education. This would serve as an investment that would hopefully pay off for black Floridians in future generations.[18]

In an attempt to downplay the influence that the Negro Convention had in the political arena of Florida, one editor of the *Florida Times Union* described this meeting as an overall failure. The writer explained that the members of the convention only desired to gain support from the new Independent Party, which, in his personal view, was largely a disaster. Obviously a southern traditionalist, the writer proclaimed, "The old crises of Ku Klux and negro supremacy are things of the past, and will soon be entirely driven from the arena of our state politics."[19]

As conservative, white Floridians lambasted the convention, black Floridians praised the meeting and its leaders for creating a plan that they perceived as advancing the community. Moreover, the black press viewed this convention as a response to the reemergence of old southern traditionalism. For example, one editor of the *New York Globe* reported shortly after the convention that the desire of the members who participated at the meeting was to maintain respect in the state, while gaining both civil and human rights., After much debate over the proper way to reach their goals, the leaders of this convention decided to push for stronger education for African Americans in the state of Florida.[20]

Black journalist and political spokesman John Willis Menard sparked the idea of a state-supported institution for advanced education for African Americans in the state. Menard's son-in-law, Thomas Van Renssaler Gibbs, had spearheaded the idea's implementation. Gibbs, also the son of the state's distinguished former superintendent of public instruction Jonathan Gibbs, achieved enactment of necessary legislation and financial support as a delegate to the 1885 Florida Constitutional Convention and as a state representative.[21]

When news that an all-black, state-supported institution would be created reached Floridians, white traditionalists acknowledged the weakness of their political leaders as it pertained to the "race questions." One conservative thinker demonized the intelligence of the black voting population in a letter to the *New York Freeman,* shortly after legislation was passed to create a state-supported education institution for African Americans. The author of this note proclaimed that "the coloreds have a great deal of political power, but they don't seem to understand it." Obviously upset with the notion of a growing black middle class, the writer argued that these classes of African Americans "render you as much service as a goose." Moreover, the writer argued, "Yet still they can dress fine, smoke fine cigars and visit frequently bad dens, and their heads are as empty as a gourd." Sentiments of this sort explain the fear that many white southerners had of African Americans in a position of authority. Moreover, images of blacks dressed in traditional Victorian garb and carrying themselves eloquently would debunk stereotypes that white southerners had previously placed on them. This breaking out of sorts also allowed southern blacks a chance to mirror the lives of middle-class whites, which also would potentially work to break down stereotypes of white superiority.[22]

While white southerners expressed their dissatisfaction with the creation and support of an institution of higher education for blacks, a question as to who would lead the school arose among the political leaders of Florida. While many black and white Floridians assumed that Thomas Gibbs would step into its presidency, white political leaders desired someone else, a fact that would carry major implications for the institution's future administrators. This came about because former Confederate general

Edward A. Perry of Pensacola had assumed the governor's chair in 1885. Perry subsequently had overseen the constitution's rewriting and generally acted to revolutionize state government with the aim of reversing Reconstruction-era trends and policies. It appears likely that Perry and his advisors mistrusted Gibbs, whose connections in black social and political circles ran to the highest levels.[23]

In these circumstances, Perry surprisingly turned to a fellow Pensacola resident to take FSNIS's helm, and he likely did so based upon advice from unexpected sources. The turn of events reflected relationships tested over decades. First, Perry's immediate predecessor as governor, William D. Bloxham, had assumed office as secretary of state and, as such, sat on the board of education. Bloxham meanwhile had enjoyed an extremely close association since the civil war's end with Leon County's state senator John Wallace. In turn, Wallace had kept close ties with his fellow black civil war veteran and one-time congressman Josiah T. Walls. Interestingly, at the time Wallace and Walls had been well acquainted for almost one quarter of a century with Pensacola attorney Thomas Tucker. The friendships trace back to the civil war when the lawyer likely taught the two public officials at the army's Mary S. Peak School in Hampton, Virginia. Wallace and Walls then were serving in Company D., Second United States Colored Infantry. At the school, Tucker and other instructors combined basic academic exercises with liberal doses of religious training. Whether Wallace and Walls retained the former cannot be ascertained, but they did not forget Tucker. Available evidence, although spotty, suggests that they recommended Tucker to Bloxham who, in turn, pressed his name upon the governor as the proper man to head the state normal school.[24]

Prior to taking the reins of FSNIS, Tucker had asserted himself as a leader in Pensacola's black community. In April 1887, shortly before he was chosen as the first president of the school, his wife, Charity Tucker, accepted a teaching position at a new public school in Pensacola for black youth. In support of his wife's new career, the lawyer gave a lecture on home training to parents "that did not know how to raise their children." This lecture was not uncommon for African Americans in the middle class, as the leaders of the race during the late 1800s desired to train their future leaders in the norms of a Victorian society.[25]

On September 24, 1887, only nineteen days after delivering his "training" address, Tucker was selected as the first president of FSNIS. Obviously reluctant to take this position miles from home in Tallahassee,

Tucker nevertheless submitted to his call to duty and arrived in the Florida capital a few days prior to the first classes. During his initial year at the new school, his wife, Charity, remained in Pensacola to hone her teaching skills.[26]

On October 3, 1887, the Florida State Normal and Industrial School for Coloreds opened its doors to fifteen students. Initially, however, admittance into this school proved difficult. According to FAMU historian Leedell Neyland, admission was restricted to persons sixteen years of age and over. Facing the challenge of educating individuals who were only twenty-two years removed from slavery, the forty-three-year-old Tucker and his new partner in education, Thomas Gibbs, "deemed necessary to examine all newcomers and place them in categories on the basis of the scores received." Therefore, the courses of study were divided into preparatory and normal school. Surprisingly, for an upstart black college during the late 1880s, the normal department courses consisted of Latin, higher mathematics, physiology, astronomy, general history, rhetoric, pedagogics, and natural, mental, and moral philosophy. On the other hand, the preparatory department courses consisted of algebra and Latin while focusing on a concise review of education practices. According to historian James D. Anderson, most black higher education during the late nineteenth century was focused on rudimentary education with an emphasis on industrial and vocational training. Therefore, Tucker's curriculum at FSNIS was totally out of step with other black educational institutions, especially southern-based black institutions during this era.[27]

With one year under his belt, Tucker began to assert himself in Tallahassee as the preeminent education leader for blacks in the state of Florida. The president gained approval from the state legislature to hire another instructor at the institution. With his first hire, Tucker appointed Laura Clark, a graduate of Wilberforce College, the first female instructor at the school. Clark lightened Tucker's teaching load by instructing English and literature courses in the preparatory department. The three instructors were, surprisingly, paid on par with staff at white normal schools in the state, with Tucker's annual salary equaling eleven hundred dollars, Gibbs's one thousand dollars, and the newly hired Clark's seven hundred dollars. This sign of confidence from state officials launched the Tucker administration into full gear, as his vision for the institution continued to grow.[28]

Building on the momentum of their new president, black leaders in the state decided to create a chapter of the Colored State Teachers Association, electing Tucker as the organization's first president on July 11, 1889. Along with Tucker, fellow FSNIS instructor Thomas Gibbs joined the new teachers association. The members of this meeting desired to place their full support behind FSNIS and other black educational institutions throughout the state, which would fulfill their mission that was begun at the state convention in 1884.[29]

While serving the entire black population in the state of Florida as their educational leader, Tucker kept his focus on the progress of FSNIS. In September 1889, the staff of the young institution released its course catalogue, a neatly printed pamphlet of sixteen pages. This catalogue revealed the number of students at the school and course offerings. Moreover, the overall purpose for this pamphlet was to assure the citizens of the state that their tax dollars were not being spent in vain. For example, the catalogue expressed that "their expense account for the year can easily be kept under $100."[30]

At the end of that academic year, the institution celebrated its third annual closing exercises. This event marked the culmination of the educational experience for the pupils, while giving the public an opportunity to see the depth of knowledge that these new intellectuals gained while at FSNIS. Almost totally conducted by the new graduates, the commencement exercise offered the audience an insightful look at their future leaders. A number of prominent figures from both races attended the ceremony, including state superintendent Major A. J. Russell and black physician William John Gunn. Governor Francis Fleming was not in attendance due to a reported illness, which kept him incapacitated for many days. Overall, the progress of the young institution surprised many people of both races.[31]

As the Tucker administration continued to flourish, black leaders throughout the state continued to support his vision for the institution. The members of the Colored Teachers Association of Florida passed a resolution proclaiming, "The members of the association will use every exertion to encourage schools and increase the attendance of the same." While Tucker received well wishes from black leaders, conservative politicians had another idea for the curriculum at FSNIS. As early as 1891, the institution began to hire more agriculture and industrial instructors, which would ultimately appease white political leaders. At the start of the academic year in 1891, the school employed W. J. Clayton, a 1891 graduate of Hampton College. Clayton trained students in the agriculture department, which marked the beginning of the end of the prominent presences of the liberal arts curriculum at FSNIS.[32]

Tucker's influence over the curriculum of FSNIS dwindled while that of Booker T. Washington, one of the most prominent leaders in black education, grew. Nonetheless, Tucker's idea of creating a prominent black middle class never faltered. This can be best described in his address to the graduates of 1895, the same year that Booker T. Washington gained national acclaim for his famous Atlanta Cotton State Exposition address. While Washington argued for blacks in the South to remain on the land that they knew, and to master skills that they had learned during slavery, Tucker encouraged his graduates to carry themselves in a respectable manner while creating a positive image that would elevate the race. Washington argued that the black population would become economically independent, and ultimately self-reliant, if they followed his plan. On the other hand, a few miles south of Tuskegee, Alabama, in Tallahassee, Florida, Tucker addressed the 1895 graduates on the importance of duty. In this address, the president informed the graduates and the audience that "to the one then who desires to serve his fellow man, duty is easily perceived and the discharge of it is attended with please." This address went on to give the charge to the young graduates to continue to work professionally while understanding their new roles in society. With the arrival of Washington's approach to black advancement in the South, Tucker's administration was all but over.[33]

For eight years, the FSNIS president served as the educational voice for African Americans in the state of Florida. Available evidence shows that prior to Washington's speech in 1895, white state politicians supported Tucker as his approach was the only one openly embraced in Florida. The goal of white conservatives was being achieved at FSNIS, as the institution was creating a "better" Negro that ultimately served the black community by better educating them. On the other hand, this radical form of education prepared these pupils to think critically about their situation and also gave them the analytical ability to devise a plan that would rescue their race from the shackles of white supremacy.[34]

After Washington's Atlanta Cotton Exposition speech that encouraged vocational and industrial education for African Americans, white conservatives later attacked Tucker's ideology as detrimental to his race. From an outsider's perspective, Washington's ideas for black education were in step with those of white conservatives, as this approach would truly create a "better" Negro that would be more equipped to serve the white community. With an in-depth analysis of Washington and his methodology for black education, one will find that his overall desire mirrored that of Tucker and others who supported classical education. For example, historian David H. Jackson Jr. reveals Washington's ideology was a ploy to ignite self-help within the black community, with the hope that it would lead to the community becoming self-sustaining. In fact, Washington adopted a survivalist approach that appeared to many black leaders, such as W.E.B. DuBois, as accommodating to the white-supremacist philosophy for black education. Clearly, Tuskegee's president gained support on a national level from white political leaders, which ultimately filtered down to local support from white conservative leaders.[35]

Not surprisingly, the tensions thus erected resulted in a troubled tenure for Tucker that, by the century's end, led him into direct conflict with the man who had acquired the state superintendent of public instruction position in 1897. That man was William N. Sheats. An Auburn, Georgia, native and graduate of Emory College, Sheats held a master's degree. He later moved to Alachua County, Florida, where he served as a high school principal for sixteen years and as county superintendent of schools for a dozen more. Significantly, Sheats had represented Alachua County as a delegate to the 1885 Florida Constitutional Convention and had authored the resulting charter's article on education. Elected state superintendent in 1892, he successfully saw to the adoption of the "Sheats Law," a statute that prohibited "white and colored pupils to be taught in the same classes." As a regionally influential educational official, Sheats became familiar with Washington and was a firm believer in the Tuskegee man's advocacy of vocational education.[36]

Importantly, Sheats clearly advocated vocational education for African Americans in the state of Florida. One result of this philosophy was to create tension between him and Tucker, which eventually cost the president of FSNIS his post in 1901. Growing support for Sheats's vocational education philosophy and Tucker's equally strong philosophy and support for classical education brought the two men into conflict. From 1897 to 1901, a second gubernatorial term for William D. Bloxham apparently blocked Sheats from acting against Tucker, but William Sherman Jennings's arrival in the governor's post in January 1901 finally opened the way for Sheats to push for Tucker's removal.

That action came in the late spring and early summer when Sheats pressed the state board of education for a decision on Tucker's removal. "He [is] not in hearty sympathy with vocational education," the official complained to its members in requesting that Tucker's tenure end. Sheats insisted further that Tucker vociferously advocated liberal arts instruction. The FSNIS president, the superintendent declared, repeatedly had announced "that [vocational education] shall not interfere with the literary work while he is head of the institution." Sheats added, "Tucker had criticized Washington and others," which he viewed as "something detrimental to the school and his race."[37]

This saga ended in the summer of 1901 as Sheats achieved his goal of having Thomas Tucker removed from the presidency of FSNIS. Tucker was replaced with someone who was perceived as focusing on industrial education, a former employee of Booker T. Washington and the Tuskegee Institute, Nathan Benjamin Young. Ultimately, Young's appointment proved more disastrous for white supremacists than Tucker's time in the office because Young, also an Oberlin College graduate, proved to be a staunch advocate of liberal arts education. At the end of Young's tenure as president of what became Florida Agriculture and Mechanical College (FAMC), he battled white political leaders on issues that pertained to the curriculum of the institution. Young ultimately lost his job in 1923 for his refusal to implement a "true" vocational education curriculum.[38]

Nonetheless, once Thomas Tucker was removed from office, he left the Deep South and moved to his wife's hometown of Baltimore, Maryland. Two years later, the educator fell ill and died in June 1903 at the age of fifty-nine. His legacy as a race and educational leader remains intact in Florida over one hundred years after his death. While little is known about his life on a national level, his influence clearly reaches throughout the country, as Florida A&M University has continued to produce prominent African American leaders.

Notes

The author would like to thank Drs. Canter Brown Jr., Titus Brown, David H. Jackson Jr., Robert Gudmestad, and Aram Goudsouzian for their support in the development of this essay.

1. W.E.B. DuBois, *The Souls of Black Folk* (New York: Random House Press, 1903), 43–62; Deborah Gray White, *Too Heavy a Load: Black Women in Defense of Themselves,*

1894–1994 (London: W.W. Norton, 1999), 21–56; Louis Harlan, *Booker T. Washington: The Wizard of Tuskegee* (Oxford: University of Oxford Press, 1983), 143–202.

2. Amilcar Shabazz, *Advancing Democracy: African Americans and the Struggle for Access and Equity in Higher Education in Texas* (Chapel Hill: The University of North Carolina, 2004), 1–25; James Anderson, *The Education of Blacks in the South: 1860–1935* (Chapel Hill: University of North Carolina Press, 1988), 1–79.

3. *Constitution of the American Missionary Association*, in American Missionary Association Annual Report 1862, Amistad Research Center, Tulane University, New Orleans, LA (hereafter AMAA); *Lancet Baltimore*, May 20, 1903; John G. Riley and Leedell Neyland, *History of Florida Agricultural and Mechanical University* (Gainesville: University Press of Florida, 1956), 12.

4. A. N. Beecher to Simon S. Jocelyn and George Whipple, July 7, 1863, AMAA.

5. E. H. Fairchild to George Whipple, Sept. 12, 1863, AMAA.

6. C. H. Churchill to the AMA, Oct. 17, 1862, AMAA.

7. George Whipple to Thomas Tucker, Oct. 18, 1862, AMAA.

8. E. H. Fairchild to Whipple, Aug. 8, 1863; AMA annual report of 1863; both in AMAA.

9. Robert E. Engs, *Freedom's First Generation: Black Hampton, Virginia, 1861–1890* (Philadelphia: University of Pennsylvania Press, 1979), 9.

10. Robert C. Morris, *Reading, 'Riting, and Reconstruction* (Chicago: University of Chicago Press, 1976); Joe M. Richardson, *Christian Reconstruction: The American Missionary Association and Southern Blacks: 1861–1890* (Athens: University of Georgia Press, 1996), 172.

11. E. H. Fairchild to George Whipple, Apr. 29, 1863, AMAA.

12. Thomas Tucker to friends of the association, Nov. 27, 1862, AMAA.

13. Clara Merritt DeBoer, *His Truth Is Marching On: African Americans Who Taught the Freedmen for the American Missionary Association, 1861–1877* (New York: Garland, 1995), 37–44; Thomas Tucker to George Whipple, Dec. 24, 1862, AMAA.

14. Thomas Tucker to George Whipple, July 15, 1865, AMAA.

15. Robert R. Barr to Leedell W. Neyland, Nov. 10, 1969. This correspondence was forwarded to Professor Neyland during his research into the creation of Florida A&M University. These notes are housed at the Carrie Meek–James N. Eaton Sr. Southeastern Regional Black Archives Research Center and Museum located on the campus of Florida A&M University (hereafter SERBA).

16. *Pensacolian*, Feb. 14, 1884.

17. *The Proceedings of the State Conference of Colored Men of Florida*, Feb. 5, 1884, Gainesville, Florida (Washington, DC, 1884), Frederick Douglass Papers, 1884, Library of Congress, Washington, DC; Jane Dailey, "Deference and Violence in the Postbellum Urban South: Manners and Massacres in Danville, Virginia," *Journal of Southern History* 88, no. 3 (1997): 556.

18. *Florida Times-Union*, Feb. 7, 1884.

19. *Florida Times-Union*, Feb. 23, 1884.

20. *New York Globe*, Mar. 15, 1884.

21. *The Proceedings of the State Conference of Colored Men of Florida*, Feb. 5, 1884, 13–15; "State Conference of Colored Men of Florida," 13–15; *New York Globe*, Feb. 16, 1884.

22. *New York Freeman*, Oct. 16, 1886.

23. Samuel Proctor, *Napoleon Bonaparte Broward: Florida's Fighting Democrat* (Gainesville: University Press of Florida, 1993), 216–39.

24. James Clark, "John Wallace and the Writing of Reconstruction History," *Florida Historical Quarterly* 67 (Apr. 1989): 409–27.

25. *New York Freeman*, Aug. 20, 1887; *New York Freeman*, Sept. 3, 1887; Stephanie J. Shaw, *What a Woman Ought to Be and to Do: Black Professional Women Workers during the Jim Crow Era* (Chicago: University of Chicago Press, 1996), 13–104.

26. *New York Freeman*, Oct. 8, 1887.

27. Riley and Neyland, *History of Florida Agricultural and Mechanical University*, 14; Anderson, *The History of Black Education*, 65.

28. Anderson, *The History of Black Education*, 65; Riley and Neyland, *History of Florida Agricultural and Mechanical University*, 14, 16.

29. *Florida Times-Union*, July 11, 1889.

30. *Florida Times-Union*, Sept. 1, 1889.

31. *Florida Times-Union*, June 25, 1890.

32. *Florida Times-Union*, June 26, 1891; *Southern Workman*, Feb. 1892.

33. Booker T. Washington, *Up From Slavery* (New York: Random House Press, 1999), 70–78; *The College Arms*, June 1895.

34. David H. Jackson Jr., *Booker T. Washington and the Struggle against White Supremacy: The Southern Educational Tours, 1908–1912* (New York: Palgrave Macmillan: 2008), 151–76.

35. *Baltimore Afro-American*, Aug. 17, 1895.

36. Procter, *Napoleon Bonaparte Broward*, 216–39.

37. State of Florida Board of Control Minutes, June 24, 1901, record group 291, series 252, vol. 3, State of Florida Archives, P. K. Yonge Library, University of Florida, Gainesville.

38. Reginald K. Ellis, "Nathan B. Young: Florida A&M College's Second President and His Relationship with White Public Officials," in *Go Sound the Trumpet! Selections in Florida's African American History*, ed. E. Canter Brown and David H. Jackson Jr. (Tampa: University of Tampa Press, 2005), 153–82.

2

African American Women and Community Medicine

Civil Rights Workers in the Age of "Self-Help"

TERESA BLUE HOLDEN

In 1903, the eminent, black scholar W.E.B. DuBois poignantly chronicled the death of his son, two-year-old Burghardt, in an essay entitled "Of the Passing of the First-Born."[1] At the time of Burghardt's death in 1899, DuBois and his wife, Nina, were living in a men's dormitory at Atlanta University (where DuBois taught) in order to live in proximity to the campus. This kept them at a distance from the African American enclave across town, where there were a small number of black doctors. After their son languished for nine days, the DuBois parents desperately sought help from these distant doctors, but care was not available for their child at any of the hospitals in Atlanta. All of the hospitals there refused to treat the city's black population. On day ten of his illness, Burghardt died of diphtheria. DuBois was crushed, and Nina would never recover from her loss.[2] Whether medical science could have helped their son is open to question, but the DuBois family realized the stark truth that their options for medical care were limited in comparison to those available to their white contemporaries. Their experience exemplifies the lack of expert medical care available to African American families at the beginning of the twentieth century. Routinely rejected by white doctors and hospitals that served the white population, black women often fended for themselves in their attempts to interpret and treat the medical needs of their families. Middle-class women like Nina DuBois were well aware that class distinctions were mostly invisible to the white population in the South. For Nina, whether or not she was economically able to pay for the medical care of her family was of no significance. The only thing that counted was the color of her skin.

At the dawn of the twentieth century, middle-class African American women, like Nina DuBois, sought greater empowerment in many aspects of their lives, including how to harness resources that would guard their own health and that of their families. Their work occurred at a time when an organized movement for comprehensive civil rights was still just an idea and black women were struggling to gain respect in the nation and empowerment in their communities and homes. Still they continued a tradition of protest and community preservation that had existed since slavery. Their efforts were deeply personal attempts to secure the basic civil right of equitable access to health services, but collectively, they engaged in acts of resistance and defiance against social structures that threatened them. Usually scholars interpret this time period as a period when black women turned inward to reform their communities through self-help activities that would raise all African Americans above white reproach. Recognizing the fact that they were also focused outwardly, continuously chipping away at public policies and social structures that kept blacks from possessing appropriate medical care, allows us to view their actions as part of a much longer civil rights movement, one that responded to the national climate without retreating.

The extensive organizing efforts of black women in clubs and churches have been well chronicled, as have been their efforts to provide health information and medical care for their families and communities, yet seldom have scholars credited them with advancing a civil rights agenda, much less one that extended influence until the latter half of the twentieth century. Their activities are most often interpreted as self-help endeavors, a bent inward rather than outward. Most scholars explain that these women turned inward to raise the race above reproach, focusing their attentions on poor, uneducated, and potentially "immoral" black women. Deborah Gray White explains, "Black club women believed they could solve the problems of the race through intensive social service, focused on home life and educating mothers."[3] This interpretation highlights the tension that existed between the relatively small minority of elite and middle-class African American women and the masses who lived in poverty. Evelyn Brooks-Higginbotham and others recognize the fact that women's organizations within church denominations focused less on cross-class differences.[4] Nevertheless, the scholarly emphasis on self-help and middle-class women's maternalism toward their sisters in poverty makes invisible the civil rights activism threaded throughout their actions. How does the interpretation of their efforts change by considering their work to be civil rights work rather than solely self-help efforts? Reinterpreting the medical activism of African American women in the Progressive Era as participation in a "long civil rights movement" allows their actions to take on new shades of meaning and importance and reveals the breadth of their influence.[5]

This chapter considers three instances in which African American women organized to improve the delivery of health services in their networks and communities and interprets their work as civil rights organizing. In publishing, Josephine St. Pierre Ruffin and the Woman's Era club of Boston protested and resisted injustice regularly. In the *Woman's Era* journal they encouraged women into nursing to help them gain control over the black community's medical care in reaction to the injustice that they faced when they depended on care by white medical professionals. Women who followed their direction and entered the career of nursing faced barriers both within the black and white communities, yet their efforts to professionalize sustained a form of civil rights agitation. Margaret Murray Washington, although an adherent to the conservative position that was embodied by her husband, Booker T. Washington, and the institution he had built, still led the Tuskegee Women's Club to counter the actions of the state that confined former slaves to abysmal conditions through convict lease and peonage. Their efforts to provide medical information and services to families caught in the web of the convict lease system have been interpreted as "self-help" and maternalistic, but they can also be viewed as resistance to governmental authority that would keep black people repressed.[6] Lugenia Burns Hope and women who along with her created the Neighborhood Union in 1908 revolutionized the health conditions of African Americans in Atlanta. Their strategies reached beyond self-help and took them to courtrooms, city council meetings, the mayor's office, and the health and sanitation departments to lobby for improvements within black neighborhoods. In all of these situations women not only reached into their communities to provide medical self-help, but they also mobilized in defiance of those who would deprive them of basic civil rights. Through doing this, they created a network of activists who set the stage for the modern civil rights movement.

In the Progressive Era, health care was the particular concern of women in the African American community because most Americans viewed household and family caretaking as women's work. Further, most believed that women were naturally more insightful than men about the health conditions of their family members. Tasked with the physical care of their families through actions like birthing, feeding, cleaning, and sewing, women engaged in activities that put them in intensely intimate contact with their loved ones. The prevailing belief in the early twentieth century was that women's role caused them to be more attuned to noticeable changes that were indicators of illness and disease. Both men and women held this belief. African American women in Atlanta, Georgia, created the Neighborhood Union (a social service organization that provided health services) in 1908 to assure that community members were linked through the neighborliness of women. They were tragically inspired by the death of a young, working-class woman who had died of an illness in her home. Her death occurred in the most progressive black neighborhood in Atlanta, on the west side, close to Atlanta University and Spelman and Morehouse colleges. The family members who lived with the woman were both men, her husband and father, and they didn't detect the severity of her illness (according to the story). Her neighbors were unaware of her deteriorating health until several days had passed. Louie Shivery, the corresponding secretary for the Neighborhood Union, related the story of this woman's death that (they believed) occurred because of the absence of "womanly care":

> After a few days, some of the more thoughtful neighbors, not having seen this woman about, called and found her very ill and greatly in need of care. They did what they could for her comfort, but in a few hours she died. Deeply grieving that at their very door and under the shadow of [Morehouse] College, a poor woman could sicken and die probably for the want of such womanly care as the neighbors could have given had they known, the College women said, "this should not be; we should know our neighbors better."[7]

This story became legendary in the Neighborhood Union and its implications were clear—if her women neighbors had intervened earlier, this young woman may not have died.

Compelled by cultural pressure to take the lead in medical advocacy, these women faced this challenge by collaborating in already existing networks and by forming new networks. Defying the hardened attitudes of most white Americans, they demonstrated early forms of civil rights organizing. The Woman's Era club of Boston did this through disseminating information that empowered black women to manage the health needs of their own families and encourage women to enter the field of nursing.

"Literary Activism"

Josephine St. Pierre Ruffin and women from Boston's Woman's Era Club began to publish the *Woman's Era* journal in 1894 to draw African American women into a community that would empower them and from which they could exert influence on many issues, including health care. Circulated nationally through a network of African American women's clubs, the journal facilitated a national conversation among black clubwomen that led to the inception of the National Association of Colored Women in 1896. Predating the Highlander Folk School (founded in 1932), the Woman's Era Club had aims that were similar, as they also sought to "eliminate stereotypes, break down barriers, develop leaders, improve the lives and social conditions of participants, and help apply the principles and spirit of democracy to everyday lives," but they were exclusively focused on supporting women.[8] One of their aims was to use rhetoric in their journal, the *Woman's Era*, which positioned African American women more positively than did the mainstream women's publications, which catered to a white audience. The journal reached all regions of the United States, and its audience was mostly African American women who belonged to women's clubs of all varieties. Using a strategy that scholar Elizabeth McHenry calls "literary activism," *Woman's Era* took as some of its early focuses the promotion of health education and encouraging women to gain professional training as nurses.[9]

Understanding the club's publishing work as "literary activism" reveals the fact that seemingly innocuous articles served an underlying purpose of subverting the dominant national narrative about African Americans. The concept of "literary activism" emerges from the thought of early clubwoman and reformer Victoria Earle Matthews, who was a regular contributor to the *Woman's Era*. In 1895, at the First Congress of Colored Women in Boston, Matthews delivered a paper called "The Value of Race Literature" that affirmed the need for black literary and intellectual works to be published and distributed as a counter to the negative and demeaning claims made by white media and intellectuals. Describing the need for African American media, Matthews explained the problem with the mainstream white media, saying, "In supporting journals, published by the dominant class, we often pay for what are not only vehicles of insult to our manhood and womanhood, but we assist in propagating or supporting false impressions of ourselves or our less fortunate brothers."[10] On the other hand, African American publications could not only provide a perspective that countered prevailing views, but they could also do so as an act of defiance. She said,

> The point . . . is the need of thoughtful, well-defined and intelligently placed [literary] efforts on our part, to serve as counter-irritants against all such writing . . . having as an aim the supplying of influential and accurate information, on all subjects relating to the Negro and his environments.[11]

These literary productions were "counter-irritants" because they grated at conventional wisdom that denied blacks the capability of being self-directing and intellectual. The *Woman's Era* exemplified this kind of "literary activism" by disseminating educational information regarding family health and by encouraging African American women to gain professional training as nurses to serve in black hospitals.

Health information was a staple of women's magazines in the late nineteenth century, but because of the circuitous path that issues of the *Woman's Era* traveled, the health information published therein reached an audience that otherwise may not have received this knowledge. Circulated through African American women's clubs, articles frequently became the subject for discussion at women's club meetings. The journal also changed hands many times within clubs and communities and thus saw circulation to women of varying classes, those who could afford to purchase a subscription and those who couldn't. Because the articles in the *Woman's Era* were published in the context of an African American publication that raised dissent and questioned injustice, the health articles may have been considered more trustworthy to black women who read them. Routinely these women and their families had experienced poor treatment from white health providers in a mostly segregated national health system.

Segregated medical care, including physical segregation in hospitals, was never the aim of black people, but it was the reality. In 1896, when segregation in public places became legal through the Supreme Court's decision in *Plessy v. Ferguson*, the decision only affirmed what was everyday practice throughout much of America, including most hospitals. Even in the North, integrated hospital wards were unusual, and frequently only one hospital in a major city or region of a state would admit African Americans. Usually hospitals that accommodated blacks placed them in the most undesirable of locations (such as attics and basements) and overtly established practices that would ensure strict segregation of supplies, as well as patients. Dr. Eugene B. Elder, who was the general superintendent of the Macon Hospital in Macon, Georgia, explained, "The negro department must always be as far from the white and executive department as possible to be under the same management." He described how to color-code the supplies for the segregated wards in this way: "The linen, gowns and every individual article of the different departments must be kept as separate as if in a different part of the city. . . . Cream and white blankets for private rooms and white wards, slate-colored blankets for colored wards."[12] Evidence that spans from Reconstruction through the twentieth-century civil rights movement illustrates that both segregation and poor care were the plight of African Americans in most white-dominated hospitals, all of which prohibited black doctors from practicing in them.[13]

Additionally, the care that African Americans received from white doctors was influenced by assumptions these doctors held about black people. African American women were well aware of the ways in which these preconceptions guided the decisions of white doctors who attended them. Rebecca Cole bluntly explained in the *Woman's Era* how white doctors treated economically poor black patients:

> On the point of deaths from [tuberculosis] . . . hosts of the poor are attended by young, inexperienced white physicians. They have inherited the traditions of their elders, and [when] a black patient [coughs], they immediately have visions of tubercles. Let him die, and though in [this] case there may be good reason for a difference of opinion, he writes "tuberculosis," and heaves a great sigh of relief that one more source of contagion is removed.[14]

Frequently, incorrect diagnoses led to inappropriate forms of treatment that resulted in deaths when black patients were in the hands of white doctors. In part, this was because black patients often were left to the least experienced doctors, because, Cole suggests, the white medical community saw black patients as expendable. Because they were aware of the great need for well-trained, insightful medical personnel, Ruffin and the women who produced the *Woman's Era* published numerous articles urging black women to enter the field of nursing.

In the first publication year of the *Woman's Era*, publisher and editor Josephine St. Pierre Ruffin and the Woman's Era Club members who produced the journal sought to inspire black women to become nurses who also could lead as nurse educators and health advocates. The vision shared in the pages of the *Woman's Era* was bigger than simply training black women to be nurses. By inspiring African American women to receive clinical training at schools that would admit them in the North, these same women could lead in the establishment of nurse training programs in affiliation with black medical schools and educational institutions in the South. Educating black women in this career field could create a ripple effect that would raise the healthfulness of African Americans throughout the country. In order to make this case, Ruffin called upon a white ally, Ednah Dowe Cheney, who was on the board of the New England Hospital for Women and Children, a Boston institution that had a nursing school that was open to black women. In an article about the hospital that appeared on the front page of the June 1894 edition of the journal, Cheney emphasized the need for black women to receive excellent training (like that they would get at the New England Hospital) so that they could be leaders in this profession. Cheney believed black nurses who were trained at the New England Hospital could lead in the development of nurse training programs in the South at African American schools and hospitals.[15]

Two months later in August 1894, another article affirmed how effective the strategy proposed by Cheney could be. Written by African American nurse Marie Louise Burgess, the article reported on the opening of the Dixie Hospital and Hampton Training School for Nurses, which was the first nurse training school for black women in the South. Burgess herself was a graduate of the nurses' training program at the New England Hospital. In her article, she invited black women between the ages of twenty-one and thirty-five to consider applying to the Hampton school, stating, "This is an excellent opportunity for young women who wish to grasp it."[16] By 1896, Burgess had moved on to become the first head nurse and supervisor of the nurses' training program at St. Agnes Hospital in Raleigh, North Carolina. In its first six months, this new hospital served 17 African American inpatients, 35 outpatients, and 223 people in their homes in the

Raleigh community.[17] The care this sparsely equipped hospital provided for the surrounding community was to patients who otherwise probably would have not received medical treatment if the hospital had not existed. Marie Louise Burgess was a prototype for exactly the type of women Ruffin hoped to inspire through articles in the *Woman's Era*.

While writers for the *Woman's Era* portrayed nursing as a dignified profession for women, the work tasks and conditions were often difficult and demeaning, underscoring the fortitude and sacrifice made by the African American women who persisted as nurses. When black women served under white supervisors they faced oppressive race prejudice, and in black institutions, money was tight and discipline was severe to repel claims of their immorality.[18] Harlem Renaissance novelist Nella Larsen trained first as a nurse and later served as the head nurse of the Tuskegee Institute's John A. Anderson Memorial Hospital in 1915. Overworked and feeling underappreciated, she left after just a year. Tuskegee medical director Dr. John A. Kenney routinely fired nurses who complained about their long hours and lack of pay.[19] Further, Tuskegee president Booker T. Washington regarded nurses not as professionals but as domestic servants who had additional training.[20] Writing for the *American Journal of Nursing* in 1910, Washington described the nurses' training program at Tuskegee and, at the same time, described black nurses in a way that was tailored to fit with and respond to white perceptions of black women. He said, "Colored women have always made good nurses. They have, I believe, a natural aptitude for that sort of work."[21] Later, in describing the work that beckoned black nurses, he said, "In the south, in the present time as in the past, the children in the best white families spend a large part of their childhood in the care and in contact with a colored nurse."[22] Given the role they would play in white families, Washington emphasized the importance of a newly created course in "child nursing and nurture" that trained the women in childhood diseases and also instructed about moral purity:

> These young women's minds should be trained; that they should possess a great store of the wholesome and beautiful lore of childhood, that they should know how to share in their games, their play, and, in all their associations with the children, to impart this lore and learning of childhood in such a way as to inspire high, pure thoughts and ideas, rather than the reverse.[23]

An assumption by white patrons that black women were prone to immorality led nursing school officials at Tuskegee and elsewhere to overtly advertise the strict discipline they maintained.[24] Tuskegee also hired out student nurses to care for white patients of white doctors in the region, a potentially exploitative but moneymaking practice that other nurse training schools also followed.[25] Nella Larsen's disappointing experience was not an isolated experience. In 1925, ten years after her stint at Tuskegee, British nurse educator Ethel Johns investigated for the Rockefeller Foundation the status of nurse education and employment that was available to black women. Her findings were so disturbing that they were never publicly released. Johns pointed to race prejudice that kept black nurses and doctors from being promoted to positions that would allow them to create change to improve conditions for other black health professionals.[26] Despite conditions that were often terrible, African American women who became nurses in this period did essential work in caring for their communities. Their very presence defied the assumptions and beliefs of the white medical establishment and represented a form of civil rights protest.

Along with attempting to infiltrate the South with well-trained black nurses, the editors of the *Woman's Era* published articles about health that acquainted readers with ways to prevent and treat disease within their families and encouraged women to care for their own health. Articles appeared that were written by nurses and other health professionals to assist women with the medical care that they provided their families. Entitled "The Nursing of Sick Children," "Typhoid Fever," "Health and Beauty from Exercise," and "Domestic Science," these articles and other articles provided medical and health education information that reflected contemporary knowledge.

All women in this time sought thorough cleanliness to gain control of disease that ravaged their families. Medical science was just learning about germ theory, and antibiotics were still forty-five years from regular use at this time. For African American women whose access to professional medical care was limited, cleanliness and proper nutrition were their best safeguards against communicable disease. In 1900, when Nina DuBois gave birth to her second child, while she was still mourning the loss of her son Burghardt, she developed an obsession with cleanliness, as she sought to preserve the health of her family.[27] Like Nina, many if not most black women experienced heightened fears because they understood the fact that their own knowledge and efforts could well be the only and final defense they had against disease. An emphasis on cleanliness pervaded many of the efforts of black women's clubs and educational institutions as they also fought hegemonic attitudes about their worth. Nannie Burroughs, who led Baptist women in the creation of the National Convention and started the National Training School for Women and Girls, called this philosophy "the three B's—the Bible, the bath, the broom: clean life, clean body, clean home."[28] This philosophy conflated spiritual belief and morality with personal hygiene and sanitation, but an emphasis on home cleanliness also reflected the extent of medical knowledge that was available to laypeople at this time.

The need for proper nutrition and an environment of impeccable cleanliness was the standard presented in a May 1894 article that appeared in the *Woman's Era* entitled "Domestic Science."[29] A close examination of the article reveals that the author, Ellen Battelle Dietrick, simply outlined the directives of Florence Nightingale's 1860 work, *Notes on Nursing: What It Is and What It Is Not,* a work that in 1894 was still considered state of the art. Both highlighted what were commonly believed to be the five most important aspects of cleanliness to promote health: (1) pure air, (2) pure water, (3) efficient drainage, (4) cleanliness, (5) light. Dietrick echoed Nightingale who had earlier stated, "Without these, no house can be healthy. And it will be unhealthy just in proportion as they are deficient."[30] She emphasized the fact that women were responsible for providing a healthy environment for their families.

While African American women felt most keenly their personal responsibility to provide for the health of their own families, they collectively strategized about breaking through boundaries that withheld health information and services from their communities. The *Woman's Era* encouraged women to take action and to gain empowerment by doing so. In an era when their barriers were more obvious than their opportunities, this message captured the imagination of the journal's readers and led them to entertain and discuss ideas about how to gain greater civil rights.

Direct Action

Along with "literary activism," black women also became directly involved with providing medical services and health education to their communities. Initially their activities were mostly not visible to people outside of their immediate locales. When clubwomen decided to formally pursue the formation of a national association at the First National Conference of Colored Women in 1895 (largely through urging that was published in the *Woman's Era*), they also asserted a claim to a public presence. By the early twentieth century, African American women had developed sophisticated nationwide networks of communication and organization through their churches and clubs. Some women's organizations were able to gain support through the philanthropy of their local black communities to take direct action to provide medical services. Others worked alongside African American educational institutions to cultivate new methods of facilitating health services, drawing upon training they had as educators and (in some cases) Progressive reformers. Some were able to harness the efforts of whole neighborhoods to gain the attention and assistance of local governments in order to raise the healthfulness of black communities and provide medical care. As they focused on providing basic access to health information and medical care to African Americans, these women sculpted a civil rights argument that would continue to take shape into the twentieth-century civil rights movement.

Even before the Progressive Era, because of the paltry medical services that were available to them, African American women began grassroots organizing to provide community health care as early as Reconstruction. In 1867, middle-class and working-class black women who composed the Daughters of Zion of Avery Chapel in Memphis, Tennessee, pooled their resources to provide a doctor for their congregation.[31] Paying two hundred dollars a year, they hired Dr. S. H. Toles, a black doctor, who cared for the medical needs of the congregation. In his first year of employment, Dr. Toles saw 260 patients, only 2 of whom died.[32] Over time women's ambitions for providing health services would grow beyond their church congregations to include their entire communities.

By 1909, when W.E.B. DuBois researched and chronicled the actions African Americans were taking on behalf of their own welfare, he noted the work of women's groups who had built hospitals. DuBois reports the fact that black women in Savannah, Georgia, were responsible for building Charity Hospital there.[33] Within six months of chartering the hospital, these women raised the funds to purchase a two-story, five-room building that became Charity Hospital and also a nurse training center. Five years later with donations of money and labor from Savannah's black community, they added two wards to the original building. Similarly, the Yates

Woman's Club of Cairo, Illinois, raised twenty-one hundred dollars over three years to buy land and construct a two-story brick hospital.[34]

Other women's clubs focused on supplying the needs of segregated black hospital wards. The Galveston, Texas, Colored Women's Hospital Aid Society organized for the purpose of maintaining the black ward of the John Sealy Hospital. Thirty members contributed ten cents each month to provide "sanitary beds" (at twelve dollars apiece) and garments for the black women's ward of the hospital.[35] Segregated wards imposed indignity on black patients. Knowing that members of their own community had made provisions for their care may have offered reassurance to these patients during their hospitalization. While some black women's clubs raised funds to build and support medical institutions that would serve African Americans, other groups innovated, molding Progressive reform strategies to match the needs they found in their communities.

Russell Plantation Settlement

The Tuskegee Women's Club adapted settlement work to a rural setting by creating the Russell Plantation Settlement. Their work stood in opposition to the surrounding white community and the state that had left leased convicts and their families to fend for themselves in brutal conditions. The Russell Plantation was a site in the vicinity of Tuskegee, where the state had settled a group of convicts and their families. Holding them on the Plantation was a way of exploiting their labor in agricultural work as part of the convict-lease system. Conditions on the Russell Plantation were wretched. The people lived in former slave cabins with outdoor, open wells and privies. Like many former slaves in the Deep South, they lacked access to good nutrition, and no schools were offered for their children.[36]

The need for health, hygiene, and nutrition information was immense in this region of Alabama. Upon agreeing to lead the formation of a school in the Tuskegee region of Alabama in 1881, Booker T. Washington visited the region for the first time. Having been born into slavery in Virginia himself, Washington was nonetheless astounded at the conditions in which "country folk" in Alabama lived. The brutality of slavery and the failure of Reconstruction, coupled with the absence of educational opportunity and the extreme poverty of the region led to an utter vacuum of knowledge within the black population about how the rest of America lived. The people of the region were sharecroppers or subsistence farmers.

They had insufficient housing, and they lacked any form of medical care. Washington was astonished to find boys through the age of fourteen naked or barely clothed.[37] Upon accepting the challenge of building a school in this region, Washington set one hard and fast rule for all of the students who initially were mostly natives of the region: if they possessed nothing else, the one item they were required to bring to school with them was a toothbrush.[38] This simple requirement set a baseline standard for personal grooming that the Institute would try to further develop in their students. It also pointed to the process of acculturation that Washington hoped the school would promote.

Margaret Murray Washington and women who belonged to the Tuskegee Women's Club sought to improve the healthfulness of convicts who lived at the Russell Plantation by creating a rural social settlement. Washington was the wife of Tuskegee founder Booker T. Washington. She and the women who were members of the Tuskegee Women's Club all had either attained a high degree of education themselves and taught at Tuskegee or were married to faculty there. Most of them were transplants (often from northern locations) to the small town of Tuskegee.[39] Often current-day historians critique Washington and other middle-class black clubwomen, saying that they sought to impose their own values and morality on poor black women. Some of this critique is merited. Middle-class and elite women recognized the fact that whites stereotyped them as no different from less educated, poor black women, who lived in a manner they considered to be crude and immoral. In the case of the Tuskegee Women's Club, the club members' access to education and experience of a broader world afforded them health knowledge that their neighbors did not possess. They demonstrated a maternal sense of mission toward their poorer neighbors through teaching them about sanitation, home cleanliness, and personal hygiene. Their class status and superior attitudes caused them to hold themselves separate from those they helped. Still both groups sufficiently overcame the barriers that separated them so that their combined efforts through the structure of a Progressive Era settlement resulted in significant improvements in the quality of life on the plantation.

Modeled after social settlements that were located in urban areas during the Progressive Era, the Russell Plantation Settlement was unique because of its rural setting.[40] The intent of the clubwomen was similar to that of workers in urban settlements, as they sought to enhance the culture of the desperately poor people on the Plantation. At most urban settlements, however, workers helped immigrants and recent migrants to retain valuable aspects of their cultures while also becoming assimilated to the environs of an American city. At the Russell Plantation Settlement women did not wish for the residents to maintain many of the elements of the culture they had developed in deprivation. Rather, they aimed for them to acculturate to middle-class standards, and in this way they extended the institutional aim of the Tuskegee. In order to accomplish this, they brought resources (chief among those resources were their own teaching skills) to attempt to overcome the lack of economic funding available. They also brought practical personal hygiene tools, like toothbrushes, to fill personal health and grooming needs that Plantation residents may not have recognized they had.[41]

Similar to other settlements, the Tuskegee Women's Club attracted Plantation residents to their work by developing clubs and offering classes for all age groups; many of their classes, however, focused on raising the health standards of the Plantation. On weekends, they offered classes in which they taught about how the unsanitary conditions compromised the residents' health. An important aspect of their work was their mothers' club. They provided childcare for mothers so that they could attend meetings at which they shared information about the health benefits of good nutrition, hygiene, cleanliness, and proper sanitation.[42] In 1911, Tuskegee medical director Dr. Kenney reported on the painstaking degree of instruction that the clubwomen provided to mothers on the Plantation. He said,

> The smallest details are looked after, as how to prepare and serve their food, how and when to bathe, how to ventilate their houses, how to care for their hair, the washing of their clothing, cleaning of their teeth, sleeping between sheets, and all such subjects as tend to improve their home conditions. The special subjects of tuberculosis and typhoid fever have been discussed before the people in the most elementary way possible.[43]

Better health resulted from their detailed instruction about minute details of personal and household care. Because the clubwomen also conducted home visits, plantation mothers were expected to demonstrate their new knowledge about their care for their families. These mothers may have experienced these efforts as invasive, but Margaret Murray Washington reported her observation that the mothers gained a sense of pride as their quality of life improved. Reflecting on their joint collaboration with the residents of the Russell Plantation, Washington stated that the residents were "a pride to themselves and a pride to those of us who have given our time."[44]

The convicts and their families who lived at the Russell Plantation were valuable to the state of Georgia for their labor, but they were also expendable to the state because their bodies themselves contained no value as property. By sparking a sense of pride in these families, the Tuskegee Women's Club brought them dignity that worked against the intentions of the state. While their actions can be viewed as maternalistic, the Women's Club also defied the government's deliberate attempt to deprive these people of their civil rights, and they acknowledged the residents' humanity.

Neighborhood Union

The Neighborhood Union mobilized the black community of Atlanta in grassroots, civil rights organizing to improve the healthfulness of their neighborhoods. Stirred by the death of her neighbor in 1908 (discussed earlier), Lugenia Burns Hope, wife of the president of Morehouse College, convened a meeting of neighbors to discuss embarking on settlement work in order to enhance the healthfulness of the community. Unlike most settlements of that era, the Neighborhood Union sought equitable access to the services of the city on their own behalf because all African Americans suffered under the strictures of Jim Crow. When women in Atlanta started the Neighborhood Union, they employed strategies of Progressive reform to do civil rights organizing in order to bring health education and medical services to the black community there.

The Neighborhood Union set out from the start to mobilize the African American community to demand change. Their charter announced their intentions, which were "to develop a spirit of helpfulness among the neighbors and to cooperate with oje [sic] another in their respective neighborhoods for the best interests of the community, city and race." In order to accomplish this cooperation they sought "to develop group consciousness and mass movements."[45] Women who began this organization didn't intend for their efforts to only be turned inward; a mass movement would have wide-reaching effects.

Lugenia Burns Hope, like Margaret Murray Washington, possessed influence and prominence in Atlanta's black community along with brilliant organizational skills and knowledge that she had gained as a volunteer at the Hull House settlement in Chicago. Before marrying and moving to Atlanta, Hope lived in Chicago and worked for an African American charity that sent her one day each week to volunteer at Hull House. There, she was able to observe firsthand and participate in the work of residents there.[46] The women who managed Hull House had developed a formula for demanding the city's attention on behalf of the poor, immigrant neighborhood they had adopted. That formula was to painstakingly gather data that they would then present to city officials to underscore their neighborhood's needs. They argued that poor conditions in immigrant neighborhoods had negative repercussions for affluent whites in the city, as well. Her experience at Hull House gave Hope the unique ability to lead this movement.

While Hope was volunteering at Hull House, Florence Kelley, a resident there, published *Hull House Maps and Papers,* a groundbreaking sociological work that provided a graphic (color-coded) depiction of the immigrant neighborhoods surrounding Hull House.[47] This document included two series of maps that Kelley had developed for the United States Bureau of Labor Statistics. One charted the nationalities of the residents surrounding the settlement house, and the second charted the income level of these same residents. Kelley and her team walked door to door and surveyed their neighbors to gain the information necessary to create the maps. Kelley's work was cutting edge and wouldn't be matched in over a decade.[48]

Women of the Neighborhood Union also began their work by surveying the people in their own neighborhood near Morehouse College. Deploying Morehouse College students to help them, they initially targeted one hundred residences. Going door to door, they gathered information about the living conditions on individual streets and shared with residents their intentions to organize. Through their initial surveys, the group gained specific, detailed information that convinced them of the need to include all of the black neighborhoods in Atlanta in their efforts.

The surveyors documented what they already knew to be true. Conditions were significantly worse in black neighborhoods than they were anywhere else in the city. A number of factors contributed to this situation. The city bypassed African American neighborhoods when improvements were made to the other parts of the city, and they left black neighborhoods to collect the various forms of refuse that were unwanted elsewhere. The city's waste disposal areas were in black neighborhoods alongside open wells. At the same time, the city avoided collecting garbage in black neighborhoods, so that it was piled everywhere. Sewer lines were not present in many black neighborhoods, and children did not have healthy places to play outside. Streets were not lit, and some areas attracted activities that were not safe for the community. Lack of proper sanitation contributed to the spread of disease.[49]

Working among their own people to solve problems that were common to all of them gave the women from the Neighborhood Union insight that was not immediately available in other types of settlement work. They accomplished their work by dividing the black neighborhoods into districts and appointing specific women to focus on the circumstances and needs of each district. Seeking members in each district from all social classes, they gained vital information from people on the ground to guide their work. Enlisting help from students at the African American educational institutions that were in their proximity (Atlanta University, Morehouse College, and Spelman College) extended their reach. Expertise that was available through the faculty at these schools informed their work. Community solidarity contributed to their success.[50]

Early on, the women began to investigate the health needs of their districts by educating themselves about disease and then applying their knowledge to their community. They sponsored talks and demonstrations by trained nurses to teach women how to care for the ill. Visiting the homes of the sick, they disseminated information about health. Within six months of the group's beginning, they sponsored a health clinic at which area African American doctors and nurses saw patients for free. Within six years, with help from officials at the segregated, black public schools they had gathered health data about black schoolchildren that demonstrated to city officials the serious health challenges of the community and led to partnerships with white agencies that could help.[51]

White residents' reaction to the Neighborhood Union was begrudgingly positive and based, in part, on fear of epidemics that were perceived to begin in black neighborhoods. When the *Atlanta Constitution* reported on the organization, the article ignored the fact that unsanitary conditions in black neighborhoods were caused by the policies of white governmental agencies. Instead, the newspaper assumed a lack of will and an inescapable inferiority had created the health problems of blacks. A February 2, 1911, *Constitution* article reported,

> The primary purposes of the [Neighborhood Union] are to elevate the moral, social, intellectual and spiritual standards in each neighborhood; to lead mothers to better care of infants, cleaner and more sanitary maintenance of their premises; to campaign everywhere against vice and disease, by appealing to individual members of the home; to organize classes or tuition in cooking, sewing and general housework. . . .
>
> It is by the purity, virility and aspiration of the home that the white race has achieved and safeguarded its civilization. . . .
>
> It is to be hoped progress will be made in these directions by this new organization. . . . The *Constitution* has many times pointed out cooperation from the superior race is called for in the degree that the white man is inevitably affected by the progress or retrogression of the negro.[52]

The opinion that the black community affected the white community—and, in fact, infected it with disease—had arisen two years previous to this article when the white Anti-Tuberculosis Association accused black laundresses of spreading tuberculosis to white families. By taking the laundry of their white patrons home with them, where they also cared for family members who were sick with tuberculosis, the association claimed, laundresses were infecting the laundry of white people with the disease and thus spreading it to the white community. This claim presented an opportunity for the Neighborhood Union to forge a partnership with the Anti-Tuberculosis Association. Ultimately, using the organizational structure of the union and the resources of both organizations, black health workers were able to take health and disease prevention information door to door in African American neighborhoods. The collaboration served the goals of both the Atlanta Anti-Tuberculosis Association (to curb the spread of tuberculosis) and the Neighborhood Union (to disseminate health information so residents could protect themselves against many diseases).[53]

With the help of the Anti-Tuberculosis League, the union gained an advocacy voice with the city, leading the city government to pass ordinances that provided clean water, garbage collection in black neighborhoods, and the destruction of outdoor privies. By 1916, the Neighborhood Union opened the first permanent health clinic for blacks in Atlanta. Black doctors and nurses volunteered their time to see patients and also to provide health education talks for residents.[54]

The Neighborhood Union harnessed the energies of the entire black community, including churches, women's clubs, men, and educational institutions. Driven by the data they gathered, they participated in political and legal processes to insist that government officials give attention to the loathsome conditions in black neighborhoods. Women in the organization made white allies to gain a foothold in white power structures. They petitioned, lobbied, and filed lawsuits. Their work began as a form of medical self-help, but it grew to become a civil rights movement that demanded equitable services from government in order to ensure African Americans had decent and healthful places for families to live and for children to go to school.[55]

The union's health initiatives directly reached beyond themselves to the next generation of civil rights workers through their work to provide healthful schools for African American children in Atlanta in a struggle that lasted from 1913 to 1921. Atlanta's board of education had left the segregated schools for black children in decrepit condition with improper sanitation and inadequate ventilation. Also overcrowding had forced these schools into double sessions so that the teachers were overworked. Further, no high school for African American young people existed. The Neighborhood Union's Women's Civic and Social Improvement Committee gained data about the number of student and teacher illness–caused absences in a school year. Armed with this information they lobbied the board of education and the city council to improve the conditions of schools that black students attended. Working with the NAACP and black ministers like Ebenezer Baptist Church minister A. D. Williams (who was the maternal grandfather of Martin Luther King Jr.), they attempted for a number of years to get a bond issue passed that would provide new schools for black students. Not until after women gained the vote through the Nineteenth Amendment were they able to mobilize enough African American voters to accomplish this goal. Within a few years Martin Luther King Jr. attended the newly built David T. Howard Elementary School and later Booker T. Washington High School, the first high school for black students in Atlanta.[56]

Even prior to the achievements of the Neighborhood Union in Atlanta, in 1913 an African American doctor from North Carolina, Dr. S. B. Jones, noted improvement to the health of black people nationally. For this improvement he recognized the work of African American institutions. Responding to claims that those of African descent were going extinct, Jones voiced dissent in an article called "Fifty Years of Negro Public Health." Adherents to social Darwinism claimed that because of inherent racial predispositions, African Americans were "dying out." Jones outlined their claims:

> At the present time arguments are being brought forward by responsible, and sometimes by irresponsible, persons that the Negro race in the United States is fast dying out. In proof of this it is claimed that the race shows an increasing death rate, a declining birth rate, the influence of alcoholic and sexual intemperance, and, in particular, a racial disposition to tuberculosis and pulmonary diseases.[57]

In response, Dr. Jones explained the disparities in disease and death rates of African Americans and whites by pointing out public policy issues that affected the African American community. He pointed to the "heartless indifference of municipalities," "economic slavery depriving an infant of its right to be well born," and "scanty hospital facilities and inadequate medical attention."[58] Ultimately, he pointed to the pioneering work of black doctors and nurses and the work of black educational institutions as a reason for improvements in the health of African Americans. Although Jones acknowledged women teachers, doctors, and nurses, he did not specifically mention the work of black women. Often invisible and rarely acknowledged in their day, African American women undergirded the medical well-being of black communities. Their efforts were acts of open defiance that protested the inferior status assigned to their community. More than that, they developed methods of mobilization, organizational strategies, and forms of direct protest that set the stage for the next generation of civil rights workers.

Nina DuBois never recovered from her son's death; her pain and her introverted nature kept her from participating in organized efforts to publicly promote health knowledge. Because of his father's essay, readers of *The Souls of Black Folk* know about the life and early death of Burghardt DuBois and the deep pain the family experienced because of his death. The disinterest of the nation's white population in the condition of America's black neighborhoods and the absence of medical services available to them necessitated that black citizens themselves take action. Early twentieth-century Americans viewed the health issues of a family to be women's concern. Because of this, African American women took the burden of their community's health upon themselves.

Black women approached this work with energy and creativity as they altered existing methods of social reform to advocate for human rights and their civil rights as Americans. The Woman's Era club of Boston built a network of communication and practiced "literary activism" to mobilize and educate clubwomen. The Tuskegee Woman's Club and the women of the Neighborhood Union applied strategies of Progressive Era reform to new environments and needs that were different from those of white Progressive women. They defied and wheedled the government as they insisted upon a quality of life that preserved a sense of human dignity in their communities. Their struggle for civil rights remains mostly hidden, but it is a legacy on which the twentieth-century civil rights movement was built.

Notes

1. W.E.B. DuBois, *Souls of Black Folk* (Mineola, NY: Dover Thrift, 1994), 127–32.

2. David Levering Lewis, *W. E. B. Du Bois: Biography of a Race, 1868–1919* (New York: Henry Holt, 1993), 226–28.

3. Deborah Gray White, *Too Heavy a Load: Black Women in Defense of Themselves, 1894–1994* (New York: W.W. Norton, 1999), 27.

4. Evelyn Brooks-Higginbotham, *Righteous Discontent: The Women's Movement in the Black Baptist Church, 1880–1920* (Cambridge, MA: Harvard University Press, 1993); Katrina Bell McDonald, *Embracing Sisterhood: Class, Identity, and Contemporary Black Women* (Lanham, MD: Rowman & Littlefield, 2007), 55–56.

5. Jacquelyn Dowd Hall, "The Long Civil Rights Movement and the Political Uses of the Past," *Journal of American History* 91, no. 4 (2005), 1234. Hall suggests that by broadening the perceived location of civil rights organizing beyond the South and lengthening the periodization of the civil rights movement to include a century (or more) before 1954 (*Brown v. Board of Education*), one can achieve greater continuity.

6. For more information on the convict lease system, see Matthew Mancini, "Race, Economics, and the Abandonment of Convict Leasing," *Journal of Negro History* 63, no. 4 (1978).

7. Jacqueline Rouse, *Lugenia Burns Hope: Black Southern Reformer* (Athens: University of Georgia Press, 1989), 65.

8. LaVerne Gyant and Deborah F. Atwater, "Septima Clark's Rhetorical and Ethnic Legacy: Her Message of Citizenship in the Civil Rights Movement," *Journal of Black Studies* 26, no. 5 (1996): 585. The first issue of the *Woman's Era* stated the purpose for the Woman's Era Club: "We the women of the Woman's Era Club enter the field to work hand in hand with women, generally for humanity and humanity's interests, not the Negro alone but the Chinese, the Hawaiian, the Russian Jew, the oppressed everywhere as subjects for our consideration, not the needs of the colored women, but women everywhere are our interest" ("Boston," *Woman's Era*, Mar. 24, 1894).

9. Elizabeth McHenry, *Forgotten Readers: Recovering the Lost History of African-American Literary Societies* (Durham: Duke University Press, 2002), 202–3.

10. Victoria Earle Matthews, *The Value of Race Literature: An Address Delivered at the First Congress of Colored Women of the United States, At Boston, Mass., July 30th, 1895*, http://brbl-dl.library.yale.edu/vufind/Record/3724631.

11. Matthews, *Value of Race Literature*.

12. Eugene B. Elder, "The Management of the Race Question in Hospitals," *Transactions of the American Hospital Association Ninth Annual Conference* 9 (1907): 127.

13. Todd L. Savitt, *Race and Medicine in Nineteenth- and Early Twentieth-Century America* (Kent, OH: Kent State University Press, 2007), 126–27; Gunnar Myrdal, *An American Dilemma*, vol. 1, *The Negro Problem and Modern Democracy* (New Brunswick, NJ: Transaction, 1996), 172; Todd L. Savitt, "Entering a White Profession: Black Physicians in the New South, 1880–1920," in *A Question of Manhood: A Reader in U.S. Black Men's History and Masculinity*, vol. 2, ed. Darlene Clark Hine and Earnestine Jenkins (Bloomington: Indiana University Press, 2001), 216; Darlene Clark Hine, "Black Professionals and Race Consciousness: Origins of the Civil Rights Movement, 1890–1950," *Journal of American History* 89, no. 4 (2003): 1280.

14. Rebecca J. Cole, "First Meeting of the Women's Missionary Society of Philadelphia" (Boston, MA), *Woman's Era*, Oct./Nov. 1896.

15. Ednah D. Cheney, "New England Hospital for Women and Children" (Boston, MA), *Woman's Era*, June 1, 1894.

16. Marie Louise Burgess, "The Dixie Hospital and Hampton Training School for Nurses" (Boston, MA), *Woman's Era*, Aug. 1894.

17. Susan Altman, "St. Agnes Hospital," in *Encyclopedia of African American History* (New York: Facts on File, 1997).

18. Darlene Clark Hine, *Black Women in White* (Bloomington: Indiana University Press, 1989), 49–50.

19. George Hutchinson, *In Search of Nella Larsen: A Biography of the Color Line* (Cambridge, MA: Harvard University Press, 2009), 93.

20. Hutchinson, *In Search of Nella Larsen*, 93.

21. Booker T. Washington, "Training Colored Nurses at Tuskegee," in *Black Women in the Nursing Profession: A Documentary History*, ed. Darlene Clark Hine (New York: Garland, 1985), 7.

22. Washington, "Training Colored Nurses at Tuskegee," 10.

23. Washington, "Training Colored Nurses at Tuskegee," 10.

24. Hine, *Black Women in White*, 49–50.

25. Darlene Clark Hine, "The Corporeal and Ocular Veil: Dr. Matilda A. Evans (1872–1935) and the Complexity of Southern History," *Journal of Southern History* 70, no. 1 (2004): 18–20.

26. Darlene Clark Hine, "The Ethel Johns Report: Black Women in the Nursing Profession, 1925," *Journal of Negro History* 63, no. 3 (Autumn 1982): 212–21.

27. Lewis, *W. E. B. Du Bois*, 252.

28. Ann Firor Scott, "Most Invisible of All: Black Women's Voluntary Associations," *Journal of Southern History* 56, no. 1 (1990): 3–22, 13.

29. Ellen Battelle Dietrick, "Domestic Science Paper No. 1" (Boston, MA), *Woman's Era*, Mar. 24, 1894.

30. Florence Nightingale, *Notes on Nursing* (Philadelphia: Edward Stern, 1946), 14–15, https://archive.org/stream/notesnursingwhat00nigh#page/n0/mode/2up.

31. McDonald, *Embracing Sisterhood*, 55.

32. Wilbert L. Jenkins, *Climbing up to Glory: A Short History of African Americans during the Civil War and Reconstruction* (Wilmington, DE: Scholarly Resources, 2002), 204.

33. W.E.B. DuBois, ed., *Efforts for Social Betterment among Negro Americans* (Atlanta: Atlanta University Press, 1909), 89; Charles J. Elmore, "Black Medical Pioneers in Savannah, 1892–1909: Cornelius McKane and Alice Woodby McKane," *Georgia Historical Quarterly* 88, no. 2 (2004). DuBois's account differs from that of Charles J. Elmore, who credits Cornelius McKane and Alice Woodby McKane with beginning Charity Hospital. DuBois differentiates between the McKane Hospital and Charity Hospital, recognizing them as two separate institutions.

34. DuBois, *Efforts for Social Betterment*, 62.

35. DuBois, *Efforts for Social Betterment*, 87.

36. Susan Smith, *Sick and Tired of Being Sick and Tired: Black Women's Health Activism in America* (Philadelphia: University of Pennsylvania Press, 1995), 27–29; Jacqueline Anne Rouse, "Out of the Shadow of Tuskegee: Margaret Murray Washington, Social Activism, and Race Vindication," *Journal of Negro History* 81, no. 1 (1996): 31–46, 33–34.

37. Booker T. Washington, letter to supporters, July 14, 1881, Papers of Booker T. Washington (The Tuskegee Collection), box 001, file 001, Tuskegee University Archives, Tuskegee, Alabama.

38. Booker T. Washington, *Up from Slavery* (New York: Doubleday, Page, 1907), 174–75.

39. Cynthia Neverdon-Morton, *Afro-American Women of the South and the Advancement of the Race, 1895–1925* (Knoxville: University of Tennessee Press, 1991), 133.

40. Neverdon-Morton, *Afro-American Women of the South*, 133.

41. Smith, *Sick and Tired of Being Sick and Tired*, 27–29.

42. Smith, *Sick and Tired of Being Sick and Tired*, 27–29.

43. Smith, *Sick and Tired of Being Sick and Tired*, 27–29.

44. Smith, *Sick and Tired of Being Sick and Tired*, 27–29.

45. Dorothy E. Roberts, "Black Club Women and Child Welfare: Lessons for Modern Reform," *Florida State University Law Review* 32, no. 3 (2005): 957.

46. Jacqueline Anne Rouse, *Lugenia Burns Hope: Black Southern Reformer* (Athens: University of Georgia Press, 1989), 139n13.

47. Florence Kelley, ed. *Hull House Maps and Papers*, https://homicide.northwestern.edu/pubs/hullhouse/.

48. Kelley, *Hull House Maps and Papers*; Kathryn Kish Sklar, *Florence Kelly & the Nation's Work: The Rise of Women's Political Culture, 1830–1900* (New Haven, CT: Yale University Press, 1995), 157, 277–78.

49. Rouse, *Lugenia Burns Hope*, 57–65.

50. Charles Hounmenou, "Black Settlement Houses and Oppositional Consciousness," *Journal of Black Studies* 43 (2012): 646, 655.

51. Rouse, *Lugenia Burns Hope*, 70.

52. Eugene Pierce Walker, "Attitudes towards Negroes as Reflected in the Atlanta *Constitution*, 1908–1918," (master's thesis, Atlanta University, 1969), 12.

53. Nancy Tomes, *The Gospel of Germs: Men, Women, and the Microbe in American Life* (Cambridge, MA: Harvard University Press, 1999), 221–25.

54. Neverdon-Morton, *Afro-American Women of the South*, 161.

55. Neverdon-Morton, *Afro-American Women of the South*, 145–62.

56. Rouse, *Lugenia Burns Hope*, 74–79; Clayborne Carson, "Introduction," in *The Papers of Dr. Martin Luther King, Junior*, vol. 1, https://kinginstitute.stanford.edu/sites/default/files/publications/vol1intro.pdf.

57. S. B. Jones, "The Negro's Progress in Fifty Years," *Annals of the American Academy of Political and Social Science* 49 (Sept. 1913): 138.

58. Jones, "The Negro's Progress in Fifty Years," 138, 140.

3

Southern Discomfort

The Rise and Fall of Civil Rights Attorney
James F. Gay, 1942–2008

JEFFREY L. LITTLEJOHN AND CHARLES H. FORD

James F. Gay served as one of the most important figures of the civil rights era in Norfolk, Virginia, but he has largely been forgotten in both academic and political circles. Gay, along with his older brother Milton, organized the sit-ins that brought down Jim Crow in Virginia's largest city, and he went on to become one of the first African Americans to graduate from the University of Virginia Law School. As a local entrepreneur and leader of the Norfolk branch of the National Association for the Advancement of Colored People (NAACP), he was even seen as a possible mayoral candidate in the 1970s. His fame finally peaked in the following decade, as he won a significant case before the U.S. Supreme Court that transformed Norfolk's local electoral practices to allow for greater diversity and inclusion in city government. Gay quickly fell from grace, however, and his fall was especially sharp and traumatic.

In 2007, a year before Gay's death, columnist Earl Swift of the *Virginian Pilot*, the area's principal newspaper, laid blame for Gay's descent into obscurity on the attorney's string of ethical lapses that had led to his disbarment in late 1993. Yet for all of his narrative prowess, Swift failed to place the rise and fall of James Gay within its proper and wider historical context. While we do not deny the self-destructive arrogance that underlay some of Gay's professional misconduct, we also appreciate the venom of Norfolk's establishment toward an outsider who successfully turned everything upside down. In fact, Gay's story is not simply a local tale about a civil rights activist falling from favor. Rather it illustrates the high hurdles that leaders of the black freedom struggle faced as they attempted to convert the political and cultural accomplishments of the 1960s into a new governmental reality in the 1980s. Along the way, Gay made many personal mistakes, but his every misstep received attention from a white oligarchy that forgave segregationists of the old order like judges Hal Bonney and James G. Martin IV and ignored the malfeasance of black politicians like city councilmen Paul Riddick and Anthony Burfoot. James Gay's sins were never forgiven, though, largely because he had effectively challenged the civic status quo, whereas many of the other transgressors simply became part of the establishment.[1]

Accordingly, in order to appreciate the meteoric nature of Gay's rise and fall, one needs to contextualize his story within the larger narrative of Norfolk's African American community and its role in the long civil rights movement. Going back to the mid-nineteenth century, thousands of enslaved African Americans across Virginia challenged the authority of their masters by fleeing to Norfolk and taking up arms with the Union army. Then, after emancipation, local freedmen declared their desire for inclusion in the new government of Virginia by issuing an *Equal Suffrage Address*, which historian Earl Lewis has called a "classic Afro-American jeremiad."[2] Later, at the onset of Jim Crow, local blacks again protested their marginalization by organizing a series of streetcar protests in 1906. Although these efforts ultimately failed, the community again challenged racially discriminatory policies in the famous teacher pay parity cases of 1939–40, in which the NAACP and the Norfolk Teachers Association successfully achieved equal pay for white and black teachers in the public school system.[3]

James Gay and his older brother, Milton, were both born in 1942, shortly after the achievement of pay parity in Norfolk's schools. The two boys grew up in a tight-knit family that lived on Chapel Street in the heart of Norfolk's African American community. Their father, Milton Sr., was a barber and a part-time custodian at the YMCA, while their mother, Thelma, performed domestic work. Despite their meager economic resources, the boy's parents placed a premium on education. They encouraged Milton and James to be upstanding Christian young men who worked hard and treated people fairly. Bishop Obadiah McInnis, the family's minister at the First Church of Christ (Holiness), repeated this lesson on a weekly basis. A well-spoken, militant civil rights activist, McInnis served on the boards of the local NAACP, Virginia Voters League, and Interracial Ministers Fellowship. His weekly sermons emphasized a broad, free-flowing reading of Scripture that taught that God had created all people in his image. Equality thus became a biblical mandate in McInnis's eyes. He preached that God rejected discrimination of all kinds and looked with disfavor on those who treated others unjustly. McInnis used this message as a natural segue to encourage his parishioners, including Milton and James Gay, to join the NAACP.[4]

Milton Jr. began his association with the NAACP during his teen years in the late 1950s. At the time, he was working at the Blyden branch of the Norfolk Public Library, where he met Roberta Robertson, the state NAACP youth advisor. Mrs. Robertson was an urbane, sophisticated woman with a strict moralistic streak. She and her husband, Robert D. Robertson, the president of the local NAACP, were staunch advocates of African American rights, and they were impressed with Milton's zeal for the cause. In fact, by 1958 Milton was serving as president of the local NAACP Youth Council, and the Robertsons asked him to accompany them on a trip to the annual NAACP convention in Cleveland. The experience was transformative. Milton heard Dr. Channing Tobias, the chairman of the NAACP board of directors, call for speedy, aggressive, and insistent opposition to segregation. He watched as Roy Wilkins, the organization's executive secretary, criticized President Dwight Eisenhower for lax enforcement of the *Brown* decision. Of greatest significance was the fact that, for the first time, Milton saw the strength and resolve of the national NAACP—his organization.[5]

Within weeks of his return from the Cleveland conference, Milton had convinced his fifteen-year-old brother, James, to join the NAACP Youth Council. "I realized somebody had to do something," James later recounted. "There was a need for students to be concerned about civil rights."[6] In fact, James joined his brother in the NAACP at a crucial moment in Norfolk's history. In the fall of 1958, Governor J. Lindsay Almond Jr. closed six of the city's public schools in order to prevent integration, and Norfolk became engulfed in a traumatic desegregation debate. Milton and James responded to the school closings by taking a number of sequential actions that, although largely imperceptible at the time, formed the basis of the student movement that emerged in the 1960s.[7]

In September, at their own initiative, the boys established the Student Cooperative Association (SCA) with their friends at Booker T. Washington High School, an all-black institution that remained open throughout the desegregation crisis. The SCA quickly drafted a petition protesting the school closings, and Milton was elected, with fellow students Melvin Quiero and Cecelia Clarke, to present the petition to J. J. Brewbaker, the superintendent of schools. The students' statement urged Brewbaker and other school officials to enforce federal desegregation orders so that "all the students in our city [may] attend public schools in compliance with the latest ruling of the Supreme Court."[8]

Although Milton's meeting with Superintendent Brewbaker produced no immediate results, he and James found the entire protest exhilarating. Indeed, they had established a civil rights organization, drafted a petition, gathered signatures, and presented a statement to the superintendent of the largest school district in the state. This was no mean feat for high school students, and they knew it. In October, the Gays' enthusiasm for the civil rights cause became increasingly intense, as they attended the state NAACP convention at Hampton Institute. At the conference, Milton was elected vice president and James was elected treasurer of the state youth conference.[9] The two boys then had the opportunity to meet one of their heroes, the renowned civil rights attorney Thurgood Marshall. In a brief but poignant meeting with the NAACP youth officers, Marshall encouraged the boys to take a leading role in the civil rights struggle in Norfolk. Later that afternoon, he presented a similar message to the twenty-one hundred people gathered at Hampton's Ogden Hall. Marshall told the audience that African Americans in Virginia were at the forefront of the campaign to topple school segregation, and he encouraged the young people of the state to get involved. The civil rights crusade "is a righteous fight," Marshall said. "Segregation is not only illegal and unconstitutional, it is downright wrong."[10]

Milton and James drew inspiration from their meeting with Marshall. Of course, they found his speech convincing, but more than that they liked his style, his panache, and his command of the legal and moral arguments regarding desegregation. The Gays hoped to master Marshall's mix of qualities and powers. As one of Milton's friends later said, "he wanted to make himself indispensable" to every group in which he participated. It was this ambition that had driven Milton earlier in the year to take a leading role in one of the youth council's principal campaigns for 1959, a statewide voter registration contest known as "Operation Citizenship."[11] Milton drafted the rules for the program with help from his brother and Patricia Godbolt, a prominent young woman who was a member of the

Figure 3.1. On October 25, 1958, the Virginia State Conference of the NAACP held its annual convention at Hampton Institute. Sixteen-year-old James Gay attended the meeting and appears in the middle photograph at the top of this newspaper story. He and the other NAACP Youth Council officers posed on the steps of Clarke Hall at Hampton following their election. *Front row (l to r)*: Jacqueline Poison of Christ Church; Mrs. J. M. Tinsley, Richmond, advisor; Miss Lucy Thornton, president, West Point; Miss Barbara Lee, Williamsburg; and Mrs. Robert Robertson, Norfolk, senior advisor. *Back row (l to r)*: Armstead G. Williams, William Giddens, and Milton Gay, all of Norfolk; Ralph Williams, Richmond; James Gay, Norfolk. Courtesy *Norfolk Journal and Guide*.

Norfolk 17—the group of African American students who desegregated Norfolk's schools in February 1959. Together, Milton, James, and Patricia designed a voter registration contest in which high school and college students would compete for national scholarships. Students were to encourage their elders to pay their poll taxes, register to vote, and go to the polls. The two students who secured the highest number of confirmed voters would receive the scholarships.[12]

Although there are no extant records to document the precise number of students involved in the voter registration contest, it seems clear that the program did encourage some young people to participate in local politics. In part, student participation was a result of the contest literature, which related voting directly to the school crisis that was then dominating local and regional news. "The reason for Operation Citizenship," the literature explained, "is that by your action you can help Save Our Schools."[13] In the spring of 1959, this message carried particular power in Norfolk. Six schools were desegregated by the Norfolk 17 in February, and a Democratic primary, seen as a public referendum on the matter, was scheduled for July. Two blocs of candidates were vying for Norfolk's open seats in the Virginia General Assembly, which was seen as the strategic battleground in the looming debate over desegregation. The first bloc of candidates, supported by the segregationist Defenders of State Sovereignty and Individual Liberties, included W. I. McKendree, a local businessman, and Hal Bonney Jr., a schoolteacher. The rival, independent bloc consisted of Henry Howell and Calvin Childress, two young attorneys, who opposed "all massive resistance candidates" and vowed to "protect and preserve public education" through desegregation if necessary.[14]

The NAACP Youth clearly supported Howell and Childress. These candidates faced a serious opponent, however, in Hal Bonney Jr. Bonney was an outspoken segregationist, a member of the Tidewater Educational Foundation, and the sole teacher in Norfolk to publicly oppose desegregation. Ironically, Bonney taught history at Norview High School, a desegregated school where seven of the Norfolk 17—including Patricia Godbolt—enrolled in February 1959. At Norview, Bonney distributed mimeographed circulars to students, which portrayed integration as a dangerous conspiracy that endangered essential southern values: hard work, moral living, and racial purity. One of Bonney's circulars—titled "The Negroes of Virginia—Have They Earned Equal Rights?"—cited pseudoscientific statistics to demonstrate the inferiority of African-descended people and the absurdity of integration. One such statement read, "Lowest 25% of whites made better grades than the highest 25% of Negroes." Outside the school, on the campaign trail, Bonney employed similar tactics to win support for his candidacy. He repeatedly cited "racial incidents" at Norview in his political speeches and described integration as a "terrible thing" that threatened "to destroy a democratic way of life."[15]

Bonney's tactics backfired, however. White moderates in Norfolk, who had grown tired of Massive Resistance, opposed his candidacy, and when word of his "Norview circulars" went public, African American leaders responded with outrage. "That a Teacher in the public school system should use the misconduct of [white] students toward a handful of Negro students for political ammunition is astounding," Vivian Carter Mason, a prominent local social worker, fumed. Rather than taking the "responsibility to re-educate and to correct the misbehavior of a handful of misguided and sorry [white] youngsters," Bonney had chosen to "[advertise] their shame." This, Mason said, was unforgivable, and she had a great deal of support.[16]

By May, Milton and James Gay had connected the Youth Council's voter registration contest with NAPAC—the Norfolk Alliance of Political Action Committees—an umbrella organization that coordinated the efforts of fifty-two smaller civil rights associations. Led by Joe Jordan Jr., NAPAC secured the support of the African American establishment in Norfolk, including Robert Robertson and Thomas Young, the editor of the region's most prominent African American weekly, the *Journal and Guide*. NAPAC also had the support of local ministers and their churches, including J. B. Henderson at Bank Street Baptist, Richard Martin at Grace Episcopal, E. Paul Simms at First Baptist Bute Street, and W. L. Hamilton at Shiloh Baptist.[17] In July, NAPAC's organizing effort paid off. Hal Bonney and his segregationist allies were defeated, while Henry Howell and Calvin Childress were selected to represent the Democratic Party in Norfolk's November elections, which they won four months later.[18]

Although the NAACP Youth Council played what can only be called a minor role in Norfolk's Democratic primary, Milton and James Gay used the election to their advantage. As they promoted voter registration and school desegregation in the spring of 1959, the boys and their friends encouraged other young people to join the local youth council. The result was a massive spike in NAACP memberships in Norfolk, increasing the local youth chapter from 172 members in 1958 to 601 members in

1959. This tremendous surge made Norfolk the leading youth office in the state, with almost twice as many members as the second-largest branch in Richmond.[19] The growth of the local Norfolk office was only part of the story, however. At the twenty-fourth annual NAACP state convention in Danville that October, Norfolk's leaders took charge of the entire state youth organization. The delegates elected Milton—now a freshman at the Norfolk branch of Virginia State College—as president of the state youth conference. In addition, James was elected as treasurer, Patricia Godbolt as assistant secretary, Wyoma Gaston as financial secretary, Melvin Fallis as editor in chief of the "Freedom Press," and Roberta Robertson as state youth advisor.[20]

Over the course of the next three months, the members of Norfolk's NAACP Youth Council accelerated their activities. On January 1, 1960, they followed Milton, their new state president, to Richmond, where they took part in the second annual Pilgrimage of Prayer for Public Schools. More than twenty-five hundred activists attended this protest meeting, which culminated in a march on the state capital led by Rev. Martin Luther King Jr., the hero of the Montgomery bus boycott and president of the Southern Christian Leadership Convention. Thirty days after the Pilgrimage, Norfolk's young people returned to Richmond for the NAACP state Membership and Planning session. This time, James Gay was in the lead. As the newly elected president of the local youth council, James headed the Norfolk delegation to the state planning session. As Norfolk's young people listened to the keynote speaker, Herbert Wright, the national NAACP youth secretary, they longed for action.[21] Little did they know that 250 miles to the south, another group of students was preparing to change the civil rights movement forever.

On February 1, 1960, four African American college students from North Carolina A&T sat-in at a Woolworth's lunch counter in Greensboro, North Carolina, sparking a direct action campaign that transformed the national civil rights movement. The Greensboro Four were not the first sit-down protesters, nor did their actions take place in a vacuum. By the dawn of the 1960s, young people around the South had organized youth councils and civil rights associations to challenge segregation in their communities. In Nashville, Tennessee, Diane Nash, John Lewis, James Bevel, and Marion Barry led one of the country's most well-organized and active student organizations. In Rock Hill, South Carolina, and Tallahassee, Florida, young African Americans joined the Congress of Racial Equality (CORE) to picket and protest against Jim Crow. Meanwhile, in Norfolk, Milton and James Gay read about the Greensboro demonstrations in the local newspaper and found the story invigorating. Here, at last, was a method to harness the pent-up anxiety and frustration that plagued the young black community in Norfolk. Here, at last, was the opportunity for direct action against Jim Crow.[22]

Within days of the first sit-in demonstration in Greensboro, Milton was coordinating a similar protest for local students in Norfolk. He called for support from his younger brother, James, a senior at Booker T. Washington High School and the newly elected president of the local NAACP Youth Council. In addition, Gay met with Eric Jones, Winston Williams, Oscar Waller, Grant Coleman, and more than a dozen other students at the Norfolk branch of Virginia State College to plan the details of the upcoming protest. When would the students demonstrate? Where would they strike? And what would they do if someone was arrested?[23]

After little more than a week of discussion, the students decided to launch their first sit-in demonstration on Friday, February 12—Abraham Lincoln's birthday. At 5:30 p.m. Milton and James Gay along with their team of thirty-six activists marched into Woolworth's department store in downtown Norfolk and sat down at the white lunch counter. It was a "chance to confront the system [of segregation] head-on in a collective manner," Eric Jones, one of the participants, remembered.[24] Although the Woolworth's store manager, L. L. Day, refused to serve the students, they remained calm and orderly. No property was destroyed, and no arrests were made. The students behaved in a focused, well-mannered fashion, sitting peacefully at the lunch counter until it closed around 6:00 p.m. As planned in advance, none of the students identified themselves or their leaders. "I'm just a citizen," one student told a newspaper reporter, while another jotted a simple note on a menu: "We want our rights."[25]

On the following day—Saturday, February 13—Woolworth's lunch counter remained closed. That afternoon, young people targeted two other stores in the downtown area: S.S. Kresge's and W.T. Grant's. Twelve students from the Norfolk branch of Virginia State moved on Kresge's, where the manager quickly closed the lunch counter to prevent demonstrations. Only one young man braved the counter at Grant's, but he was ignored by waitresses and left shortly thereafter.[26]

Then, as quickly as they began, the sit-ins in Norfolk seemed to end. During the course of the following workweek, not one African American

Figure 3.2. On February 12, 1960, thirty-eight young African American demonstrators held a peaceful lunch counter protest at the Norfolk Woolworth's Store on Granby Street. Milton Gay led the demonstrators, many of whom had schoolbooks with them, while others were dressed in ROTC uniforms from the Norfolk branch of Virginia State College. Courtesy *Virginian-Pilot*.

student demonstrated at the city's downtown lunch counters. Norfolk's white leaders were ecstatic at the development. They hoped to avoid the nightmare that was taking place in Portsmouth, their sister city across the Elizabeth River. There, on Tuesday, February 16, dozens of white toughs—some carrying hammers and wrenches—attacked sit-in demonstrators and African American bystanders in the parking lot at the mid-city shopping center. The following day, twenty-seven people were arrested when a crowd of three thousand gathered for another showdown. "One highschooler was found to have a loaded .22 caliber pistol," the newspaper reported. "Two had chains. Another carried a switchblade knife. All four were white." While Portsmouth's segregationist mayor, B. W. Baker, called for order and calm, the city's orgy of violence appeared in the pages of *Life* magazine.[27]

At the *Virginian-Pilot*, editors found the developments in Portsmouth startling. "The possibilities of serious public disorder among high school whites and high school Negroes, particularly as disclosed in Portsmouth . . . are important enough to bring into play all possible restraining influences," the editors wrote. The paper called on Norfolk's civic leaders and school officials to prevent the local situation from "degenerat[ing] into open clashes and public violence." Should young African Americans continue to oppose the segregation of the city's lunch counters, the editors said, they should pursue traditional lines of protest. They should write editorials, join the NAACP, or litigate their cases in the court room. They should not, however, continue the sit-ins. The *Pilot* came out in direct opposition to these demonstrations, arguing that they "may lead . . . to public difficulties and dangers" of the first degree. Now was not the time for heroics and radicalism, the editors suggested, and it was instead "a time for intelligence"—"for restraint and good sense."[28]

Milton, James, and the other participating students agreed that this *was* a time for intelligence and good sense, but they had no intention of bowing to Jim Crow. On the contrary, they had only postponed their sit-in activities in order to form the Student Relations Association (SRA) and coordinate their movement so that its members would conduct themselves according to the highest standards of nonviolent behavior. Indeed, when the Norfolk students resumed their sit-ins on Saturday, February 20, they did so in a deliberate and exacting manner. Shortly after noon, seventy-five African American youths entered Kresge's downtown department store. As the students occupied the seats at the white lunch counter, manager A. P. Hunt announced that the store was closing for the day. He rushed the students, customers, and employees out the front entrance and then locked the building to prevent any further protest. The SRA had won its first tactical victory; Kresge's lunch counter was closed.[29]

During March, the sit-in protests continued as African American students occupied the lunch counters at Woolworth's, Kresge's, and Grant's. The demonstrators were neither served nor arrested, but their presence caused a sharp decline in white patronage.[30] When interviewed about the demonstrations, sit-in leader Milton Gay called for talks between the protesters and the variety store managers.[31] Although he refused to elaborate on the nature or objectives of these proposed talks—seeking to maintain a diplomatic, conciliatory air—Milton's brother, James, was not so reticent. "During the past few weeks," James wrote in a March editorial in the *Virginian-Pilot*, "students have been conducting sitdown demonstrations at various restaurants, and the management refused to serve these students simply because they were Negroes." This was not only discriminatory, James argued, it was un-American: "Negroes have helped to defend America in every war since the American Revolution. Yet the Negro has not been allowed to enjoy the American ideal of equality for all." The sit-down demonstrators meant to right this wrong, to exact justice through their own direct action protests. "Remember," James said, "the young educated Negro will not be satisfied with second class citizenship. He has proven that he is willing to go to jail if necessary, in order to secure the blessings of equality for himself and others in his race."[32]

White political leaders responded to this newfound black militancy in a variety of ways. On the national scene, President Dwight Eisenhower pursued a policy of calm detachment. In a March press conference, the president said that he was "deeply sympathetic" toward the protesters and "deplore[d] any violence" used against them. But, he insisted, the sit-ins were local issues to be handled by local governments. "I certainly am not lawyer enough or wise enough in this area," Eisenhower said, "to know when a matter . . . violate[s] the constitutional rights of the Negroes." Eisenhower's apparent confusion was not shared by his predecessor, the former president Harry Truman. On April 18, at a press conference in Ithaca, New York, Truman derided the sit-in protesters, declaring that their entire movement was orchestrated by the Communist Party. "You never can tell," Truman said (as only he could), "where you'll find their fine Italian hand, and it's not Italian—it's Russian."[33]

At the state level, Virginia governor J. Lindsay Almond Jr. called for an immediate end to sit-in demonstrations that were sweeping through the state. He believed that the protests were illegal: they violated the personal property rights of business owners, and they endangered standards of racial decorum throughout the state. On February 24, the Almond administration proposed three new anti-trespass bills, which were meant to halt the sit-in demonstrators in their tracks. In less than twenty-four hours, the General Assembly passed the measures by unanimous vote, with a good deal of "moderate" support. Norfolk's Edward Breeden Jr., Portsmouth's William Spong Jr., and Lynchburg's Mosby Perrow Jr.—all well-known liberals—signed on as sponsors of the legislation.[34] On February 25, Governor Almond signed the new bills into law, providing for a maximum penalty of one year in jail, a thousand-dollar fine, or both, for trespassing, encouraging others to trespass, or conspiring with others to trespass on private property.[35] Although Robert Robertson tried to make light of the situation—saying that the new laws would not "stop Negroes from seeking their constitutional rights,"—the legislation clearly put protesters at increased risk for arrest.[36] In fact, local police departments around the state used the new legislation to lock up dozens of sit-in activists who trespassed on private property when they refused to leave restaurants or other places of business.[37]

The new anti-trespass laws were extremely controversial, however, even among whites. In Norfolk, the editors of the *Virginian-Pilot* noted that the state would "be lucky if bills enacted so fast and with so little attention do not show constitutional or other flaws."[38] A more serious criticism came from Ellis James, a white pro-school advocate and the named litigant in the school desegregation suit *James v. Almond*, who called the new laws "harsh and punitive." Had the state of Virginia learned nothing from the failed policy of Massive Resistance? he asked. It strained belief to imagine that the General Assembly and the governor now proposed to arrest and imprison young people who dared to ask for equal treatment at lunch counters and libraries. To those white citizens in Norfolk who supported the anti-trespass legislation, James had one thing to say: "The Virginia Negro today is a citizen coming of age. Obviously, he doesn't want or seek paternalism in government or economic life. He simply wants fair and equitable treatment and the elimination of discriminatory practices based solely on color."[39]

Despite moderate white support in the *Virginian-Pilot* and occasional assistance from whites at lunch counters, African American students bore the brunt of the sit-in struggle. In April, Norfolk's black community tightened ranks behind the young protesters. At the *Journal and Guide*, publisher P. B. Young characterized the demonstrators as "dignified and non-violent" students, whose "exemplary conduct is matched only by the reasonableness and Americanism of their objectives."[40] Robert Robertson shared Young's assessment. When the protests began, he issued a statement on behalf of the local and state chapters of the NAACP, promising to "furnish whatever support is necessary, legally and otherwise, to help these courageous youths in their efforts to make American democracy a living reality."[41] In early April, Norfolk's NAACP executive council acted on Robertson's promise, issuing a resolution urging African American customers to boycott downtown stores that practiced racial discrimination.[42]

The boycott was publicized at churches and community functions, and the NAACP printed hundreds of leaflets to support the protest. As African American pressure mounted in the downtown district, however, white leaders in the city struck back. Police Chief Harold Anderson remembered that the sit-in demonstrations and downtown boycott created "an ugly era." "It wasn't a pleasant thing at all," he said, "and it wasn't good for the picture of the city."[43] As students marched through the streets carrying protest signs and singing songs, police officers used K-9 dogs to monitor the demonstrations and maintain order.

Although arrests in Norfolk remained infrequent, in mid-April, eight high school students and two college men were taken into police custody for distributing NAACP leaflets as part of the boycott campaign. The young men were charged with violating section 3–1 of the Norfolk city code, which made it unlawful to distribute materials "liable to litter the streets."[44] James Gay, the president of the Norfolk NAACP Youth Council, was among those who were detained. At the time of his arrest, he and his friends Alfred Edmunds, Eric Jones, and James Reeves were standing in front of W.T. Grant's on Granby street. As the students went about their task—distributing handbills—a policeman approached and arrested the young activists. The students were then taken to the police station, booked, and fingerprinted, and their parents were called to pick them up.[45]

Word of the arrests soon filtered out to the community. Joseph Jordan and Evelyn T. Butts, two local African American activists, alerted Robert Robertson at the NAACP. Robertson was furious that the young men were charged with such a ridiculous crime. Indeed, their first amendment right to freedom of speech protected their activities, he declared. NAACP attorneys Victor Ashe and J. Hugo Madison agreed. They argued that the students had a fundamental—constitutional—right to distribute materials that advised patrons to avoid stores that practiced racial discrimination.[46]

Shortly after the arrests, Robertson issued a statement on behalf of the NAACP, declaring that the city's police crackdown would not halt the African American boycott.[47] In fact, the arrest and subsequent conviction of the student protesters energized the black community. Ministers implored their congregations to avoid shopping at downtown stores, while civic leaders demanded an end to segregation at restaurants on Granby Street. Meanwhile, high school and college students continued their downtown demonstrations as pressure against segregation mounted throughout the South.

Although sit-in demonstrators throughout the nation remained unaware of the federal government's activities on their behalf, on June 1, 1960, U.S. attorney general William Rogers met with national representatives of Woolworth's, Kresge's, Grant's, and other major variety stores. Rogers encouraged the representatives to begin the desegregation of lunch counters at national chain stores. He said that desegregation was important "because the standing of the United States as a leader of the free world suffers as the result of acts of racial discrimination." After the meeting, national chain store executives instructed their local managers to speak with public officials in their towns to determine the most efficient and peaceful way to eliminate segregation.[48]

In late July, Norfolk's variety store managers made the decision to desegregate lunch counters at Woolworth's, Kresge's, and Grant's. Seeking to introduce the change with as little excitement as possible, the managers requested a conference with three of the region's leading African American ministers, Henry W. B. Walker, James A. Askew, and S. L. Scott Jr., the president of the Metro Baptist Ministers Conference. The store managers informed the ministers that they had decided to offer service to all customers at their lunch counters, regardless of race. The implementation of the decision would take place on July 23, 1960, and the ministers were to be the first people served.[49]

Although Norfolk's student protesters discovered that desegregated seating would be introduced at the downtown variety stores, they were not included in the negotiations. At the time, Milton Gay was diplomatic about the situation. He praised the ministers and their congregations for supporting the sit-ins. "The church has played its role in facilitating this change," Gay declared, "by allowing students to speak to congregations . . . [and] planning the implementation of the decision to desegregate."[50]

Later, however, Milton and his brother, James, expressed their anger at the way in which Norfolk's students were treated. Milton remembered that the students were "totally ignored." "We felt it was out of retaliation," he said. The store managers "were just saying, 'You students will not make us integrate. We will be the ones to decide who will sit down at the counter.' We felt that we had fought the battle, and someone else was getting the credit."[51] In the twenty-first century, James Gay continued to feel this way. "The students were left out," he remembered. "The store managers and ministers sought the credit—they ignored the students and their leaders."[52]

Despite the controversy over credit, Norfolk's downtown lunch counters desegregated on July 23. Students who were privy to the development rushed to Woolworth's to participate in "Operation 4 O'clock," when the counters opened to African American patrons. Milton Gay, James Reeves, Oscar Waller, and James Stanton were among those students who sat down to inaugurate a new day of race relations in Norfolk. Reflecting on developments that day, Francis M. Mantz, another student protester, summarized the sit-in movement and its achievement. "The students [did] not fight for self-seeking purposes or for personal advancement," Mantz said. "They [spent] their time and energies in the cause for desegregation because they [believed] it to be right and proper."[53]

The students inspired by the brothers Gay, therefore, kept on going. Although Milton left the area for various mission trips and then graduated in 1964, James would carry on with his local activism. In 1963, as Mayor Roy Martin and the city of Norfolk grappled with the logistics of desegregation, James formed the Student Committee against Discrimination (SCAD) at the local division of Virginia State College. This committee steered an independent path between the more conservative approach favored by the NAACP, the *Journal and Guide*, and most black ministers and a new blend of legal and popular theater pushed by a trio of radical black attorneys—Joseph Jordan, Edward Dawley, and Leonard Holt. The students' independent path did not preclude them from collaborating with all of the various factions under the umbrella of the civil rights

Figure 3.3. Executive committee of the Virginia State Youth Conference of the NAACP in November 1961. *Crisis,* April 1962. *Seated (l to r)*: Marcus Delk, Mildred Springs, Melvin Fallis Jr., James Benton Jr., Milton F. Gay Jr., Faye Young. *Standing*: Mrs. Robert Robertson, state youth chairperson; Marvin Lake; Winston Williams; James Gay; and Herbert Wright, NAACP youth secretary. Courtesy *Crisis.*

movement, however. While keeping their eyes on the prize of legal equality, this pragmatic advocacy did not mean accommodation with obstructionist municipal leaders. For instance, in the summer of 1963, James Gay appeared in a long-running conflict with Mayor Martin, which foreshadowed the intensity of his struggles with Norfolk's oligarchy to come.[54]

The trouble began in June, when Gay appeared before Mayor Martin and the city council with a petition bearing some 1,115 signatures requesting immediate reforms in the way the city handled racial matters. Gay and his allies wanted the city to adopt ordinances requiring businesses licensed by the city to offer equal accommodations, access, and job opportunities regardless of race. In addition, the petitioners requested immediate desegregation of schools and the appointment of teachers and administrators without regard to race. Mayor Martin and his fellow council members categorically rejected these requests and sent Gay on what they hoped would be a fruitless fact-finding mission to document other municipal efforts to end racial discrimination. In addition, Martin sought to insulate his council from future charges of prejudice by delegating all future questions of systemic discrimination to the newly created biracial Citizens Advisory Committee (CAC).[55]

Undeterred, Gay appeared before the first CAC meeting to consider racial issues on July 8. There, he presented Martin's requested evidence and more. Along with P. B. Young Jr., the editor of the *Journal and Guide*;

James L. Staton, a teacher at Booker T. Washington High School; and housewife Evelyn T. Butts, a representative of the Oakwood Civic League, Gay offered documentation on recent anti-discrimination legislation in Louisville, Philadelphia, Kansas City, and San Antonio. Consequently, CAC decided to set as its initial objective negotiations with downtown hotel owners who had not yet desegregated their premises and services. Another outcome of this effort was the appointment of attorney Hilary Jones as the first African American on the Norfolk school board in August 1963. Around the time that Jones was appointed, a bevy of Norfolk hotel owners announced that they would desegregate immediately.[56]

Buoyed by his recent successes, James Gay then led a cohort of local students to the historic March on Washington in August 1963. Returning to town with renewed confidence, he supported a close friend, Marvin Gay (no relation), who led a mass walkout at Booker T. Washington High School in September to protest conditions at the dilapidated school.[57] Meanwhile, James pursued a chemistry degree at the Norfolk division of Virginia State College and continued to complain of the "snail-like pace of desegregation" before the city council. In May 1964, he had yet another showdown with Mayor Martin, an encounter that exposed the very personal and nasty backlash intended for anyone who revealed the real intentions of city leaders. In a relatively detailed and sympathetic editorial in the *Journal and Guide*, editor P. B. Young Jr. showed his disgust at the councilmen's strategic decision "to castigate, ridicule, and abuse Mr. Gay." Young reported that Mayor Martin himself "led the assault on Mr. Gay" by dismissing him as someone who had never been in business and by using the dialectical code word "Nigra" repeatedly in his diatribe. Most "disappointing," if not surprising, to Young and his readership was the turning of would-be ally Sam T. Barfield, a supposed moderate who had been elected only with black votes in 1960. Barfield deemed Gay's marches and protests as "juvenile and ridiculous" and went on to lecture the college senior that "we have a responsibility to the white people in this city, too." Gay followed up Barfield's barrage by reminding him of how well entrenched and long-lived the Jim Crow system was in Tidewater, to which Barfield snapped, "Do you want the world all at once?" Gay had the last word here, though, and responded, "I'd like to enjoy some of these things you enjoy before I'm dead and gone." Young noted that Barfield, like most outsiders in Norfolk politics, had "made his peace with powers in City Hall and had 'joined the club.'" In contrast, Gay would never be a

Figure 3.4. On February 2, 1965, James Gay led students from the Norfolk campus of Virginia State College into the city's Central YMCA to integrate the facility for African Americans. Don Costa Seawell, an African American student, had been kicked out of the facility because of his race days earlier. Although this effort was not initially successful, the Central Y did soon desegregate its services. Courtesy *Virginian-Pilot*.

clubbable man, even if he would help to open up that charmed circle for many others.[58]

In the spring of 1965, at the suggestion of NAACP veteran G.W.C. Brown, Gay applied to law schools at the University of Virginia, Harvard, and Washington and Lee. After enjoying a busy summer with the Moral Rearmament program in Brazil alongside a grandson of none other than the late Mahatma Gandhi, James had brother Milton drive him to the University of Virginia to begin his legal studies.[59] In his initial year in Charlottesville, James participated in voter registration drives and supported congressional candidate George Rawlings in his successful 1966 primary bid to unseat Judge Howard Smith, an implacable foe of the Civil Rights Act of 1964. Although Rawlings lost in the general election to his Republican opponent, Gay recognized the significance of the connection between high politics and grassroots civil rights activism. In fact, in 1967, he successfully ran for the presidency of the statewide Young Democrats, becoming the first African American to ever hold the post. As head of the organization, Gay pushed for a number of resolutions, including the creation of a state fair employment practices commission and the repeal of Virginia's miscegenation laws. Commenting on the inevitable relationship between mainstream politics and civil rights achievements, Gay knew that "we could not succeed without becoming involved in politics," even if politics would never be the same with the engagement of himself and other advocates. Accordingly, Gay practiced what he preached by becoming the first African American elected to the flagship university's student council.[60]

After graduation from the University of Virginia in 1968, James returned to Norfolk, where his brother Milton had become curate at Grace Episcopal Church, the chosen place of worship for many black leaders. After briefly going to work at Allied Chemical Corporation's Latin American division in New York City, James became legal counsel, executive director, and then president of the Tidewater Area Business League, which helped to prepare local blacks to become entrepreneurs and corporate managers. He was so successful in this mentoring and networking that he became the director of the National Business League's Project Outreach. While pursuing his own business opportunities, he never ignored politics. For instance, he supported the first wave of African American candidates for local and statewide offices, including his Norfolk State College (now Norfolk State University) professor William P. Robertson Jr.; he also supported the ongoing initiatives to save and upgrade his alma mater, Booker T. Washington High School.[61]

James Gay's approach to business could be as disruptive as his involvement in politics and advocacy. His fearlessness, occasional abrasiveness, and sense of loyalty—which had carried him through dealings with Mayor Martin and company—got him into trouble in the business world as the 1970s wore on. Devotion to family, seen by others as needless nepotism, played a central part in Gay's rise and fall. Here, his position at Coastal Pharmaceuticals is particularly instructive. Gay accepted a job with the interracial wholesale drug company in 1970 in hopes that he could help to turn the struggling operation around. On the surface, Gay's position with this firm was an extension of his political and social activism. The largest customer of this company was the federal Veterans Administration, and Vietnam veterans of all backgrounds were the primary beneficiaries

Figure 3.5. On May 8, 1967, the *Virginia Weekly* featured an article on James Gay, shown here. At the time, Gay attended the University of Virginia Law School and served as the president of the Young Democrats association. Courtesy James Gay Papers, Norfolk State University Library.

of its efforts to provide cheap, reliable drugs. Friends of Gay recalled the good things that he did with Coastal, expanding the business from a tiny operation with one full-time employee to a large firm with over seventy workers. Problems, however, quickly mounted at the firm with financial losses running to a reported seventy thousand dollars a year by 1977. In addition, there were a bevy of complaints about questionable business practices and nepotism involving Gay's own family. For instance, Gay's mother, Thelma, served as the supervisor of packaging, while his wife's uncle, Carl Jeter, worked as office manager. This cycle of internal patronage went beyond the confines of the firm and extended even to the businesses with which Gay traded. In one of his most egregious lapses of judgment, Gay secured an order of discounted air conditioners from Aqua Dynamics, Ltd., a company headed by his father, Milton Gay Sr., and then sold them at a large profit to Ghent Arms Nursing Home, a subsidiary of Coastal Pharmaceuticals. Although no legal charges were filed in the case, Coastal's board of directors fired an unrepentant Gay in 1977.[62]

With his self-inflicted wounds from Coastal still fresh, Gay concentrated his efforts on the local political scene. In 1982, he made a run for city council along with Ballentine grocer, Herbert M. Collins. The two men publicly proclaimed that they were not running against anyone, and cited support from both the grassroots and the black middle class. They won the coveted support of the Norfolk Democratic Party Committee by stressing the economy over more controversial social issues such as court-ordered busing. Their two African American rivals, incumbent Rev. Joseph Green and challenger Evelyn T. Butts, also gingerly avoided the third rail of cross-town busing, but they stressed their own long records of civil rights accomplishments. In the end, Green, the most well connected and well financed, won reelection, while Gay, Collins, and Butts lost their bids. Gay and Collins attributed their defeat to Norfolk's at-large council elections and immediately set about getting rid of them legally via the Voting Rights Act. Green and Butts initially supported the idea of a ward voting system, but Butts, in particular, changed her mind and became a steadfast defender of the at-large council system.[63]

James Gay served as the local attorney of record on the suit, *Herbert M. Collins Sr. v. City of Norfolk*, which was officially filed on behalf of the local NAACP and seven Norfolk residents in August 1983. The suit alleged that the city's at-large councilmanic elections, which had been in place since 1918, illegally diluted the voting power of the black community by privileging white, wealthy candidates from the west side of Norfolk who could afford to run citywide. A recent change to section 2 of the 1965 Voting Rights Act allowed Gay and the NAACP attorneys to downplay any discriminatory intent on the part of Norfolk's political leaders and to instead argue that the at-large system resulted in a racially discriminatory political system. This legislative change proved crucial as the case moved forward, since the evidence clearly demonstrated that Norfolk's African

American community was woefully underrepresented on city council. According to the 1980 census, Norfolk had a voting age population of 201,366, of whom 64 percent were white and 31 percent were black. Yet since the implementation of the at-large election system in 1918, only two African Americans had been elected to city council—Joseph Jordan Jr. in 1968, 1972, and 1976 and Reverend Joseph N. Green Jr. in 1978 and 1982. Prospects for the case looked good, as other Virginia cities, including Hopewell, Richmond, and Petersburg, had been forced to abandon their at-large voting systems due to threats of legal action and popular pressure by local constituents.[64]

Despite the initial optimism, federal district court judge J. Calvitt Clarke Jr. ruled for the city of Norfolk in 1984, citing the recent May 1 election of the African American Reverend John Foster of Shiloh Baptist Church to city council. According to Clark, Foster's election showed that more than one African American candidate could win election to city office. Moreover, Clarke found that Gay and his allies failed to "establish that the political processes leading to the election of the members of the city council were not equally open to participation by the black citizens of the city." Indeed, Clark said, "the city's black citizens had an opportunity equal to that of other members of the electorate to participate in the electoral process and to elect representatives of their choice." Frustrated by Clarke's decision, Gay and his colleagues appealed to the Fourth Circuit Court, which, in 1985, confirmed the district court's ruling in favor of the city. A subsequent appeal to the U.S. Supreme Court succeeded, however, and in July 1986, the high court vacated and remanded the case to the Fourth Circuit. This led to another referral, in which the circuit court sent the case back to the district court. On February 3, 1988, the district court again ruled in favor of the city, and it took a further appeal to the Fourth Circuit in August 1989 for Gay and his allies to achieve their first clear-cut victory. The city immediately appealed this decision to the U.S. Supreme Court, which denied certiorari in October 1990, finally ending the case once and for all. In March 1991, Norfolk's city council proposed the following to the Department of Justice: five racially mixed yet geographically consistent wards with two equally mixed superwards. The council, as before, would choose the mayor from its own ranks. Norfolk would not have an elected mayor until the twenty-first century, but the efforts of Gay and his colleagues did help make the municipal government more concerned about neighborhoods outside of the wealthy west-side sections of Ghent and Larchmont. It was a lasting contribution that cannot be underestimated, for which Gay became president of the local branch of the NAACP in the late 1980s. He was at the top of his game, but not for long.[65]

At the height of this hard-fought and ultimately successful campaign, James Gay ran into familiar, self-inflicted problems of managing money and relationships. This time, the resulting wounds would prove deadly. Gay's latest round of scandals started when his brother Milton passed away suddenly in the Maryland suburbs of Washington, DC, in February 1987. James filed a petition with the Orphans' Court of Prince George's County, Maryland, to become the executor of Milton's estate, since his brother and his wife had separated. In the petition, however, Gay erroneously identified himself as a resident of Maryland, a misrepresentation that, along with numerous failures to submit required reports and inventories of the estate, led to his removal as the executor of his brother's estate. Then, in a related matter, Gay misappropriated several thousand dollars from a $23,913 life insurance policy that his brother had left for his children. As executor of the money, Gay paid himself $3,807 as a fee and was alleged to have spent thousands of additional dollars without consulting the beneficiaries of the estate, resulting in the financial suspension of his own niece from the University of Virginia for a term. These improprieties were followed by other similar cases in which Gay defrauded clients and friends or failed to fulfill his professional duties as an attorney. Most egregious was his neglect of an equal opportunity employment lawsuit in which he let a statute of limitations lapse in order to get a quick settlement that would benefit himself over his client. This type of behavior betrayed his social ideals and years of activism on behalf of the black community in Norfolk. Indeed, the State Bar Association found that this pattern of obvious misconduct and the complete lack of any remorse as more than ample grounds to disbar Gay formally in February 1994. Here once again, Gay broke the rules and saw himself as above the law: in politics, he appealed to the courts to change the rules and laws that he did not like, but, in his professional practice, such arrogance was a big liability—hurting the very family and community that he had always tried to help.[66]

Gay never rebounded from this disgrace. The depths of his professional and communal exile cannot be exaggerated—alienated from key family members, he ended up taking solace at the Reverend Jim Downing's All God's Children's Church, which was adjacent to the Tidewater AIDS Crisis and then (after 2001) Community Taskforce—a storefront church that

Figure 3.6. When James Gay returned to Norfolk in the 1970s, he ran a local law office and served as head of the Norfolk branch of the NAACP. Courtesy *Norfolk Journal and Guide*.

had and still has a heavily gay and transgender congregation. It was a far cry from hobnobbing with Norfolk's black elite at Grace Episcopal. His health deteriorated in the 1990s as well: a series of strokes brought on kidney failure and then dialysis. He continued to blame his predicament on city fathers who had it out for him because of success in the ward suit, and he never apologized for his own mistakes that had eclipsed his own considerable political legacy. When he died in 2008, old supporters in the press tried to gloss over his legal difficulties, but no one could ignore the steep fall he had endured.[67]

James Gay's creativity and passion in advocacy transformed the political and social landscape of Norfolk forever. He was a most effective and unusual undergraduate and sustained an impressive record of success into middle age. Winning the ward suit against Norfolk's well-entrenched oligarchy took a lot of chutzpah and bravado. But those very same qualities led him to make professional decisions that were decidedly unprofessional. He paid a very heavy price for his criminal behavior, and that price was probably greater than it should have been because of resentment or jealousy of his record of previous achievements. Nevertheless, in the long run, the civil rights won by James Gay outweigh his civil wrongs.

Notes

1. Earl Swift, "James Gay Awaits Kidney Transplant, Chance at New Life," *Virginian-Pilot*, Jan. 7, 2007, http://hamptonroads.com/node/204281. On Hal Bonney, see Mylene Mangalindan, "Hal J. Bonney Jr.—A Benchmark in Bankruptcy, the Federal Judge, a Complex Man Known for His Command of the Courtroom, Straight-Shooting Legal Opinions and Longtime Service in the Community, Is Stepping Down after Nearly 25 Years," *Virginian-Pilot*, Jan. 15, 1995; Denise Watson, "Former Segregationist Learns Respect for the Rule of Law," Oct. 1, 2008, http://hamptonroads.com/2008/09/former-opponent-integration-learns-respect-rule-law. On James G. Martin, see Amy Waters Yarsinske, *The Martin Years: Norfolk Will Always Remember Roy* (Gloucester Point, VA: Hallmark, 2001), 79–84. On Paul Riddick, see Harry Minium, "Feds Claim Norfolk Councilman Owes $246,000 in Unpaid Taxes," *Virginian-Pilot*, Jan. 19, 2012, http://hamptonroads.com/2012/01/feds-claim-norfolk-councilman-owes-246000-unpaid-taxes; Bill Sizemore, "Riddick Touts 22-Year Record in Norfolk Re-election Bid," *Virginian-Pilot*, Apr. 29, 2014, http://hamptonroads.com/2014/04/riddick-touts-22year-record-norfolk-reelection-bid; Harry Minium, "Riddick Offers No Apologies," *Virginian-Pilot*, May 1, 2012, http://hamptonroads.com/2012/05/column-paul-riddick-offers-no-apologies; "City Elections 2014 | Norfolk Results," *Virginian-Pilot*, May 6, 2014, http://hamptonroads.com/2014/05/city-elections-2014-norfolk-results. On Anthony Burfoot, see Jillian Nolin, "Election | Anthony Burfoot Elected Norfolk Treasurer," *Virginian-Pilot*, Nov. 6, 2013, http://hamptonroads.com/2013/11/election-anthony-burfoot-elected-norfolk-treasurer.

2. Earl Lewis, *In Their Own Interests: Race, Class, and Power in Twentieth-Century Virginia* (Berkeley: University of California Press, 1991), 11.

3. On the streetcar protests, see "Jim Crow Law Works Smoothly," *Virginian-Pilot*, June 15, 1906; "Is Great Falling Off in the Negro Traffic," *Ledger-Dispatch*, June 15, 1906; "Negroes Boycott Street Cars; Use Wagon," *Virginian-Pilot*, June 26, 1906; "Negroes Prepare for Boycott of Street Cars," *Virginian-Pilot*, July 15, 1906; "Jim Crow Bus Line Operating," *Virginian-Pilot*, Aug. 24, 1906; "Jim Crow Bus Line Is Not Big Success," *Virginian Pilot*, Aug. 29, 1906. On teacher pay-parity cases, see Jeffrey L. Littlejohn and Charles H. Ford, *Elusive Equality: Desegregation and Resegregation in Norfolk's Public Schools* (Charlottesville: University of Virginia Press, 2012), 8–47.

4. James Gay, interview by Jeffrey L. Littlejohn, Norfolk, Virginia, Feb. 21, 2007. See also, "Bishop McInnis to Take Up New Work in Chicago," *Journal and Guide*, Oct. 28, 1961.

5. James Gay, interview by Jeffrey L. Littlejohn, Norfolk, Virginia, Feb. 21, 2007. For coverage of the NAACP meeting, see Russell Porter, "Rights Plea Made by N.A.A.C.P. Head," *New York Times*, July 9, 1958; Russell Porter, "N.A.A.C.P. Urges Negro Voters to

Back Liberals, Not a Party," *New York Times*, July 14, 1958; Russell Porter, "Eisenhower Gets Integration Plea," *New York Times*, July 13, 1958.

6. James Gay, quoted in Bob Yuhnke, "Jim Gay YD State Pres.," *Virginia Weekly*, May 8, 1967.

7. Littlejohn and Ford, *Elusive Equality*, 80–113. See also Alexander S. Leidholdt, *Standing before the Shouting Mob: Lenoir Chambers and Virginia's Massive Resistance to Public-School Integration* (Tuscaloosa: University of Alabama Press, 1997); and Forrest R. White, *Pride and Prejudice: School Desegregation and Urban Renewal in Norfolk, 1950–1959* (Westport, CT: Praeger, 1992).

8. "In Talk with Superintendent: 'Let All Students Go to School,' BTW Pupils Ask," *Journal and Guide*, Oct. 4, 1958.

9. "Program, 24th Annual NAACP State Convention," Oct. 9–11, 1959, NAACP Papers, part 27, series A, reel 19.

10. John I. Brooks, "Marshall Hits State on Schools," *Virginian-Pilot*, Oct. 13, 1958; "26th Annual NAACP Meeting the Best in State's History," *Journal and Guide*, Oct. 18, 1958. (This article title incorrectly identifies the number of the state convention, which the NAACP program itself notes is the twenty-fourth annual convention.)

11. Memo to Members of Executive Boards, Virginia State Conference—NAACP from the Executive Secretary, Lester Banks, Dec. 1958, NAACP Papers, part 19, series D, reel 6. See also Lester Banks to Milton Gay Jr., Dec. 4, 1958, NAACP Papers, part 19, series D, reel 6. Milton and James traveled to Petersburg for the executive board meeting of the Virginia NAACP Youth Councils on November 15, 1958. At the meeting, the board put forward a bold program for the following year. It voted to hold a statewide voter registration contest, to begin a vigorous 1959 membership drive, and to begin publishing a newsletter. Milton was elected to chair the committee in charge of the suffrage contest, which would award two national scholarships that summer. For information on the scholarships, see Herbert L. Wright to Milton Gay, Feb. 24, 1959, NAACP Papers, part 19, series D, reel 6. One of the scholarships was to the 1959 Encampment for Citizenship Program, which was to be held at the Fieldston School in New York City from June 28 to Aug. 8, 1959. The second scholarship was to the 1959 Experiment in International Living project with preference to the Ghana or Israel study tours. That spring, Milton won the NAACP voter registration contest and received a scholarship to attend the "Encampment for Citizenship," a summer youth program that emphasized civic responsibility and cultural tolerance.

12. See W. Lester Banks to Milton Gay, Dec. 4, 1958, NAACP Papers, part 19, series D, reel 6; and Memo, "Operation Citizenship," Mar. 1959, NAACP Papers, part 19, series D, reel 6.

13. Memo, "Operation Citizenship," Mar. 1959, NAACP Papers, part 19, series D, reel 6.

14. "Politics in High Gear," *Journal and Guide*, Apr. 18, 1959.

15. "A Little Smoke, but No Fire," *Journal and Guide*, June 6, 1959; "Name-Calling Admitted: Cover-Up of Race Incidents at Norview Denied by Perdue," *Virginian-Pilot*, May 26, 1959.

16. Vivian Carter Mason, "Integration and Politics: The People Have 'Had It,'" *Journal and Guide*, June 6, 1959; Richard B. Martin, "When the Enemy Is Hurt," *Journal and Guide*, June 6, 1959.

17. Thomas L. Dabney, "Use Ballot For Freedom," *Journal and Guide*, May 2, 1959.

18. "5,000 Colored Voters Went to the Polls Tuesday: Electorate 'Informed,' Intelligent Confusion at a Minimum; Moderates Win Endorsement," *Journal and Guide*, July 18, 1959. See also "Election Contested, Suit to Void Vote Called Flimsy, 4400 Negro Ballots Are Protested, Defender Candidate Heads Group Trying to Use Old Ruling," *Journal and Guide*, Aug. 1, 1959.

19. "Statement of Virginia Youth Memberships," NAACP Papers, part 19, series D, reel 6. Richmond had 309 members. None of the other 58 branches in the state had more than 150 members.

20. "Meet Your State Leaders," *Freedom Press* 1, no. 3 (1959), NAACP Papers, part 19, series D, reel 6. See also "Program, 24th Annual NAACP State Convention," Oct. 9–11, 1959, NAACP Papers, part 27, series A, reel 19. For information on Laura Greene see "NAACP: The Virginia Defender," July–Aug. 1960, vol. 1, no. 3, NAACP Papers, part 19, series D, reel 6.

21. Herbert L. Wright to Gloster Current, Feb. 8, 1960, NAACP Papers, part 19, series D, reel 6.

22. William H. Chafe, *Civilities and Civil Rights: Greensboro, North Carolina, and the Black Struggle for Freedom* (New York: Oxford University Press, 1981); Howard Zinn, *SNCC: The New Abolitionists* (Boston: Beacon Press, 1964); David Halberstam, *The Children* (New York: Random House, 1998); Aldon Morris, "Black Southern Student Sit-In Movement: An Analysis of Internal Organization," *American Sociological Review* 46 (Dec. 1981): 744–67. For sit-ins before Greensboro see Carl L. Graves, "The Right to Be Served: Oklahoma City's Lunch Counter Sit-Ins, 1958–1964," *Chronicles of Oklahoma* 59 (1981): 152–66; Gretchen Cassell Eick, *Dissent in Wichita: The Civil Rights Movement in the Midwest, 1954–72* (Urbana: University of Illinois Press, 2001); and Ronald Walters, "Standing Up in America's Heartland: Sitting in before Greensboro," *American Visions* 8 (Feb./Mar. 1993): 20–23.

23. James Gay, interview by Jeffrey L. Littlejohn, Norfolk, Virginia, Feb. 21, 2007; Oscar Waller, telephone interview by Jeffrey L. Littlejohn, June 10, 2007; Grant Coleman, telephone interview by Jeffrey L. Littlejohn, July 1, 2007.

24. Eric Jones quoted in Cindy Schreuder, "Color Barrier Fell 25 Years Ago," *Virginian-Pilot* and *Ledger Star*, Mar. 24, 1985.

25. "Sitters Move On Norfolk—Portsmouth Also Hit; Elizabeth City Tense," *Virginian-Pilot*, Feb. 13, 1960.

26. "Sitters Hint at Cool-Off," *Virginian-Pilot*, Feb. 16, 1960.

27. For information, see William Connelly, "White and Negro Students Fight Briefly at MidCity," *Virginian-Pilot*, Feb. 17, 1960; William Connelly, "Crowd Mills; 27 Arrested—No Violence Recurs at Shopping Center," *Virginian-Pilot*, Feb. 18, 1960.

28. "Responsibility at the Lunch Counter," *Virginian-Pilot*, Feb. 18, 1960; "Who Stands Up for Law and Order?" *Virginian-Pilot*, Feb. 19, 1960. See also "Trespass Acts in a Hurry," *Virginian-Pilot*, Feb. 26, 1960, which states that "the mass demonstrations

... have outlived any usefulness they possessed ... and can degenerate into new and serious difficulties."

29. "Sitdown Protests Spread," *Virginian-Pilot*, Feb. 21, 1960.

30. "Sitdowns Giving Way to Boycotts," *Virginian-Pilot*, Mar. 4, 1960.

31. "Sitdowns Giving Way to Boycotts."

32. James Gay, "A Negro Student Speaks," *Virginian-Pilot*, Mar. 4, 1960.

33. Harry Truman quoted in Clayton Knowles, "Truman Believes Reds Lead Sit-Ins," *New York Times*, Apr. 19, 1960.

34. "Senate Rushes Trespass Bills: Governor Asks Moves to Discourage Sitdowns," *Virginian-Pilot*, Feb. 25, 1960. Senator Fred Bateman of Newport News, who ushered the bills through the General Assembly, said that the new restrictions did not mean that the state would enforce segregation in stores and eating establishments. Rather, he argued that the state would "protect the rights of the private property owner to conduct his business as he might legally choose" ("Stiff Trespass Laws Signed by Governor," *Virginian-Pilot*, Feb. 26, 1960).

35. "Stiff Trespass Laws Signed by Governor."

36. "Protesters March, Library Closes," *Virginian-Pilot*, Feb. 28, 1960.

37. See for example Peter Wallenstein, *Blue Laws and Black Codes: Conflict, Courts, and Change in Twentieth-Century Virginia* (Charlottesville: University of Virginia Press, 2004), 114–41.

38. "Trespass Acts in a Hurry."

39. Ellis James, "The Negro in Public Life," *Virginian-Pilot*, Mar. 7, 1960.

40. "Commendation," *Journal and Guide*, Apr. 2, 1960.

41. "Cooling Off Hinted in Sitdown Activity," *Virginian-Pilot*, Feb. 16, 1960.

42. "Convicted of Passing Out Handbills, Pupils Appeal," *Journal and Guide*, Apr. 23, 1960.

43. Harold Anderson quoted in Schreuder, "Color Barrier Fell 25 Years Ago."

44. On Thursday, April 14, Donald M. Giddens and William E. Thorton Jr., both students at the VSCN, were arrested for distributing NAACP leaflets in downtown Norfolk. Judge Llewelly S. Richardson of municipal court assessed the two college students fifteen dollars each on April 15 ("Distribution Will Go On, Robertson Says," *Journal and Guide*, Apr. 16, 1960). Meanwhile, Juvenile Court judge Alfred W. Whitehurst fined the three boys ten dollars each on April 18. They were arrested Friday night (April 15) while passing out handbills in front of W.T. Grant's on Granby Street. The boys were released into custody of their parents. ("Students Appeal Litter Penalties," *Virginian-Pilot*, Apr. 20, 1960).

45. James Gay, interview by Jeffrey L. Littlejohn, Norfolk, Virginia, Mar. 16, 2007.

46. "Lunch Counter Protest Appeals on Way for 10," *Journal and Guide*, Apr. 30, 1960.

47. "Distribution Will Go On, Robertson Says"; "Lunch Counter Protest Appeals on Way for 10."

48. William P. Rogers quoted in "Executives Meet with Attorney General—He Stresses Voluntary Nature of Moves—Towns Not Listed," *New York Times*, Aug. 11, 1960.

49. "In Norfolk Lunch Counter Desegregation Effort: Ministers, NAACP, Students Worked Together," *Journal and Guide*, Aug. 6, 1960.

50. Milton Gay quoted in "In Norfolk Lunch Counter Desegregation Effort."
51. Milton Gay quoted in Schreuder, "Color Barrier Fell 25 Years Ago."
52. James Gay, interview by Jeffrey L. Littlejohn, Norfolk, Virginia, Mar. 16, 2007.
53. "In Norfolk Lunch Counter Desegregation Effort."
54. "Norfolk Pushes 3-Prong Drive Toward Rights," *Journal and Guide*, June 22, 1963; Bob Yuhnke, "Jim Gay YD State Pres.," *Virginia Weekly*, May 8, 1967.
55. "Council Rejects Students' Pleas; Racial Problems Boil: Rocky Start for Advisory Group," *Journal and Guide*, June 29, 1963.
56. James Gay, interview by Jeffrey L. Littlejohn, Norfolk, Virginia, Mar. 16, 2007; Bill Sauder, "Anti-Bias Agenda Set," *Ledger-Dispatch*, July 8, 1963.
57. On the Booker T. Washington walkout, see Littlejohn and Ford, *Elusive Equality*, 114–16.
58. "The Councilmen and the Student," *Journal and Guide*, May 9, 1964.
59. James Gay, interview by Jeffrey L. Littlejohn, Norfolk, Virginia, Mar. 16, 2007; Obie McCollum, "Looking On in Norfolk," *Journal and Guide*, June 12, 1965.
60. Bob Yuhnke, "Jim Gay YD State Pres.," *Virginia Weekly*, May 8, 1967.
61. James Gay, interview by Jeffrey L. Littlejohn, Norfolk, Virginia, Mar. 16, 2007; "TABL Brightens Area's Business Picture: Provides Financial, Technical Assistance for Minority Firms, Better Business Opportunities for Black People Is Primary Purpose of Local Organization," *Journal and Guide*, Mar. 18, 1972.
62. "Reorganization Interracial: Gay Elected President of Pharmaceutical Co.," *Journal and Guide*, Jan. 17, 1970; "Coastal Pharmaceutical Board Okays Expansion," *Journal and Guide*, Feb. 21, 1976; Marvin Leon Lake, "President Unseated in Drug Firm's Dispute," *Virginian-Pilot*, May 9, 1977.
63. Milton A. Reid, "Two More Seek Council Seats," *Journal and Guide*, Feb. 24, 1982; "Democrats Endorse Gay, Collins; Green, Butts Respond," *Journal and Guide*, Apr. 7, 1982; Bill Nachman, "Campaign Rifts Brew in Norfolk," *Journal and Guide*, Apr. 7, 1982; "Support Grows for Ward System," *Journal and Guide*, May 19, 1982.
64. Tammie Smith, "City Faces Large Civil Rights Battle; Suit Filed for Elimination of At-Large Elections in Norfolk," *Journal and Guide*, Aug. 17, 1983; Collins v. City of Norfolk, 605 F. Supp. 377 (E.D. VA 1984); Collins v. City of Norfolk, 768 F.2d 572 (4th Cir. 1985); Collins v. City of Norfolk, 478 U.S. 1016 (1986).
65. Collins v. City of Norfolk, 605 F. Supp. 377 (E.D. VA 1984); Collins v. City of Norfolk, 768 F.2d 572 (4th Cir. 1985); Collins v. City of Norfolk, 478 U.S. 1016 (1986); Collins v. City of Norfolk, 816 F.2d 932 (4th Cir. 1987); Collins v. City of Norfolk, 679 F. Supp. 557 (E.D. VA 1988); Collins v. City of Norfolk, 883 F.2d 1232 (4th Cir. 1989); City of Norfolk v. Collins, 498 U.S. 938 (1990). For press coverage, see "Norfolk Voters Will Elect under 7-Ward System," *Journal and Guide*, June 12, 1991; Leonard E. Colvin, "Court Orders Norfolk City Officials to Design New Ward System," *Journal and Guide*, Jan. 9, 1991; Leonard E. Colvin, "At-Large Outlawed: Norfolk Voting System Ruled Barrier, Unfair," *Journal and Guide*, Aug. 23, 1989, 1; and Leonard E. Colvin, "Ward Voting System to Change Norfolk Politics," *Journal and Guide*, Nov. 7, 1990.
66. Order of the Virginia State Bar Disciplinary Board in Virginia State Bar, Ex Rel. Second District Committee v. James F. Gay, docket no. 81–37, June 9, 1982; Order of

the Virginia State Bar Disciplinary Board, in Virginia State Bar, Ex Rel. Second District Committee v. James F. Gay, docket no. 87-0279, Apr. 26, 1989; James Gay v. Virginia State Bar, Ex Rel. Second District Committee, 239 Va. 401 (VA Supreme Court, 1990); Order of Administrative Suspension before the Virginia State Bar Disciplinary Board in the Matter of James Ferbee Gay, docket nos. 90-020-0095, 90-020-0783, 90-020-0848, 90-020-1072, Sept. 9, 1996; Order of Revocation before the Virginia State Bar Disciplinary Board in the Matter of James Ferbee Gay, docket nos. 90-020-0095, 90-020-1072, 90-020-0848, 90-020-0108, 90-020-0783, Feb. 24, 1994.

67. Leonard E. Colvin, "James F. Gay: Helped Reform Elections in Norfolk," *Journal and Guide*, Apr. 23, 2008; Harry Minium, "Activist Took First Steps on the Path to Council's Diversity," *Virginian-Pilot*, Apr. 27, 2008.

4

Revisiting the Urban Revolts of the 1960s

York, Pennsylvania—A Case Study

PETER B. LEVY

> That was a time when racism was everywhere.... What the people felt was going on in the southern counties, it wasn't only going on down there, it was going on right here.
>
> Stephen Freeland, 2003

Shortly after sundown on July 21, 1969, Lillie Belle Allen, age twenty-seven, of Aiken, South Carolina, was murdered in York, Pennsylvania, in the midst of nearly a week of racial turmoil at the tail end of a decade of civil unrest. The day before, Allen and her family set out for Brooklyn, New York, where her older brother Benjamin had migrated years before. She planned a brief stop in York along the way to visit her sister Hattie. As Allen drove northward the nation celebrated mankind's first successful moon landing and Neil Armstrong's unprecedented lunar walk. Unbeknownst to Allen, racial tensions had boiled over in York shortly before she departed Aiken. By the evening of the twenty-first, dozens of men and women, black and white, had already been shot, including Officer Henry Schaad, a rookie policeman. (He would later die from the gunshot wound he incurred on July 18.) Yet Allen and her family had little if any sense that they were in danger when they set out to buy some food after a relaxing day in the countryside at her brother-in-law's favorite fishing spot. As they approached the railroad tracks that crossed North Newberry Street, Hattie, who was driving her father's Cadillac, recalled seeing a white man with a gun pointed in their direction. "Lord," she yelled, "they're getting ready to shoot!" In a panic, Hattie tried to turn the car around. When she proved unable to do so, Lillie Belle Allen stepped out of the car with the intention of taking over the driving from her sister Hattie. But no sooner had she stepped out of the car than she was met by a fusillade of gunshots. The gang of whites who shot at Allen had mistaken her and the vehicle she was in for another car, which they feared was occupied by young black men whom they had been battling since the most recent turmoil had begun. Allen was the quintessential innocent bystander; she was in the wrong place at the wrong time and, as one reporter put it, in the "wrong car."[1]

Largely ignored by the press and historians and conveniently forgotten by York's citizens, Allen's murder and the riots that surrounded it captured international attention over thirty years later when in mid-May 2001 its two-term mayor, Charlie Robertson, was arrested and charged with murder in connection with Allen's death. From as far away as Alberta, Canada, to London, England, the story that a mayor of a U.S. city had killed a "preacher's daughter" made headlines. As *Newsweek* reported, "Mayor Charlie Robertson of York, Pa., should have been a shoo-in this fall for a third term. For the past decade, York has cheerfully prospered under his leadership, and the town of rolling green hills and integrated neighborhoods is still undergoing a $100 million building boom. But . . . last week, just as the mayor was celebrating a tight Democratic primary victory, police put him in handcuffs." Specifically, authorities claimed that Robertson, who had been a police officer in 1969, had supplied the bullets that others had used in Allen's murder and inspired white gang members to defend their turf, which included North Newberry Street. The mayor acknowledged that he had shouted "white power" at a gathering in a nearby park the night before Allen's shooting, but he denied that he had provided one gang member with a 30.06 rifle and encouraged him to "kill as many niggers as you can." He also rebuffed suggestions that he had stated that if he "wasn't a cop [he'd] be leading commando raids against black neighborhood," as attested to by one witness. A week after he was indicted, Robertson reluctantly agreed to withdraw from the race for mayor, leaving behind a city that he had served first as a police officer and then as a government official for over thirty-five years. Calling the decision the "most painful I have ever made in my life," Robertson vowed to defend himself, accusing the Republican district attorney and the Republican-owned local newspaper with pursuing the case to further their ambitions. Ten other white men were indicted for Allen's murder alongside

Robertson. Subsequently, two black men were indicted for the murder of Office Henry Schaad, whose case, like Allen's, had gone unsolved for over thirty years. (In part because the specific charges against him were harder to prove, Robertson was not convicted but all of the other defendants in both cases were.)[2]

* * *

In a ten-year period between 1960 and 1970 America experienced over 750 riots or uprisings (defined as involving at least thirty participants and personal injury, property damage, or both). Upward of 525 cities were affected, including nearly every city with a black population over fifty thousand. Of the 100 largest cities in the nation, at least 88 experienced rioting.[3] As contemporaries from Martin Luther King Jr. to H. Rap Brown observed, and as most historians have agreed, these rebellions demonstrated the inadequacies or shortcomings of the civil rights movement, waking up the nation to the fact that the enactment of the Civil Rights Act of 1964 and the Voting Rights Act of 1965 did not signify the fulfillment of the black freedom struggle. In recognition of these shortcomings, King, the Student Nonviolent Coordinating Committee (SNCC), and others reoriented their efforts in an attempt to speak to and for the riot participants. The uprisings challenged the primacy of nonviolence as a means to overcoming racial inequality, bolstered the Black Power movement, and boosted the fortunes of the New Right. Just as significantly, they demonstrated that race was not a southern problem but rather one that knew no regional boundaries.[4]

All this said, our understanding of the urban revolts of the 1960s, especially when compared to other aspects of the civil rights movement, remains underdeveloped. Most problematically, the vast majority of scholarship focuses on rioting that took place in large cities—Watts, Los Angeles, in 1965 and Detroit, Michigan, and Newark, New Jersey, in 1967—when in fact more revolts took place in midsize communities, with between twenty-five thousand and one hundred thousand residents, than took place in big cities. In addition, nearly all research has examined revolts that took place before 1969. Because York's revolt took place during the summer of 1969 and because its population stood at approximately fifty thousand, this study allows us to begin to rectify these shortcomings and to consider the degree to which place and time shaped the nature of the revolts and to a lesser extent their causes and consequences. Finally, both York's size and the availability of an extraordinary amount of source material—ranging from contemporary news coverage and state investigatory reports to more recent trial transcripts and oral histories—allows us to arrive at a more intimate feeling for the urban revolts of the era than usual.[5]

* * *

Because the roots of the unfulfilled expectations and frustrations of African Americans who migrated north began in the South, our journey to understand York's riot begins with a brief detour to Aiken, South Carolina, years before Lillie Belle Allen commenced her summer trip. Between 1920 and 1970 hundreds of thousands of South Carolina's blacks left their "native" soil, joining millions of other African Americans in the Great Migration to the North (also West and urban South). Following the railroad lines, a significant percentage of these migrants ended up in Pennsylvania. Of those who moved to York, a disproportionate number came from Aiken and Bamberg Counties in South Carolina. They were pushed out by an array of well-known factors, ranging from poverty and unequal education to political powerlessness and the indignity of Jim Crow. But one factor stood out: white violence. Aiken was a Ku Klux Klan stronghold. Its members regularly terrorized blacks, making sure that they stayed in their "place," namely on the bottom and silent.[6]

A particularly notorious lynching in 1926 drove home this feature of white supremacy. As the NAACP's Walter White wrote in *Rope and Faggot*, the brutal triple murder or lynching of Bertha, Damon, and Clarence Lowman, of Aiken, on October 8, 1926, was conducted with the full knowledge of the "members of the South Carolina legislature, relatives of the Governor, lawyers, farmers, business men, and politicians," not to mention the newly minted sheriff, who was an open leader in the Klan. The triple murder occurred about a year after law enforcement officials had engaged in a shootout at the Lowmans' property, which had resulted in the death of the local sheriff. Remarkably, an appellate court exonerated the Lowmans of the sheriff's death. But whites cared less about the guilt or innocence of the Lowmans than they did about sending a message to all regarding the proper place of blacks in South Carolina. By the time of the shootout, Sam Lowman, the son of slaves and the patriarch of the family, had learned to read and write and become a self-sufficient farmer, an owner of a Ford touring car, and a registered voter. Put somewhat differently, he and his family were guilty of demonstrating "too much independence," and for this reason Bertha, Damon, and Clarence Lowman were lynched.[7]

Twenty years later in the immediate aftermath of World War II white supremacists in the region again used the weapon of violence to remind blacks of their second-class status. In this instance, Sergeant Isaac Woodard, a World War II veteran who was headed home after three years of serving his country, was "beaten with a nightstick and blinded" by Aiken's chief of police. As with the Lowman lynching, a trial followed, though this time the sheriff was the defendant. Not surprisingly justice again proved it was *not* color blind, as a jury—to the cheers of a jam-packed courtroom—acquitted Sheriff Linwood Shull of all charges. Internationally, Woodard's case, along with those of a handful of other black soldiers who were viciously attacked upon their completion of the service, became a cause celebre. Folk singer Woody Guthrie, for one, released a song entitled "The Blinding of Isaac Woodard." And President Harry Truman appointed his Commission on Civil Rights in part in reaction to this atrocity. But for African Americans who resided in Aiken, these acts were small solace and they had little if any impact on their daily lives.[8]

Whether the Lowmans' lynching or Woodard's blinding affected members of Lillie Belle Allen's extended family remains unclear. But white violence certainly was one of the forces that pushed black residents of Aiken to join the Great Migration, and the promise of a more just society was just as certainly one of the factors that pulled them northward. It would be naïve to suggest that African American migrants expected the North to be a place of milk and honey, but, at the least, they believed they were escaping law enforcement authorities who were one and the same with the Ku Klux Klan. York, like the other cities, also attracted Aiken's blacks by offering economic opportunities that were unavailable in the South. In 1950, for instance, the median per capita income of blacks in York was nearly double what it was for blacks in Aiken County, $1,353 versus $758. In other words, blacks believed that changing their geographical home would enhance their place in American society.[9]

While we do not know how Aiken's blacks first learned that there were jobs in York, during the 1920s and even more so during World War II and after, the "White Rose City," as it was known, had a wide array of openings, especially in its many manufacturing establishments, such as American Chain and Cable, and Schmidt and Ault Paper, all of which paid much better than work in South Carolina. True, not all of York's firms opened their doors to blacks and many blacks were relegated to low-skilled and poorly paid service positions, such as porters, custodians, and day laborers. Nonetheless, the pull of these jobs, along with the relative greater sense of social freedom that existed in the North compared to the South, was strong enough to ensure a steady stream of newcomers. As a result, the black population in York grew steadily from under 2,000 in 1920 to over 6,500 fifty years later, a 300 percent increase. Even though they constituted a much smaller percentage of the total population than in Baltimore and Philadelphia, which lay to the south and east, respectively, of York, blacks in York built a vibrant community, which included black churches, fraternal associations, and social clubs. Crispus Attucks, a social service association named after the black revolutionary hero who died at the Boston Massacre, for instance, played a central role in the life of much of York's African American community. The NAACP established a branch in York with the goal of eradicating Jim Crow in the city's schools and facilities. Just as importantly blacks developed close interpersonal ties that helped them grapple with economic hardships during the Depression and after. Or as Eric Kirkland, whose parents migrated from Bamberg, South Carolina (the county adjacent to Aiken), in the mid-1920s noted, "we were all like one big family."[10]

This said, in the areas of housing, recreation, employment, education, and especially relations with the police and "city hall," York's many blacks found that they had migrated to a promised land that wasn't. As of 1970, blacks constituted 13 percent of York's population, with the vast majority living in two of the city's sixteen census tracts, 10 and 7 (see figure 4.1). Housing in census tract 10, which as of 1960 was the only majority-black tract, was, in a word, abysmal. Out of a total of 1,121 housing units in this tract in 1960, nearly a third were rated as either deteriorated or dilapidated. The medium value of units in the tract in 1970 stood at sixty-one hundred dollars, a third less than the city average, and the vast majority of blacks in the city could not afford to own a home. Instead they were compelled by economic circumstances and de facto segregation to live in rental units, many of which lacked adequate heating, plumbing, or both. Urban renewal, sometimes termed "negro removal" by civil rights activists, left blacks fending for a declining stock of the urban housing that they could afford and that realtors and rental agents were willing to show them in the first place. The destruction of the Codorus Street and the Frey Ave

Figure 4.1. York, Pennsylvania, census tracts by race, 1960.

communities, two centers of black life, a byproduct of the city's limited urban renewal program, left close to two hundred black families looking for a place to live in a housing market that already inadequately met their needs.[11] To make matters worse, throughout the era, city hall proved unresponsive to the black community's call for better housing, applying for federal funds for public housing reluctantly if at all and enforcing housing codes just as ineffectively.[12]

To make matters worse, the housing travails of York's black community occurred in the midst of a suburban boom, and in York County, as elsewhere in the 1950s and 1960s, the suburbs were virtually all-white. In 1960, 99.9 percent of those who lived in York's suburbs were white; ten years later the number stood at 99.6 percent. In contrast to the deteriorating and overcrowded housing in the inner city, homes in the suburbs were replete with modern amenities and saw their values steadily increase. This suburban boom was fed by the out-migration of whites from York. After changing city boundaries have been adjusted for, the city lost 8,464 whites between 1960 and 1970, continuing a trend that had begun in 1950. The fact that the city's white population, starting from a peak of 56,699, had fallen to 43,556 just half a year after York's riots belies the common belief

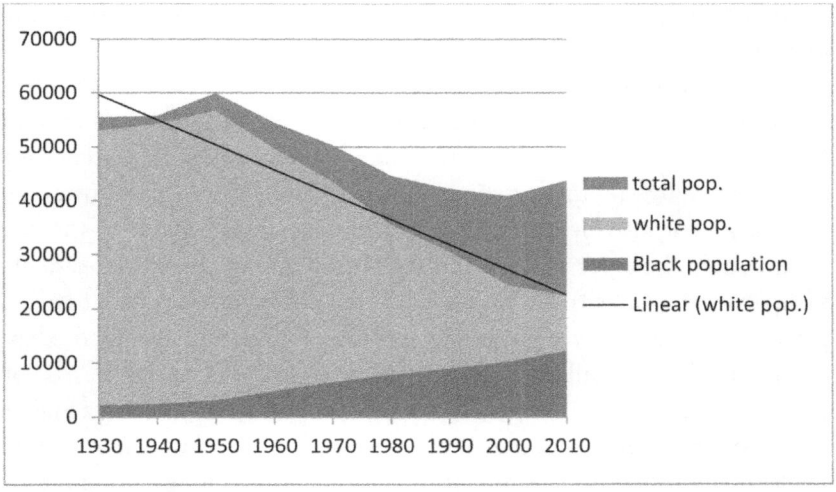

Figure 4.2. York, Pennsylvania, population, 1930 to 2010.

that the riots caused white flight, unless one assumes that the vast majority of those who fled did so in the last five months of 1969 (see figure 4.2). What these demographic statistics tend to mask is that a significant segment of the white population that remained in the city suffered from some of the same housing problems as York's black population and may have underlain a good deal of the white anxiety of the period. For instance, census tract 16, where the Newberry Street Boys who were associated with Allen's murder resided, tied with census tract 10 for last in terms of "substandard" housing. As of 1960, over half of the homes in this tract were rated as deteriorated or dilapidated, a significantly greater proportion than in tract 10.[13] Just as significantly, housing prices in the city faced downward pressures at a time when homes were becoming the primary investment of many Americans.

While the overall employment situation in York through most of the 1960s remained strong (which helps explain the continued in-migration of blacks to the city), persistent discrimination at the workplace combined with shifts in the labor market, both spatially and occupationally, added to the growing frustrations of many black Yorkers and perhaps of some younger white city residents. Throughout this era, York remained a blue-collar town, especially for men. Partly fueled by defense spending and by the competitiveness of many of the firms located in the region, manufacturing jobs grew at a steady pace, from 36,160 in 1960 to 42,292 in 1970, a 20 percent increase. An even faster rise in white-collar and service work combined with the fact that York had a relatively diverse mix of industries—from machinery and metal fabrication to paper and food production—resulted in low unemployment rates, 3.2 percent for the city in 1970.[14] Yet these statistics masked the economic circumstances for many African Americans. Unemployment rates for blacks in the city were double those for whites, and twice as many of the city's residents were unemployed as those who lived in the suburbs. Blacks held lower-paying jobs, earning on average well less than whites. In 1970, the median income for black families in York stood at $6,118, well under $8,762 for county residents, in spite of the fact that black women worked at a higher rate than their white counterparts. One reason for this disparity was outright discrimination. A survey of ninety-nine employers conducted in 1961 found that 75 percent did not have any black employees and 10 percent declared they would not hire blacks "under any circumstances." While the Civil Rights Act of 1964 made such blatant discrimination illegal, blacks in York still encountered road barriers to obtaining skilled and well-paying jobs. The Pennsylvania Human Relations Commission, for instance, observed "striking examples of Black college graduates denied employment at commensurate skill levels" and businesses did not afford blacks equal chances for "advancement" once they obtained a job.[15]

Moreover, even in manufacturing, many of the best paying and more secure jobs were located in new plants outside the city, making it more difficult for York's blacks to secure employment. Along the same line, blacks tended to work at older, less productive, and ultimately less profitable firms (or branches), thus placing them at greater risk for seasonal layoffs and, in the long run, making them more susceptible to deindustrialization. With lower rates of education (see below), blacks were not as able as whites to buffer themselves from the changing economy by finding employment in the more rapidly growing sectors of the economy. They had also accumulated fewer savings to weather downturns. This proved particularly true for blacks who lived in census tracts 7 and 10, where the poverty rate stood at 34 percent, more than triple the city average and almost seven times higher than in the county overall.[16]

Somewhat similarly, even though blacks enjoyed much better educational opportunities in York than they did in the South, unequal education remained the rule. Until *Brown v. Board of Education*, blacks in York attended segregated elementary schools—either James Smallwood or Aquilla Howard. After *Brown*, these schools were closed. Still, racial discrimination pervaded the system. McKinley Elementary School, which was 54 percent nonwhite in 1968, did not have a gym or library and the student-to-teacher ratio was higher than at the "white" schools. At Hanna Penn Junior High School, which was integrated, the Human Relations Commission found "a racist attitude on the part of teachers," as evidenced by "frequent recourse to corporal punishment." At William Penn High School (WPHS), black faculty and staff were underrepresented, making up only 3 percent of the employees, whereas black students composed 23 percent of the student body. Guidance counselors steered blacks away from attending college, and black students were disproportionately placed in low level classes. In 1967, for example, only fourteen of four hundred nonwhite students took the College Board examination. Sam Manson recalled that an "overwhelming number of Black students were assigned to . . . special education and low academic level classrooms in the basement also known as the dungeon of the building." Nonetheless, the educational system proved more responsive to black demands for reform than did other sectors of York society. Most notably, in the immediate aftermath of Martin Luther King Jr.'s assassination, black students at WPHS forged a protest movement that won significant concessions from the city, from the hiring of more black staff and teachers to the introduction of African American history into the curriculum.[17]

The 1960s were an era of heightened expectations as well as poor relations between blacks on one hand and the police and city hall on the other. After holding investigatory hearings due largely to complaints of police abuse, the Pennsylvania Human Relations Commission (PHRC) concluded that "the Police Department of the City of York" seemed more concerned with maintaining "the status quo than maintaining the peace." The PHRC observed that the police department's use of the canine corps displayed the racist attitudes of many on the force and substantiated the black community's view that the police used dogs "to instill fear in Black Youths."[18] Countless attempts to get "city hall," especially York's Mayor John Snyder, to address the black community's concerns about the police got nowhere. In the summer of 1963, following the mauling of two black men who were already in custody by police dogs, blacks staged a protest at city hall. Coming in the immediate aftermath of the vicious use of German shepherds in Birmingham, Alabama, which generated a national outcry, one might have thought that Mayor Snyder would have rethought his decision to deploy police dogs. Instead, Snyder defended their use, which in turn led to repeated instances of abuse, black protest, and Snyder's insistence on the value of the canine corps.[19]

Even though York averted riots during the long hot summer of 1967 and in the spring of 1968, following Martin Luther King's assassination, the city experienced a series of mini-riots or disturbances in the summer and fall of 1968, all of which grew out of and displayed the long-standing grievances of the black community, particularly regarding the police and the irresponsiveness of "city hall." The first occurred in mid-July when police ordered fifty black youths to leave Penn Common Park and arrested two for refusing to obey their orders. Rather than bringing the confrontation to a close, the situation escalated, culminating with shots being fired by a police officer. At first the police denied they had fired their guns; subsequently, Police Chief Landis explained that Patrolman Wayne Toomey fired into the air, as a warning, though he acknowledged that this too violated police procedures. Both the shooting, which witnesses claimed nearly struck a nearby resident, and the police obfuscation angered the community, with one black man angrily accusing Landis of harboring "racists in your outfit." News that the incident was precipitated by the police decision to enforce a curfew ordinance that had recently been annulled angered many residents even more, with one youth adding, "Why do they have to disperse a group of blacks? What's wrong with congregating in the park?"[20] In the immediate aftermath of the shooting, some stores were trashed, gunshots were exchanged, and the police were put on high alert.

The second mini-riot, which took place in early August 1968, proved more serious than the first. This "riot" was precipitated by a confrontation between Chester Roach, a middle-aged white man who lived above Hoffman's Meat Market, at 226 South Penn Street, a mere block from where Schaad would be shot the following year. While accounts of the altercation varied, it appears that the trouble began when Roach yelled at youths for making too much noise outside of his window at approximately 11:30 at night. Apparently, when the youths yelled back, Roach began firing at them first with a pellet gun and then with a shotgun, striking ten, at least one seriously. When police arrived they largely ignored black complaints and did not place Roach under arrest. When tensions flared, the police deployed two recently acquired armored trucks and upward of two-thirds of the police force in full riot equipment. Black anger over the shooting and police response reached new heights. "This is open warfare," declared one youth. "Whitey made his statement last night. He said, 'I hate you niggers and I'm going to kill you.' So baby if whitey is going to start shooting, you better bet I'm firing back." Another teen stated that he had "never thought very much about the black power philosophy but that the Penn [Roach] street shooting changed his mind," adding, "if he had been black do you think the cops would have left him there firing a gun? Man, if a black man had been in that house the cops would have bombed him out.... But it was a white man. And ... they were probably glad that he was just shooting some niggers that the cops wouldn't have to shoot themselves."[21]

The third mini-riot took place in the fall of 1968 following a football game between York's William Penn Senior High and Cedar Cliff High, from Camp Hill, a predominantly white suburb of Harrisburg, about twenty miles north of York. After the game, fights broke out between some of the fans, and then, as the crowd spilled into York's downtown area, more disorder broke out. York's city police exacerbated the situation by selectively sicking their police dogs on black youths. By night's end, at least seven had to be hospitalized for dog bites. Reverend Adam Kittrell declared that the dogs attacked "a number of the youths" who were "doing nothing." Police asserted that those bitten had refused to obey their orders to clear the area. Yet one newspaper story clearly suggested otherwise. According to the *York Gazette and Daily*, Calvin Stokes, a fifteen-year-old black youth, was stopped by police as he was walking home from the game, allegedly for jaywalking in front of a car. While two policemen ushered Stokes toward their police car, a third policeman, Nevin Barley, who had a notorious reputation in the black community, sicked the dog on Stokes. After being badly bitten by Barley's German shepherd, Stokes was thrown into the patrol car, with police allegedly terming him "one of those smart niggers." The police also took umbrage at a reporter for the *York Gazette and Daily*, Arthur Magida, who sought to take photographs of the action. He claimed that they sicked a police dog on him and broke his camera. Incredibly, the police countered that Magida had thrown the camera down on the ground and broken it himself. (Throughout the era, York had two newspapers: the *York Dispatch* and the *York Gazette and Daily*. The latter was by far the more liberal of the two papers and was the home newspaper of syndicated political cartoonist Walt Party Miller, who was famous for his left-leaning political cartoons on civil rights and the Vietnam War.)[22]

While some longtime York residents recall the riots as one long continuum, in fact a significant lull took place between the third mini-riot in September 1968 and the eruption of virtual warfare in July 1969. To understand the latter development, we need to consider both some of the external and internal forces that help explain its severity. Outside of the city of York, the nation was in the midst of its most tumultuous times since the civil war, including a massive wave of urban revolts following Martin Luther King Jr.'s assassination, intense protests at colleges and universities over the Vietnam War and a variety of other campus issues, feminist demonstrations against sexism at the Miss America pageant in Atlantic City, and violent confrontations between police and largely young activists in the streets of Chicago during the Democratic National Convention. These developments emboldened those on both ends of the political spectrum, nationally and locally. Rather than accommodate calls for peace and calm, a growing number of blacks and whites (including some members of the police force) embraced increasingly confrontational rhetoric and behavior. One way we can glean York's shift away from the consensus or centrist mood of the early and mid-1960s is to briefly examine its political history. Whereas President Johnson won 70 percent of York's vote in 1964, four years later 55 percent of the electorate supported Nixon or George Wallace. And in 1972, even though registered Democrats continued to outnumber Republicans, the city completed its rightward swing, giving the Nixon-Agnew ticket 68.2 percent of their vote. While race was not the only issue driving York's voters to the right, it should be noted that in 1968, 9 percent of the city voted for George Wallace, a symbol of Jim Crow. In the city's Ninth Ward, which was overwhelmingly white and Democratic, Wallace won nearly 17 percent of the vote.[23]

Congressman George Goodling's career similarly displayed the shift away from centrist politics in the region. First elected to Congress in 1960 as a moderate "Eisenhower/Rockefeller" Republican—he voted for the Civil Rights Act of 1964—Goodling lost to Nathaniel Craly, a Democrat, in 1964. In 1966, Goodling won back his seat and henceforth went out of his way to become identified with white backlash. He described the poor people's march, which Martin Luther King Jr. had been busy organizing on the eve of his assassination, as "the most disgusting sight I had ever seen" and disputed the claim that "chronic poverty" existed in America.[24]

Like Spiro Agnew, Goodling's political neighbor who enjoyed a meteoric rise from Baltimore County executive to the vice presidency in less than four years, Goodling rejected claims that white racism caused the riots and calls to spend more money on poverty programs. Indeed, Goodling embraced Agnew at the state convention of the Young Republicans at the Yorktown Hotel in the fall of 1968, where the vice presidential nominee slammed the Johnson administration for funding militants and enabling anarchists. (Congressman William Goodling, George Goodling's son, would serve as a character witness for Charlie Robertson in 2002, describing Charlie and his brother Wibie—who was also a police officer—as "lifelong friends.")[25]

At the grassroots level, evidence of white backlash abounded. When WPHS's principal, Dr. O. Meredith Parry, allowed black students to stage a walkout following Martin Luther King Jr.'s assassination, one teacher not only protested that the students should have been forced to attend class, disciplined, or both, but he also added that "the auditorium would have to be fumigated because of the all-black assembly." During the Pennsylvania Human Rights Commission (PCHR) hearings in York, Corporal Peter Chantiles went out of his way to disrupt its proceedings, openly calling the entire hearings "useless" and warning one of the witnesses, "You better get your goddamn facts straight . . . [or] I'll fix you." When Director of Public Safety Jacob Hose was asked whether Chantiles would face discipline for his public outburst, Hose responded that Chantiles was there "as a private citizen [and] I don't know how you'd keep anybody out who wanted to come in."[26]

Rather than accept the PHRC's call for police reform, the Citizens' Council of York demanded an end to the "coddling [of] lawless elements in the community." Residents of the Salem Square neighborhood, which abutted the West End, demonstrated that they had no intention of kowtowing to black demands. "They're trying to take over this county and we're not going to let them," one resident of the Salem Square neighborhood informed a newspaper reporter. "White people are roaming about Salem square with weapons waiting for any Negro to leave his cordoned off ghetto," explained another white man. "The police had better get in charge of this situation or we will."[27] Somewhat similarly, whereas civil rights groups in York demanded the suspension of Officers Toomey and Chantiles, one white teenager applauded them for having fired at black youths. "I wish I'd [been] out there with Toomey," the white teen explained, "blasting away at them niggers with a .30-20. I'd have gotten about 20 of them." Seeing York as fertile territory, Roy Frankhouser and George Houser, leaders of the KKK in Pennsylvania, planned a "robed march" in York for November 12, 1968. An early freak snowstorm, however, prompted them to call off the march. Nonetheless, some assert that York County's Klan leader, Albert Lentz, helped organize the "white power" rally that took place in the midst of the July 1969 riots.[28]

And then there were the white gangs of York. On one level, York's youth gangs, most notably the Newberry Street Boys, the Girarders, the Swampers, and the Yorklyn Boys, were social in nature. They joined together neighborhood youths who hung out at their "club houses," played sports (and drank), and proudly wore their colors and insignias at school and on the streets. On another level, the gangs represented the prevalence of de facto racial segregation and served as conveyors of white-supremacist attitudes. These white gangs attacked blacks who ventured into "their" neighborhoods, with the explicit purpose of keeping them from "getting their foot in the door." Randy Graham recalled that as a sixteen-year-old white gang member he went to the York Fair looking for blacks to fight: "They were black. We were white. If there were blacks somewhere, we were fighting them." Only years later did Graham express deep regret for his attitudes and actions, but at the time, he observed, he had been taught that blacks were not equal and he did not question this claim. The gangs also sought to keep white youths from crossing cultural boundaries that either explicitly or implicitly undermined white solidarity. Craig Ilgenfritz, a white youth who grew up in the predominantly black Frey's Avenue neighborhood and favored "black" music, like Marvin Gaye, recalled being chased and beaten by members of the Newberry Street boys because of his association with blacks, or as Ilgenfritz put it because they saw him as a "flip over of Uncle Tom."[29] One particular boundary that the white gangs fiercely guarded was the one between the sexes. More specifically, they did not tolerate interracial dating. Members of the Girarders, for instance, called Mark Eissler, a white York College student who was dating a black women, a "nigger lover" and then nearly knocked him unconscious. York police, as well, were known to threaten black men seen with white women in town.[30]

While white gang members were known to fight each other, during periods of racial turmoil, they put aside whatever rivalries they might have had. Rick Knouse, one of the codefendants in the Allen murder trial and a member of the Girarder gang, testified that when the trouble started in July 1969 members of the Newberry Street gang "came and asked for help in their neighborhood, and so we went over there." Whites associated with the Girarders and Yorklyn Boys, who did not live in the Newberry Street neighborhood, gathered with the NSBs at a white power rally the night before Lillie Belle Allen was killed and joined forces with them the day of her murder. On both occasions they shared a common racially charged language, referring to blacks as "niggers" and championing "white power." During the same time period, members of York's police force, many of whom lived in these same white neighborhoods, saw nothing wrong with arming white youths to defend "their neighborhoods," which they defined in racial not spatial terms. Or as one anonymous NSB member put it, "the gang had been under the advisement of the police department since the trouble started." They had told people that the police "wouldn't interfere with their defending their turf," because, simply stated, the "cops are on our side."[31]

At the same time as a growing body of the white population demonstrated its commitment to maintaining the racial status quo, segments of the black population were growing more frustrated and committed to exploring militant approaches to challenging it. Even before the mini-riots of the summer of 1968, a number of York's blacks had begun to turn away from "traditional" civil rights organizations in favor of more radical ones. In 1966, Lionel Bailey and Theodore Holmes formed a local branch of the Congress of Racial Equality (CORE), which had recently jettisoned its commitment to nonviolence and interracialism. The local branch invited James Farmer to speak at a rally at the Alcazar Ballroom in downtown York, where the longtime CORE leader described York's housing "as bad as I have ever seen." Visiting York was like rereading Ralph Ellison's *The Invisible Man*, Farmer observed, because the "Negro in York is invisible, swept under the rug." In addition to supporting the chapter's call for better housing Farmer endorsed CORE's demand that the city create a police advisory board to address the numerous cases of police abuse.[32]

In the wake of the first mini-riot, a cluster of about thirty-five black adults and youths met at Bobby Simpson's home and formed a new all-black organization, which initially took the name the York City Youth. The group employed militant rhetoric, with Simpson asserting, "We are going to give this white power structure their last chance, and if they think they have seen something this past week, they ain't seen nothing yet."

At the same time, this new group, like the better-known Black Panther Party, focused much attention on the bread and butter concerns of the black community, like establishing better recreational facilities.[33] When the chamber of commerce reached out to the black community by holding an open discussion session, black residents proved far less accommodating to the white elite than in the past. Rather than wait for one more report or hearing, one black resident declared that blacks needed to "arm to protect themselves." Still another black resident warned that if the city didn't rectify existing conditions "the entire city will explode."[34]

During the same time period, black militants also challenged the traditional leadership in the black community. Noting that blacks lacked political representation, Ocania Chalk, who owned a bookstore that sold books on African and African American history, exhorted blacks to "agitate, agitate, agitate. . . . You don't have . . . a representative . . . or judges or people sitting on City Council. All you've got is agitation." Chalk also formed a slate that sought to take control of Crispus Attucks, which he contended kowtowed to white financiers and "Uncle Toms." While this challenge failed, it probably nudged more mainstream black leaders to adopt a more militant tone themselves.[35] A number of black businesspeople, for example, established the Association for the Advancement of Black-Owned Businesses. Describing liberal white efforts as "bankrupt," it pledged to aid "black enterprises that will benefit the community in terms of jobs, housing, and care for the young, sick and elderly."[36]

In mid-May 1969 the Black Unity Movement (BUM), an outgrowth of CORE and the York City Youth Organization, held its first meeting at the Crispus Attucks Center on the anniversary of Malcolm X's birthday. At its inaugural event, Bill Thompson, a Black Power spokesperson from Reading, Pennsylvania, discussed Malcolm X's emphasis on black unity, which Thompson insisted underlay the goal of "social, political, economic, but most important of all, military power." At the same meeting, "The Black Players," an-all black theater group from William Penn Senior High, presented its rendition of African American history, including an emotional depiction of the near-lynching of Elizabeth Eckford on the day that Central High School in Little Rock, Arkansas, was slated for desegregation in the fall of 1957. Many of the founding members of BUM had experienced run-ins with the police, and some of them would later admit to having armed themselves in the midst of turmoil in 1969.[37]

In spite of the growing polarization of the nation and the city, many

Yorkers remained convinced that the White Rose City remained immune to the turmoil that was sweeping the nation. Most notably, the York Chamber of Commerce published a history of Greater York that totally glossed over the community's racial divide. The book described York as a beautiful balance of the old and new, where citizens had deep ties to the region and were welcoming of newcomers. The photographs in the book displayed clean-shaven working men laboring away in the community's factories, smartly dressed women shopping at newly opened malls, and smiling children studying at school. Although 1968 was one of the most tumultuous years in American history, the York book told outsiders that the city remained untouched by these developments. The first black person to be pictured in the book was a Ugandan foreign exchange student. And the only other two images of people of color were of black youths frolicking at a summer camp and of blacks and whites bowling together.[38]

To an extent, this booterish view of York, common among small and midsize business leaders across the nation, provided cover for city officials, especially Mayor Snyder, who refused to disband the canine corps or implement other meaningful reforms. Other key institutions and figures, from the *York Dispatch*, which informed readers that national experts had determined that "no more major riots" were to be expected, to Congressman Goodling, who insisted that the summer's turmoil could be traced to a "small minority" of the population, similarly allowed the city to ignore the PHRC's strongly worded recommendations that it implement key reforms in the areas of employment, housing, recreation, and police-community relations immediately.[39] Relative calm in the spring and early summer of 1969 suggested that they might be right. But in truth, this proved simply the proverbial calm before the storm.

* * *

At a bit after 7 p.m. on July 17, 1969, Clifford Green, a twelve-year-old black youth, checked into the York hospital to be treated for facial burns. He informed hospital authorities that members of the Girarders had set him afire. Temperatures had been excessively high for days in South Central Pennsylvania, so oppressive that the local utility company had called on its customers to limit their use of electricity in order to avert a possible brownout. Booming thunderstorms and strong rains on the evening of July 17 broke the heat wave but not before Green's accusation, which he later recanted, set off a firestorm that consumed the city for nearly a week. Later that same night fights broke out between black and white youths near Farquhar Park, a few blocks away from where Lillie Belle Allen would be murdered several days later. Afterward, a cluster of young blacks smashed the windows of a cigar shop that served as the Newberry Street Gang's clubhouse. Less than an hour later, two black youths, Taka Nii Sweeney and John Washington, were shot and wounded. This incident, coupled with the fact that the response of the police to the shooting was measured at best—they neither questioned nor arrested anyone at the time—angered the black community even further. (Robert Messersmith, a leader of the NSBs, was later arrested, charged, and convicted of this shooting.)[40]

In the words of Judge William Nealon, "a night of terror followed." Nineteen whites were wounded, either by gunshots or by projectiles, such as bricks and rocks, many in the heart of the black community. A bit after 3 a.m. on the morning of July 18, a group of black youths pulled alongside John Smith's car as he was driving home from work. As he recalled over thirty years later, they "stuck a gun out the window and shot." The shotgun blast struck Smith under the chin. Fortunately, the shot was not fatal. A few hours later, Mrs. Madelyn Bowman, a white woman, was struck by a brick, fracturing her jaw. Not long afterward, Dean Coffman was driving to work at National Biscuit when he encountered a crowd of thirty at the corner of Penn and College, who shot out his front windshield. A smattering of firebombs were thrown into buildings owned by white businessmen, as well, though no appreciable looting was reported.[41]

As the sun set on the evening of July 18, larger crowds gathered in the heart of the black community and attacks on passersby resumed. At 10:30 p.m. "Big Al," one of York Police's two armored vehicles, was dispatched to assist firemen not far from Penn and College. While there, Stanford Gilbert, who was riding home from work on his 1956 Triumph Thunderbird motorcycle, was shot and nearly killed. As he testified years later, he had never had a problem in the neighborhood before; in fact, he had consumed a drink or two at Sam's Café, a local hangout, with some of his black biker buddies. But on this occasion, he was shot in the back and knocked unconscious.[42]

In response, "Big Al," which was occupied by three police officers, including Henry Schaad, drove by the Penn and College intersection. A number of black observers testified years later that the policemen in the armored vehicle yelled, "Niggers, get off the corners, go to your homes."

The surviving policemen denied heaping any such abuse on the crowd of at least twenty to thirty blacks, many of them armed. Regardless, shots rang out. More than one witness recalled Stephan Freeland exclaiming, "I hit the mother fucker," though few if anyone knew or believed that his bullet had pierced the armor of the vehicle that Schaad was in. Officer Ronald McCoy recalled hearing a loud noise, "like boom." Not until Schaad stated that he had been shot did McCoy realize that the noise he had heard came from a gun—later identified as a .34-40 Krag rifle—and that its bullet had penetrated the plating of the armored vehicle and fatally wounded his fellow officer.[43]

Violence intensified following Schaad's shooting. Less than two hours afterward, two black males, Clarence Ausby and Bennie Carter, were wounded while sitting inside their home by police who, upon hearing of the attack on their fellow officer, decided to take revenge. Two young black children, Lynn and Jeannette Register, ages two and eight, respectively, were hit by gunshots outside of the Parkway homes where they lived, allegedly by police gunfire. Bobby Simpson recalled hearing the armored vans rumble up the street and then the sound of gunshots entering his home. "The unrelenting beating of bullets," writes Kim Strong, brought their young son, Mark, "running into their parents' bedroom," where Simpson "pulled him to the floor" until the firing stopped five to ten minutes later. White gang members firebombed the home of Mr. and Mrs. Frank Meyers, the only blacks to live in the Cottage Hill/North Newberry Street neighborhood. When the Meyers' neighbor Clifton Kohler, who was white, reported the incident to police, officers responded that they couldn't do anything about it. Ernestine Rankin, a black woman, was shot at while driving her Cadillac at North Newberry and Gay, virtually the same spot where Allen would be shot and killed the following day. So too were Louis Multry and Mitchell Edwards, who fled their car after it was peppered by gunshots fired by white youth. Meanwhile, authorities arrested Lionel Bailey, a longtime civil rights activist, on charges of curfew violation, in spite of the fact that a top city official had authorized him to walk the streets in order to try to cool things. While he was in custody, "racial slurs and threats" were directed at him by police. In the midst of the tumult, York's mayor John Snyder declared a state of emergency, imposed a curfew, and requested support from the state police.[44]

On Sunday, July 20, as hinted at above, at least one hundred white youths, most members of York's various white gangs, gathered at Farquhar

Park about four blocks north of NSB's headquarters to discuss, as one witness recalled, "how they were going to protect their neighborhood." Rather than chase them out of the park, as they had done in the past, a handful of York police, including Charlie Robertson, rallied their spirits with "shouts of white power." Some of those assembled recalled that the police emboldened them by displaying Officer Schaad's blood in "Big Al" and telling them that if they "had guns or ammunition to bring them down to Newberry Street." As Stewart Aldinger, one young member of the NSBs put it, the police left the clear impression that they sided with the white youths, as did the police decision not to disarm any of them when they gathered in the Newberry Street neighborhood, armed with rifles and shotguns, the following evening. (In a region where hunting was popular, guns were ubiquitous.)[45]

The violence culminated with the aforementioned shooting of Lillie Belle Allen, after which Mayor Snyder requested support from Pennsylvania's governor Raymond Shafer, who mobilized the National Guard. They arrived over six hundred strong, astride armored personnel carriers. Though tensions remained high, the violence essentially subsided. By the time that the final guardsmen departed on July 28, police reported that at least twenty-eight people had suffered gunshot wounds, including two fatalities; at least a dozen other men and women were seriously injured by objects that had been thrown at them. One hundred and eight individuals were arrested for curfew or firearm violations. While York experienced little looting, numerous businesses were set ablaze, and York's firefighting force had to risk life and limb to keep entire sections of the community from burning to the ground. All told, based on the most extensive and widely used quantitative data set, York experienced the fifteenth-most intense riot or urban revolt out of over five hundred that occurred in the nation between 1963 and 1972, and if one were to adjust this data set for population size, York experienced one of the most severe uprisings of the era.[46]

As with disorders in other cities, those in York did not occur all over the city. Rather, battles between blacks and whites, including between the police, who were overwhelmingly white, and blacks, were concentrated in four sections of the city, foremost in the southwest quadrant of the city, sometimes referred to as the West End or as Penn-College, and secondarily in the Cottage Hill Road–North Newberry Street neighborhood, approximately six blocks north of the intersection of Penn and College.

These were the locales where Officer Schaad and Lillie Belle Allen, respectively, were killed, and in the immediate aftermath of the disturbances large caches of arms were confiscated from homes in these areas.[47]

During the Lillie Belle Allen trial over thirty years later, defense and prosecuting attorneys agreed to over one hundred stipulations that laid out countless acts of violence and arson. What they disagreed over was whether the defendants, Robert Messersmith, Greg Neff, and Charlie Robertson, were criminally responsible for Lillie Belle Allen's death. (Six other defendants pled guilty in exchange for lesser sentences.) In both murder trials, the primary defense was that so many individuals had participated in the shootings that it was impossible to assign culpability to any of the accused. Likewise, in the Officer Schaad murder trial, Michael Wright, the brother of one of the defendants, Leon "Smickel" Wright, landed a bombshell when he testified that at least fifteen to twenty people (young black men) had shot at the armored vehicle, including himself. Michael Wright had nothing to gain and everything to lose by admitting that he had fired shots that might have killed Schaad; he hadn't been charged with the crime, and neither prosecuting nor defense attorneys expected him to make this claim. Upon cross-examination, defense attorneys tried to suggest that Michael Wright's testimony was motivated by his desire for the limelight. But Wright, himself, made it clear that he and he others had fired because they had grown tired of mistreatment by the police and determined that it was time to defend their homes and neighborhood.[48]

While none of the attorneys in Allen's case probed the deeper causes of the violence nor tried to place York into a broader understanding of the urban revolts of the era, it is doubtful that they would have disagreed significantly with the Kerner Commission's finding that the riots of the era had grown out of the failure of America to "make good" on its promises. As noted above, blacks departed the South with the hope that by migrating to the North they would enhance their opportunity to enjoy a better place, or social and economic space, in society. Like black migrants to other cities, however, they found that the barriers to achieving the American dream remained high, and they grew increasingly frustrated with their inability to garner significant reforms. The failure of reformers of all stripes to convince Mayor Snyder to cease deployment of the canine force or to create a police review board remained a case in point. Without a doubt young black men proved the most willing, in the long run, to attack whites who ventured into their community, engage in armed clashes with the police and white gang members, or both—in part because they themselves were the group most likely to experience confrontations with the police and with white gangs. Blacks who rebelled in 1969 did not do so because they were "seeking the thrill and excitement occasioned by looting and burning," conservative understandings of the riots notwithstanding.[49] Whether York also provides a degree of evidence for a handful of geospatial analyses of the urban revolts of the era remains problematic. Max Herman, among others, has argued that rioting most often took place in communities experiencing "ethnic succession." Other social scientists similarly suggest that rioting took place in cities that were approaching a demographic tipping point. Yet as late as 1970, blacks composed only 13 percent of York's population, suggesting that concerns about ethnic succession—into "white" neighborhoods, jobs, and government, should not have been a factor.[50]

What makes York's revolt somewhat unique is that it witnessed direct clashes between blacks and whites, which, according to most historians was not the case elsewhere. York did not experience a "commodity riot"; while some arson took place, the upheaval mostly resembled the race riots of the earlier part of the century, where blacks and whites clashed following confrontations over physical spaces, such as recreational sites and access to public housing. Moreover, white citizens were not passive figures in York's revolt. Perhaps emboldened by Richard Nixon's call for "law and order," which many read as a not-so-subtle form of white backlash, and to a lesser extent by George Wallace, whose third-party campaign for president enjoyed considerable support north of the Mason-Dixon line, they rallied around the cry of "white power," determined to maintain the racial status quo that, in York, as in the South, had always entailed white privilege, if not outright white supremacy.[51]

That the police sided with white gang members rather than serving as impartial and detached public servants fits well with many analyses of the rioting of the sixties. In the immediate aftermath of York's revolt, one of the city's six black policemen (out of ninety-six) resigned, accusing the force of systematic racism, including "unnecessary use of firepower" during the riots and the indiscriminate use of the canine force throughout the era. With the support of the NAACP, a cluster of blacks filed a class action suit, calling for the state to take over the city's police force due to its history of racism. While Judge Nealon rejected the plaintiff's call to place the police under receivership and outside control, he did find much that disturbed him, and it was in his 1969 ruling that Charlie Robertson's association with white power first appeared, not in the newspapers over thirty years later.[52] Yet it should be remembered, as York director of public safety Jacob Hose put it, the "police didn't create the ghetto."[53]

While Nealon did not excuse the rioting, he concluded with the hope that "a new atmosphere of trust and confidence between the York police and the black community would be most welcome and would go a long way to avoid any future senseless blood baths." Whether this would take place must (due to constraints of space) remain the subject of future work. Suffice it to say, in spite of some extraordinary efforts to create a genuine dialogue between whites and blacks in the wake of the 1969 riot—in the form of community "Charettes"—neither in York nor in most of America did the racial divide diminish significantly in the post-riot period.[54] White flight, particularly white middle-class flight, from the city, continued to take place: York's white population fell from 43,556 in 1970 to 24,416 in 2000 (see figure 4.2 above). When coupled with key economic changes, from the decline of downtown shopping districts and rise of suburban shopping malls (which began in York prior to the riots) to "deindustrialization," this flight led to the increasing concentration of poverty in the urban core. As urban expert David Rusk reported in a comprehensive analysis of the York region, between 1970 and 1990, poverty rates increased in twelve out of sixteen census tracts in York, and the income gap between the city and the largely white suburbs widened.[55] Racial polarization also continued apace in the political realm. (Barack Obama won less than 39 percent of the countywide vote in 2012 even though he carried the city of York and the state of Pennsylvania.)

But rather than seeing the riots as a pivotal point in the community's history, as many in York and elsewhere are wont to do, it would be more appropriate to conceive of the urban revolts as a consequence rather than as a cause of the racial divide and to consider the revolts a by-product of rising and unfulfilled expectations (which helps explain their prevalence in the 1960s compared to recent times where expectations have been dampened by years of economic stagnation). In other words, the riot of the summer of 1969, which might better be described as a black uprising and a white counter-revolt, had both long- and short-term causes that can most simply be summarized by the word "place." From the moment blacks joined the Great Migration they sought to change places, geographically, economically, socially, and politically. They sought to break down the boundaries that had restricted them to a second-class life, and they saw the move to York as a means to achieving this end. White Yorkers reluctantly accepted blacks into the community as long as they maintained their place, physically within the black section of town, socially and economically on the bottom of the ladder, and politically disempowered. Various mechanisms were employed to maintain this racial order, from the steering of blacks to certain residences—which in turn affected what schools their children attended—to the advice blacks received from guidance counselors to the actions of white gangs who harassed blacks who entered "their" neighborhoods. But as in many other communities across the nation, it was the police who played a central role in keeping blacks in their "place," clearing them from local parks at night, sicking dogs on them, and rallying white residents to defend "their neighborhoods" while not providing equal protection to York's black residents.[56] Ironically, Charlie Robertson, who became the face of white resistance, displayed a far greater commitment to overcoming this history in the years that followed the 1969 revolt than did many others who not only fled York but also gave up on the vision articulated by Lyndon Johnson in 1964 of a nation that had great cities and left no citizens behind.

Notes

Epigraph source: Testimony of Stephen Freeland, Commonwealth of Pennsylvania v. Stephen D. Freeland and Commonwealth of Pennsylvania v. Leon F. Wright, Court of Common Pleas of York County, York, PA, Mar. 2003.

1. William Keisling, *The Wrong Car: The Death of Lillie Belle Allen: A Police Murder Mystery* (Yardbird, 2007), Kindle edition; Testimony of Hattie Dickson, Commonwealth of Pennsylvania v. Robert N. Messersmith, Gregory H. Neff, Charles Robertson, et. al., Court of Common Pleas of York County, York, Pennsylvania, Oct. 2002.

2. William Costopoulos and Brad Bumsted, *Murder Is the Charge: The True Story of Mayor Charlie Robertson and the York, Pennsylvania, Race Riots* (Philadelphia: Camino Books, 2004). For international coverage of Robertson's indictment, see "Another 1960s Race Death Trial," *Weekend Australian*, May 19, 2001; "Old Wounds of Racism Reopened," *Globe and Mail* (Canada), May 18, 2001; and "Mayor Fights Poll—and Murder Charge," *London Guardian*, May 18, 2001. For national coverage, see Amy Worden, "Mayor of York Withdraws from Race," *Philadelphia Inquirer*, May 25, 2001; "Indicted York Mayor Says He Won't Step Down," *Philadelphia Inquirer*, May 18, 2001; and "3 Agree to Testify in Racial Killing," *Philadelphia Inquirer*, June 26, 2001. For contemporary coverage of the riot, see "Gunfire Renews as Cyclists Scatter People in York, Pa.," *New York Times*, July 21, 1969; "Woman Killed in York, Pa.," *New York Times*, July 22, 1969; "Calm

Prevails in York, Pa., as Guard and Police Patrol," *New York Times,* July 24, 1969; and "Strain and Calm in York, PA: Guard and Curfew Restore Order on the Surface," *New York Times,* July 27, 1969.

3. Gregg Lee Carter developed the most thorough data set on urban rioting; see Gregg Lee Carter, "In the Narrows of the 1960s U.S. Black Rioting," *Journal of Conflict Resolution* 30 (Mar. 1986): 115–27; and Gregg Lee Carter, "Explaining the Severity of the 1960s Black Rioting" (PhD diss., Columbia University, 1983). See also Lemberg Center for the Study of Violence, *Riot Data Review* (Waltham, MA: Brandeis University, 1968). This essay will use the terms "riots," "uprisings," and "urban rebellions" and "urban revolts" interchangeably.

4. For interesting contemporary views on the impact of the riots see C. Vann Woodward, "After Watts—Where Is the Negro Revolution Headed," *New York Times Magazine,* Aug. 29, 1965; and Julius Lester, "Black Revolution Is Real," *The Movement,* Sept. 1967. On the myth of southern exceptionalism, especially in modern times, see Matthew Lassiter and Joseph Crespino, eds., *The Myth of Southern Exceptionalism* (New York: Oxford University Press, 2009).

5. The two best contemporary studies of the urban revolts of the 1960s are National Advisory Commission on Civil Disorders, *Report of the National Advisory Commission on Civil Disorders* (Washington, DC: GPO, 1968); and Robert Fogelson, *Violence as Protest: A Study of Riots and Ghettos* (Garden City, NY: Doubleday, 1971). The sociological literature on the rioting of the era is vast. See especially Daniel J. Myers, "Racial Rioting in the 1960s: An Event History Analysis of Local Conditions," *American Sociological Review* 62 (Feb. 1997): 94–112; and Seymour Spilerman, "The Causes of Racial Disturbances: A Comparison of Alternative Explanation," *American Sociological Review* 35 (Aug. 1970): 627–49. For a brief review of the literature on the urban riots of the era, see Heather Ann Thompson, "Rethinking the Politics of White Flight in the Postwar City: Detroit, 1945–1980," *Journal of Urban History* 25 (Jan. 1999): 163–98. On the impact of the riots, see William Chafe, *The Unfinished Journey: America since World War II* (New York: Oxford, 2003), 366–68; and Irwin Unger, *Turning Point: 1968* (New York: Scribner, 1988). One of the few works to look at rioting in a small or midsize community is Andrew Goodman and Thomas Sugrue, "Plainfield Burnings: Black Rebellion in the Suburban North," *Journal of Urban History* 33 (May 2007): 568–601. The only comprehensive study of the rioting that took place following Martin Luther King Jr.'s assassination in 1968 is Clay Risen, *A Nation on Fire: America in the Wake of the King Assassination* (Hoboken, NJ: John Wiley & Sons, 2009).

6. I. A. Newby, *Black Carolinians: A History of Blacks in South Carolina from 1895 to 1968* (Columbia: University of South Carolina Press, 1973). On the migration of South Carolina's blacks to the North see "IN MOTION: The African-American Migration Experience," Schomburg Center for Research in Black Culture website, http://www.inmotionaame.org/home.cfm;jsessionid=f830167081139479995226 0?bhcp=1, especially the charts linked to "The Great Migration (1916–1930)" and "The Second Great Migration (1940–1970)"; and Isabel Wilkerson, *The Warmth of Other Suns: The Epic Story of America's Greatest Migration* (New York: Random House, 2010). On the migration of African Americans in York, see Jim Kalish, *The Story of Civil Rights in York, Pennsylvania: A*

250 Year Interpretive History (York, PA: York County Audit, 2000), 20–21. For the story of one migrant, see Voni B. Grimes, *Bridging Troubled Waters* (York, PA: Wolf, 2008).

7. Walter White, *Rope and Faggot* (New York: Arno, 1969), 29–33; Elizabeth Robeson, "An 'Ominous Defiance': The Lowman Lynchings of 1926," in *Toward the Meeting of the Waters: Currents in the Civil Rights Movement in South Carolina during the Twentieth Century*, ed. Winfred B. Moore Jr. and Orville Vernon Burton (Columbia: University of South Carolina Press, 2008), 65–92; Newby, *Black Carolinians*.

8. Mary Dudziak, *Cold War Civil Rights: Race and the Image of Democracy* (Princeton: Princeton University Press, 2000), 23.

9. Median income statistics can be found in U.S. Bureau of the Census, *U.S. Census of Population: 1950: South Carolina* (Washington, DC: GPO, 1951); and U.S. Bureau of the Census, *U.S. Census of Population: 1950: Pennsylvania* (Washington, DC: GPO, 1951).

10. Teresa McMinn, "Codorus Street Reunion Plans to Give People a Look Back—and Ahead," *York Daily Record*, July 22, 2012, http://www.ydr.com/ci_21127933/codorus-street-reunion-plans-give-people-look-back; Panel Discussion on Codorus Street Community, Feb. 8, 2014, York County Heritage Trust; Debora Hamm, interview by the author, Baltimore, MD, Dec. 20, 2013.

11. York Planning Commission, "An Analysis of Socio-economic Factors and Housing," 1973, HUD Papers, RG 207, box 2541; and York Planning Commission, "York County Comprehensive Plan: Population," 1970, HUD Papers, RG 207, box 1857; both in National Archives, College Park, MD.

12. Pennsylvania Human Relations Commission (hereafter PHRC), "Investigatory Hearing Report, 1968," Raymond P. Shafer Papers, General File, MG209, carton 42, Pennsylvania State Archives, Harrisburg, PA.

13. York Planning Commission, "An Analysis of Socio-economic Factors and Housing"; and York County Planning Commission, "Comprehensive Plan," 1978; both in HUD Papers, RG 207, box 405.

14. York County Planning Commission, "Comprehensive Plan," 1978; U.S. Bureau of the Census, "Census of Population and Housing, 1970: Census Tracts, Final Report PHC (1)-237 York, Pa. SMSA," (Washington, DC: GPO, 1972).

15. York County Planning Commission, "Comprehensive Plan," 1978; U.S. Bureau of the Census, *Census of Population and Housing, 1970* (Washington, DC: GPO, 1971); PHRC, "Report."

16. York County Planning Commission, "Comprehensive Plan," 1978; U.S. Bureau of the Census, *Census of Population and Housing, 1970* (Washington, DC: GPO, 1971); PHRC, "Report."

17. PHRC, "Report"; Dwayne Wright, "Black Pride Days, 1965–1970: A Critical Historical Ethnography of Black Student Activism, Curricular Reform, and Memory at William Penn Senior High School in York, Pennsylvania" (PhD diss., University of Georgia, 2005), Manson quoted on p. 82; Jeffrey Werner, "A Peaceful Mourning: The York High Students' Reaction to Martin Luther King's Assassination and Its Significance When Contrasted with York City" (senior thesis, York College, 2008, in author's possession).

18. PHRC, "Report." For an early example of police misuse of dogs see *York Gazette*

and Daily (hereafter *YGD*), July 20, 1963; and Kalish, *The Story of Civil Rights in York*, 44–77.

19. Kalish, *The Story of Civil Rights in York*; PHRC, "Report"; PHRC, "Press Release," n.d., Raymond Shafer Papers, General File, MG 209, carton 42; "Mayor's Dog Probe Fizzles, but He's for Them Anyway," *YGD*, June 7, 1968. In "The Grapes of Wrath," a retrospective exploration of the roots of the 1969 riots, Debbie Noel provides a keen sense of the rhythm of police abuse, black protest, and city hall irresponsiveness (*York Dispatch*, Sept. 21, 2005).

20. "Cops Shoot While Chasing Teenagers, Residents Say," *YGD*, July 12, 1968; "Police Chief Says Patrolman Fired Shot and It Was a Mistake," *YGD*, July 13, 1968; "Series of Events Thursday Led to Firing by Police," *YGD*, July 13, 1968; "Curfew Blamed in Disorders; Officials Say No Law Exists," and "Rock Throwing and Assaults and Fire Mar City Weekend," both in *YGD*, July 15, 1968; "Buckpassing by City on Disorders Feared," "York Police Put on 12-Hour Shifts," "2 Firebombs Came in Midst of False Alarms," and "Ghetto Leaders Form Committee to Avoid Crisis," all in *YGD*, July 16, 1968; "Black Adults, Youths Hold Discussion of Recent Acts," "2 Persons Swear They Saw Toomey Fire His Pistol," "Police Harassment Is Blamed for Violence by Black Youth," all in *YGD*, July 17, 1968; "Black Council Plans to Repair Damages; Will Give City a 'Last Chance to Act,'" *YGD*, July 19, 1968; "Disorders Began When Teenagers Were Cleared from Park by Police," *YGD*, July 22, 1968; "Warning Shots Out of Line, Police Say," *York Dispatch*, July 13, 1968; "Rid 'Problem Police' Negroes Prod Hose," *York Dispatch*, July 15, 1968.

21. "Police in Riot Dress Patrol York after Shooting of 11 Persons," *YGD*, Aug. 5, 1968; "Black Youths Angry after What They Feel Was Attack," *YGD*, Aug. 5, 1968; "Policeman Ordered Suspended," *YGD*, Aug. 6, 1968; "20 Hurt as New Violence Rakes West End Area," *York Dispatch*, Aug. 5, 1968; "Key Developments in York's Latest Disturbance," *York Dispatch*, Aug. 6, 1968.

22. "10 Injured, 15 Held in Disorder after York Football Game," "Leaders Describe Police Dog Actions against Black Youth," and "Reporter Bitten by Police Dog, Camera Smashed," all in *YGD*, Sept. 21, 1968; "Black Youth Bitten by Dog Tells of Police Encounter," and "Another Newsman in Police Court," *YGD*, Sept. 23, 1968; "10 Injured as Disorders Sweep Mid-city in Wake of Grid Game," *York Dispatch*, Sept. 21, 1968.

23. Vote totals come from George R. Brittingham Jr., ed., *The Pennsylvania Manual, 1968–69*, vol. 99 (Harrisburg: Department of Property and Supplies, 1969).

24. On Agnew see Peter B. Levy, "Spiro Agnew, the Forgotten Americans, and the Rise of the New Right," *The Historian* 75 (Winter 2013): 707–39; "Yorkers Skeptical on March Results; Disappointed at Talk with Goodling," *YGD*, June 20, 1968.

25. "Agnew Raps Youth Involved in 'Unconscious Anarchy,'" *YGD*, Sept. 6, 1968; Testimony of William Goodling in Commonwealth v. Robert Messersmith, et. al.

26. "Chantiles Berated for His Conduct at Racial Hearing," and "Superiority 'Attitude' Causes Race Tension State Hearing Is Told," both in *YGD*, Aug. 29, 1968; "Disorders Here Laid to 'Small Minority,'" *York Dispatch*, Sept. 18, 1968.

27. "Salem Square Whites Voice Reactions to Civil Disorders," *YGD*, Aug. 7, 1968.

28. "Public Safety Director Hose 'Severely Reprimands' Toomey," *YGD*, July 27, 1968; Jacob Whiteford, "Watts Meets Mayberry: Rioting in York, Pennsylvania, and Its Place

among Urban Upheavals of the 1960s" (senior thesis, York College, undated, in author's possession); Federal Bureau of Investigation, "Memorandum: Hooded Ku Klux Klan March," Nov. 5, 1968, and "Memorandum: Hooded Ku Klux Klan March, York, PA," Nov. 12, 1968, in FBI Records, 157-3239-3 and 157-3239-4, respectively, RG 65, box 187, National Archives, College Park, MD; Marlin Cutshall, "Personal File on White Supremacists in York, PA," in author's possession.

29. Craig Ilgenfritz, interview by the author, York, Pennsylvania, June 11, 2014; Debbie Noel, "The Grapes of Wrath"; Karen Rice-Young, "Ten Days: The '69 Riots in York, PA: An Oral History" (senior thesis, York College, Apr. 24, 1992, in author's possession).

30. "Student Assaulted by 'Gang in York,'" *YGD*, Sept. 12, 1969; Craig Ilgenfritz interview.

31. Commonwealth of Pennsylvania v. Charlie Robertson, et. al., especially opening statements and testimony of Steven Noonan, Robert Stoner, Steven Rinehart, Stewart Aldinger, Frederick Flickinger, Greg Bowwer, Richard Hansford, Dennis McMaster, and Rick Knouse. For the anonymous oral history see Karen Rice-Young, "Ten Days." This admission is particularly valuable because it was made years before the investigation of Allen's murder was reopened and all sorts of confessions started to be made, some, perhaps, under duress.

32. "CORE Head Finds York Slum Typical of Northern Cities," *YGD*, Jan. 17, 1966; Philadelphia SAC to J. Edgar Hoover, Jan. 18, 1966, Federal Bureau of Investigations Philadelphia Office, case file 157-PH-1711-v. 1, record group 65, box 58; Theodore Holmes, "Letter to the Editor: White Racism Needs Treatment," *YGD*, June 25, 1968; "Militant Leader with a Past," *York Dispatch*, online edition, Mar. 9, 2003.

33. "City Officials Commandeered Armored Truck," *YGD*, Aug. 2, 1968.

34. "Chamber of Commerce Listens to Negro Complaint," *York Dispatch*, Aug. 7, 1968.

35. Chalk quoted in Olysa Townsley, "When the Bubble Burst: Understanding the York Race Riots through the Lens of a Community Resistant to Change" (senior thesis, York College, May 2010, in author's possession), 8; "Benefit Concert for Poor People's March," *YGD*, June 18, 1968; "Yorkers Skeptical on March Results," *YGD*, June 20, 1968. One can find evidence of a possible gender division, with young black men more inclined to adopt Black Power rhetoric and garb and black women more committed to grassroots organizing that they hoped would result in better housing and economic benefits. See for example "Public Housing Grievances Voiced by Community Group," *YGD*, June 13, 1968.

36. "York Negroes Form New Body for Economic, Political Growth," *YGD*, Aug. 13, 1968; "Yorker Named to Area Office Aiding Negroes," *YGD*, Aug. 14, 1968.

37. "New Black Group to Hold Program," *YGD*, May 15, 1969; "Malcolm X Honored at Crispus Attucks," *YGD*, May 19, 1969.

38. Lynn Smolens Taub, *Greater York in Action* (York, PA: York Area Chamber of Commerce, 1968).

39. "No More Major Riots Expected," *York Dispatch*, Sept. 16, 1968; "Disorders Here Laid to 'Small Minority,'" *York Dispatch*, Sept. 18, 1968; PHCR, "Press Release," n.d.

40. Rhoda Barton and Lewis Johnstone, v. Eli Eichelberger, Mayor, City of York, et al., 311 F. Supp. 1132; 1970 U.S. Dist. Lexis 12284, especially Judge Nealon's Finding of Fact;

"Policemen, 7 Others Wounded By Gunfire on York's Streets," *YGD*, July 19, 1969; "Boy's Fabricated Story of Being Set Afire Touched Off Clashes of Gangs," *YGD*, July 19, 1969; Debra Noel, "The Grapes of Wrath"; "Fear and Fury: The Riots of 1969: Special Report"; "State Police Report: Disorder, York, Pennsylvania," Sept. 8, 1969, Governor Shafer Papers, MG209, 9-1136, carton 98, folder 1; "Operational Report: Civil Disturbances—York, Pennsylvania, 22–28, July 1969," Governor Shafer Papers, MG209-1136, carton 98, folder 3; Commonwealth v. Stephen Freeland; Commonwealth v. Leon Wright, Court of Common Pleas of York County (2003), especially testimony of Anthony Brown and Taka Nii Sweeney. See also Commonwealth v. Robert Messersmith, et al., especially testimony of Taka Nii Sweeney, Michael Sipe, Arthur Messersmith, and Stipulations Read into the Record by District Attorney Thomas Kelley.

41. Barton v. Eichelberger; Commonwealth of Pennsylvania v. Stephen D. Freeland, especially testimony of John Smith, Dean Goffman, and Josephine Giuffrida.

42. Commonwealth of Pennsylvania v. Stephen D. Freeland, especially testimony of Stanford Gilbert.

43. Commonwealth of Pennsylvania v. Stephen D. Freeland, especially testimony of Richard Rasco, Donald McCoy, Michael Wright, and Sherman Spells.

44. "Fear and Fury: The Riots of 1969: Special Report"; "State Police Report: Disorder, York, Pennsylvania"; "Operational Report: Civil Disturbances—York, Pennsylvania, 22–28, July 1969"; Barton v. Eichelberger; "Gunfire Renews as Cyclists Scatter People in York, Pa."; Mark Scolforo, "148 Might Testify: DA Calls 11 More for '69 Riots Case," *York Dispatch*, Sept. 12, 2002; Commonwealth v. Robert Messersmith, especially testimony of Alexis Kay, Sherman Spells, and Louis Multry and Stipulations Read into the Record by District Attorney Thomas Kelley; Kim Strong, "1969 York Riots: As He Lay Dying," *York Daily Record*, http://www.ydr.com/story/archives/2010/02/12/1969-york-riots-as-he-lay-dying/74452732/, accessed Jan. 4, 2013; Laurie Lebo, "Spells Details '69 Run-in with Messersmith," *York Dispatch*, Aug. 25, 2005.

45. Commonwealth v. Robert Messersmith, especially Testimony of Robert Stoner, Stewart Aldinger, Frederick Flickinger, Theodore Halloran, Robert Traettino, Thomas Smith, and Rick Lynn Knouse, and Grand Jury Testimony of Gregory Neff, read into record by Rodney George.

46. "Policemen, 7 Others Wounded By Gunfire on York's Streets"; "Boy's Fabricated Story of Being Set Afire Touched Off Clashes of Gangs"; Debra Noel, "The Grapes of Wrath," *York Sunday News*, July 25, 1968; "Fear and Fury: The Riots of 1969: Special Report"; "State Police Report: Disorder, York, Pennsylvania"; "Operational Report: Civil Disturbances—York, Pennsylvania, 22–28, July 1969." See also Barton v. Eichelberger.

47. Data from *U.S. Census of Population 1970* (Washington, DC: GPO, 1971); GIS map in Brandon MacDonald, "White Flight: Examining Demographics and Deindustrialization in York, Pennsylvania" (senior thesis, York College, May 14, 2014), in author's possession.

48. Commonwealth vs. Robert Messersmith, especially Opening Statement by Peter Solymos, Closing Statement of William Costopoulos, and Stipulations Read into the Record by Thomas Kelley. Since Mayor Robertson was not accused of actually firing shots, Costopoulos had an easier task of challenging those who claimed that his client

had supplied either ammunition or the gun that had killed Allen; see Commonwealth v. Stephen D. Freeland and Commonwealth v. Leon F. Wright, especially testimony of Michael Wright.

49. *Report of the National Advisory Commission on Civil Disorders*; Edward Banfield, "Riot for Fun and Profit," in *The Unheavenly City: The Nature and Future of Our Urban Crisis* (Boston: Little Brown, 1968), 185–209. Thomas Sugrue, *Sweet Land of Liberty: The Forgotten Struggle for Civil Rights in the North* (New York: Random House, 2008), 348–55, provides an excellent overview of the competing understandings of the urban revolts of the 1960s. For an outstanding collection of "contemporary" studies of the urban revolts see Kenneth Kusmer, *The Ghetto Crisis of the 1960s: Causes and Consequences*, vol. 7 (New York: Garland Press, 1991).

50. Max Herman, *Fighting in the Streets: Ethnic Succession and Urban Unrest in Twentieth-Century America* (New York: Peter Lang, 2005); Janet L. Agu-Lughod, *Race, Space, and Riots in Chicago, New York, and Los Angeles* (New York: Oxford: 2007).

51. Paul A. Gilje, *Rioting in America* (Bloomington: Indiana University Press, 1996), presents the most comprehensive discussion of rioting in U.S. history. See also Alan Spear, Review of *Violence in the Model City: The Cavanaugh Administration, Race Relations, and the Detroit Riot of 1967*, by Sidney Fine, *Public Opinion Quarterly* 54 (Winter 1990): 633–36.

52. Barton v. Eichelberger; Karen Rice-Young, "Ten Days."

53. "Housing Conditions in York's Ghetto Tied to Disorders," *YGD*, July 18, 1968.

54. For a discussion of the "Charrettes," see Raul Urrunaga, "The York Charrette, April 19–27, 1970," *Journal of York County Heritage*, Sept. 2011; Jim Kalish, *The Story of Civil Rights in York*; and Melissa Tyrell, "An Understanding Begins," *York Daily Record*, June 25, 1999.

55. "The Rusk Report on the Future of Greater York," *York Daily Record*, Nov. 20, 1997.

56. PHRC, "Report."

5

"What We Eat Is Politics"

SNCC, Hunger, and Voting Rights in Mississippi

MARY POTORTI

In Mississippi, the setting of many of the most celebrated and traumatic episodes of the civil rights era, activists quickly realized that the tactics that brought the modern struggle's earliest and most publicized triumphs could not meaningfully address the problems of the rural South. The sit-ins that won significant concessions in southern cities after 1960, inspiring the formation of the Student Nonviolent Coordinating Committee (SNCC), promised little reward to poor blacks who, even if seated at a restaurant or lunch counter previously reserved for whites, could rarely afford anything on the menu. Consequently, activists with SNCC and other civil rights organizations working in the state under the coordination of the Council of Federated Organizations (COFO) realized that protection of the right to vote stood as the most pressing need and most promising movement strategy for black Mississippians.[1] Only the franchise could harness latent black political power to force tangible improvements in the daily lives of Mississippi's hungry poor. Ruthlessly policing the racial status quo, Mississippi officials and vigilantes worked to impede voter registration drives and other black advances with threats and acts of brutal violence—shootings, lynchings, arson, and mysterious disappearances that left an uncounted number of black corpses floating in local waterways. More subtle than such flagrant criminal attacks, threats of economic retribution—termination by white employers, eviction by white landlords, loss of credit from white institutions—loomed ominously in the minds of the black poor who had the most to gain from winning the vote but who could least afford the very real costs of working to secure it. More than any other locale in which the movement operated, the socioeconomic landscape of rural Mississippi made painfully apparent the manner and extent to which hunger and food insecurity operated as implements of black political disfranchisement. Civil rights organizers quickly recognized that political rights had little meaning for people whose material deprivation or poor health limited their range of practical options to those most likely to keep them alive. Movement leaders thus aimed to ameliorate the political and corporeal hunger of black Mississippians by using food to fuel their political and ideological aspirations, encouraging poor sharecroppers to demand their share of the American banquet.

Analyzing the long civil rights era through the lens of food politics establishes new frameworks for understanding struggles to explode racist views of black personhood, to resist systemic deprivation and political marginalization, and ultimately to challenge the role of the capitalist democratic system in perpetuating inequality. It also expands understandings of "activism" and "civil rights," efforts and aims that, particularly for poor black Mississippians, often entailed great personal risk and sacrifice. As the Mississippi story reveals, hunger and near-starvation impelled the consideration, response, and action of a range of groups in ways that demands for integrated public schools and lunch counters, fair housing and employment, and legal protections did not. The food politics of the black freedom struggle therefore shed light on the political dimensions of hunger and the human dimensions of organizing, illustrating that before a constituency can move toward higher aims, the most basic material needs of its people must be met.

The physical deprivation and suffering endured by African Americans in the plantation South has been recounted in numerous important scholarly works.[2] In addition to documenting the natural trials of life in agriculture, historians have detailed the manner in which white landowners from the antebellum period through the 1960s manipulated federal agricultural policies to their own financial benefit and their workers' economic, political, and bodily peril.[3] Less acknowledged or understood have been the responses of organizers and the hungry poor to the challenges posed by state-sanctioned food insecurity, hunger, and malnutrition. SNCC, the guiding force of COFO, lived and died with grassroots organizing. From its initial Mississippi campaign in McComb in 1961, SNCC organizers endeavored to dwell among the people, surviving on subsistence wages, staying with local families, and exposing themselves to the hazards of life in the rural South. In moving among the people, SNCC field staff quickly realized that those at the Mississippi grassroots were "dirt poor."[4] As early as 1962, when the town of Greenwood in Leflore County cut off federal food aid in retribution for voter registration work, SNCC recognized the importance of daily sustenance—of food—to their struggle to bring meaningful change to African Americans in Mississippi.

SNCC's approach to food aid, what many activists termed its "welfare programs," evolved drastically between late 1962 and early 1964.[5] Beginning with the so-called Greenwood food blockade and the subsequent "Food for Freedom" campaign—a nationwide effort to gather food and funds for distribution to destitute Mississippi sharecroppers—SNCC staff, many drawing on their own experiences of hunger, saw the potential of food programs as "social work," a means of holding people over until the food crisis subsided or could be addressed through official, democratic channels.[6] The surprising voter registration upsurge in Leflore County in response to SNCC's local food relief efforts encouraged the organization, for a time, to view food as political incentive, emboldening black Mississippians to risk their lives and livelihoods by registering to vote. In doing so, organizers sought to reverse the generations-old white practice of manipulating food access to maintain an abundant, docile black workforce, the foundation of white economic domination. If a lack of food stifled movement, SNCC reasoned, then the promise of food could incite it.

Following the short-term successes of the initial food campaign in Greenwood, which proved to the community SNCC's commitment to addressing grassroots struggles, some voices within the organization began questioning the efficacy of this work. If organizers intended for food aid to enable people to hold on, to remain present in the struggle in body if not always in mind and spirit, some wondered whether it did not also hinder prospects for a true restructuring of the social order. Certainly people needed to eat—and most SNCC staff and volunteers voiced genuine empathy and compassion for the hungry poor—but some feared that satiated people might become complacent. While many within the organization viewed food as fundamental to the freedom fight, more radical voices among its leadership began by the end of 1963 to argue SNCC's social work counteracted its ultimate objective of social transformation.[7]

Much of the strife endured by black Mississippians in the twentieth century can be traced to the years after emancipation and the emergence of sharecropping, a race-based economic order that, in the wake of slavery, became the bedrock of white economic power in the Cotton Belt.[8] In sharecropping arrangements, farmers, or "croppers" (most often black, but sometimes white), contracted with white landowners to live on and farm their land, in return splitting the harvest in "shares." Under this system, the farming year fell into two phases. During the "furnish," croppers relied on white landowners' credit for shelter, food (typically cornmeal, fat pork, and molasses), clothing, farming equipment, tools, mules, seeds, fertilizers, and other commodities needed to work and survive until the second phase, the "harvest."[9] In contrast to tenant farmers, who paid cash to rent farmland and thus enjoyed some degree of autonomy, sharecroppers forcibly contracted to make all purchases through the plantation commissary, which regularly charged prices 10 to 25 percent higher than market value.[10] At harvest time, landlords deducted items credited to croppers' accounts from their share of the yield, which typically came to half the value of their annual cotton production. Like many social institutions of the Deep South, the sharecropping system held immense potential for abuse.[11] Rarely could croppers clear enough money at the end of the harvest to emerge with any profit. More often they finished the season in debt. Though they possessed the legal freedom to move to other plantations, sharecroppers regularly lacked the economic means to do so. At the turn of the twentieth century, the majority of southern black farmers—75 percent—lived as sharecroppers or renters.[12]

Beyond the economic function of maintaining a low-paid, docile workforce, enriching white planters at the economic and physical expense of black laborers, sharecropping and other forms of tenancy served vital political and social functions as well. Given the financial dependence of most blacks on white employers and the totalizing demands of the chopping and harvesting seasons, the children of black farmers often worked beside their parents. As a result, they seldom completed grade school.[13] Coupled with the damning uncertainties and demands of farm life, the shameful quality of black education in the Jim Crow South bred widespread intergenerational poverty, as children seldom gained the knowledge or skills necessary to forge a life beyond the cotton fields.[14] In relegating black farmworkers to the fringes of economic viability, the neo-plantation system made it virtually impossible for them to take economic risks or to assert themselves politically, as the subtlest suggestion of defiance threatened devastating consequences.

At about the time the sharecropping system began to take hold, re-solidifying the socioeconomic oppression of African Americans following the brief promise of the Reconstruction years (1865–1877), white Mississippi politicians swiftly maneuvered to obstruct the black political agency portended by passage of the Fifteenth Amendment in 1870, which guaranteed all male citizens the right to vote.[15] An 1890 convention amended the state constitution, implementing two key provisions that would serve to disfranchise generations of black Mississippians. First, delegates instituted a two-dollar poll tax to be paid annually for two years before an individual could vote in local or state elections.[16] The second prerequisite, a literacy test, represented an especially despicable device for stifling black political impulses given the deplorable status of black public education.[17] Because the power of white political authorities and legislators depended on black oppression, policymakers had no practical incentive to improve black schools. This cycle of miseducation, illiteracy, and political paralysis proved exceedingly effective in inhibiting latent black political action. As a final failsafe, local registrars (always white) wielded ultimate authority to pass or fail applicants.[18] For the next seventy-five years black electoral participation, for all intents and purposes, did not exist in Mississippi.

While black disfranchisement was the de facto policy across the state, the unique social and economic conditions of the Delta region amplified the oppressive influence of political marginalization on the daily welfare of African Americans.[19] The storied Yazoo-Mississippi Delta sits between the Mississippi River to the west and the Yazoo River to the east, though in colloquial use "the Delta" often refers to Mississippi's entire northwest quadrant. This region houses some of the most fertile soil on earth and for years produced greater quantities of high-quality cotton than anywhere else in the world. The advent of the cotton gin in 1790 greatly reduced the time and labor required to separate the plant's valuable fibers from its meddlesome seeds, thus making cotton farming—and race slavery—exponentially more profitable.[20] The subsequent emergence of a cotton aristocracy reliant on forced black labor shaped the trajectory of the Delta's racialized socioeconomic order. Because cotton farming depended on plentiful unskilled labor, white planters actively discouraged outmigration, and most blacks in the Delta continued to earn their living in cotton agriculture into the 1950s.[21] Though Mississippi's black population, like that of the South in general, thinned during two periods of mass exodus spurred by the world wars, the Delta in the mid- to late 1950s maintained a strong African American majority, including some of the most densely concentrated black populations in the state.[22]

The Delta coincided roughly with Mississippi's second congressional district, represented since 1941 by Democratic congressman Jamie Whitten, chair of the House Appropriations Subcommittee on Agriculture, Rural Development, Food and Drug Administration, and Related Agencies.[23] The region likewise produced the Citizens' Council, a network of white supremacists that actively, and at times violently, resisted integration in the wake of the Supreme Court's 1954 *Brown* decision.[24] Variously celebrated and denounced as "the most Southern place on earth," the Mississippi Delta at mid-century constituted a field of extremes, one that cultivated lavish wealth and crushing poverty, federal largesse and utter abandonment, racist terrorism and nonviolent protest.[25] Organizer Stokely Carmichael, who spent the summers of 1962 and 1963 canvassing prospective voters in Greenwood, refuted the perception that poverty alone defined the region.[26] "The Delta was in fact very, very rich. It produced great wealth," he observed. "It was agribusiness on a gigantic scale, highly productive, heavily government subsidized, and based almost totally on the equivalent of slave labor. . . . It was only *the people* who were poor. Dirt poor."[27] Sunflower County, for example, was home to both legendary sharecropper-turned-freedom-fighter Fannie Lou Hamer of Ruleville and commanding U.S. senator James O. Eastland, a wealthy cotton planter from nearby Doddsville and a fervent enemy of communism and civil rights.[28] The remarkable polarities of the Delta spurred the ire of activists and inspired their efforts to mobilize. "There in the Mississippi Delta's vast, almost eerie flatness of cotton lands," Carmichael reminisced, "in its small hamlets and rural churches, on its dark, dusty plantation back roads; from its fetid jails and the cattle prods and blackjacks of brutal 'polices'; in the drive-by shootings and midnight bombings of night-riding Klansmen—I saw the best and worse [sic] of which human beings were capable."[29] SNCC organizers faced a daunting task when they arrived in the Delta in 1962. Executive Secretary James Forman expressed great admiration for the courage of Bob Moses, statewide head of SNCC's voter registration work, and "his band of guerilla fighters" who put themselves on the line to try to bring change to the Delta. "They were resisting a tyranny imposed over hundreds of years," Forman affirmed. "They were writing history with their lives."[30]

Focusing the attention of civil rights supporters on the alliances among southern lawmakers, white planters, and the Department of Agriculture (USDA), movement organizers used Mississippi as a lightning rod, a tragic illustration of federal abuses and excesses at their most extreme. Despite the avowed (if not always active) position of the White House in support of civil rights, the agricultural policies of the Kennedy and Johnson administrations in fact reinforced the entrenched power of Mississippi's white-supremacist planting class. County officials made most decisions affecting the lives of African Americans, particularly those mired in poverty, and did so generally with the tacit approval of those holding statewide elected offices.[31] Unsurprisingly, officials responsible for administering federal relief programs exhibited little concern for the needs of the black poor. Diminishing their sense of self-worth and dignity by forcing the hungry to accept the status quo, beg for food, or face starvation (and sometimes all three at once), the white-supremacist system in general and the biased, degrading welfare system in particular circumscribed the political and economic agency of the black poor. By mandating that people focus their energy and resources on brute physical survival, white leaders and their proxy institutions diminished black capacities to concentrate on higher pursuits or long-term aims. And that, it seemed, was their intent.

Scholars of southern history, and of American race relations and food politics more broadly, have documented the use and abuse of food as a device to control black labor since the time of slavery.[32] Perhaps even more so after emancipation, manipulation and monopoly of the food supply enabled those with land to maintain authority over labor. Beginning with the New Deal, the nation's farmers benefited from federal subsidies, price supports, loans, and acreage-reduction plans, all of which aimed to ensure that, regardless of market forces, farmers could earn a living from the land.[33] The advent of a federal surplus commodity distribution program during the 1930s likewise protected these interests, as distribution of surpluses to the poor offered a politically popular way to relieve the troublesome glut without diminishing the profits generated by agriculture. If federal food programs improved social welfare, they did so incidentally, a by-product of policies designed to safeguard the prosperity of American farmers.[34]

This reality inevitably shaped the character of federal food aid, as most monthly commodity allotments consisted primarily of starches (almost invariably in overstock) with little in the way of protein, vitamins, and minerals. Program participants usually received flour, cornmeal, rice, dried milk and other dairy products, and occasionally some canned meat, but never fresh fruits or vegetables, which created difficulties for storage and transport.[35] Government commodities arrived in nondescript packaging with no instructions for storage or preparation. Of course, products that recipients did not have the facilities or knowledge to store or prepare offered little bulwark against hunger and malnutrition. Even more problematically, supplies often ran out midway through the month, leaving families to scavenge or go without during the long days before they retrieved the next month's supply. Barriers to access exacerbated the program's nutritional deficiencies, as local governments first had to request federal food aid for their jurisdiction and then bore responsibility for the costs and administration of distribution. In many cases, officials simply chose not to participate in federal food programs rather than accept the expense and hassle. In some localities that technically did participate, people had to walk up to twenty-five miles to retrieve their allotments, as few areas offered decentralized distribution points.[36] The cost and time of transportation thus often rendered the program impractical for those most in need.

Official insensitivity, hostility, and outright bias compounded the practical obstacles to obtaining commodity food aid. Though funded by federal dollars, commodity distribution, like other welfare programs, fell under the jurisdiction of state welfare offices and the direct administration of county officials generally unsympathetic to the plight of the hungry.[37] In addition to setting standards for eligibility, county agents wielded authority to certify participants. This system allowed planters to continue to pay starvation wages throughout the year while the federal government, in effect, fed their workforce. In fact, some county governments only supplied federal commodities during the winter months, ensuring that once the cotton season began, farmworkers had no choice but to return to the employ of opportunistic landlords, lest they and their families go hungry. Despite the numerous painful shortcomings of federal aid, the physical and economic survival of many poor Mississippians relied upon it. Recognizing this, landowners and local officials dually responsible for registering voters and administering federal food aid colluded to deploy provisions in a manner that perpetuated black economic dependence. The majority of black residents avoided rankling local authorities so as not to risk being cut from the program without any means of redress.

Unsurprisingly, white leaders deemed voter registration a particularly egregious offense.

In one notable demonstration of courage and defiance, Mary Oliver Welsh and Daisy Griffin, elderly black women from Humphreys County at the lower edge of the Delta, testified before the U.S. Civil Rights Commission in February 1965 that the country registrar, G. H. Hood, had verbally abused and threatened them when they attempted to register as voters. Both women relied on federal surplus commodities and "before going to the courthouse," the commission report noted, "had expressed concern to civil rights workers in Belzoni [the county seat] that an attempt to register would cost them their commodities."[38] Welsh reported that the county registrar "told me I was going to get in trouble, and he wasn't going to give me no commodities. That's what he said. . . . After I went there and he scared me so bad, I didn't go back to see was I passed or no."[39] Griffin and others likewise attested that the registrar had mentioned their reliance on commodities when they went to register. Official manipulation of residents' fear of hunger thus served not only as retaliation but as intimidation as well, as administrators wielded the much-needed commodities to bully those otherwise undeterred from pursuing their right to vote. Though the devious nature of this process intentionally obscured the actual number of individuals dropped from the program for attempting to register, the imminent threat of hunger very likely kept thousands of local people from rocking the boat. County authorities wedded to a southern tradition based on the oppression and subjugation of black Americans therefore continued to hold the lives of poor blacks in their hands. The white economic noose around the necks of thousands of blacks in the Delta minimized the likelihood that they would accept the economic and physical perils entailed in supporting any efforts to challenge the entrenched race-based social order.[40]

For decades, this arrangement worked to the economic advantage and racial privilege of white planters, who maintained their political clout in areas where blacks vastly outnumbered them. By the early 1960s, conditions for black Mississippi farmers were worse than they had been in generations.[41] Despite complex federal efforts to constrict agricultural productivity, technological advances continued to produce unprecedented bounties. Many landowners also stipulated that all arable soil be dedicated to cotton cultivation, allowing none for food plots or subsistence gardens. With the mechanization of cotton production nearly complete by the end of the 1950s, landowners less often leased their land, instead preferring to hire day laborers during the harvest.[42] Unprotected by federal labor regulations until 1966, farm laborers who managed to find work averaged just three dollars per day during the cotton season from April to December, earning an annual income of about six hundred dollars (in 1961–62 dollars). These conditions ensured that the cotton labor force, especially sharecroppers, teetered on the edge of calamity, leading a hand-to-mouth existence that dashed any hopes of accumulating savings. Mired in a cycle of hunger and hopelessness, poor families had limited mobility in every sense—physically, socioeconomically, and politically.

While the stringent voting regulations set in place in 1890 had largely shut down black political participation in the state, the open and ominous threat of economic reprisal tightened the white chokehold on the black community to be ready in the event that local blacks entertained ideas of organizing. Most black Mississippians soon knew, for example, the story of Fannie Lou Hamer's ill-fated attempt to register to vote on August 31, 1962.[43] When she defied the orders of her landlord, B. D. Marlowe, to return to the county courthouse to rescind her application, he promptly evicted her from the plantation where she and her husband had lived and worked for eighteen years.[44] Word spread about cases like hers, eliciting indignation but often dampening enthusiasm for political action. Evictions and firings not only thwarted the potential for individuals, now homeless and hungry, to assert themselves in defense of their rights, but they also served as a warning to others on neighboring farms and in surrounding communities that any intimation of political resistance would evoke immediate repercussions. For years, this system was astoundingly effective in neutralizing threats of black political power.

Several developments converged in the early 1960s to disrupt this state of affairs. As the mechanization of cotton agriculture in the late 1950s fueled widespread unemployment in the Delta, civil rights groups began to move into the state. After SNCC's first wide-scale voter registration drive, held in the southwestern city of McComb in 1961 and 1962, organizers honed in on the Delta for new and more vigorous efforts to secure the franchise in an area not greatly changed since emancipation.[45] Bob Moses, director of SNCC's Mississippi voter registration project, saw that the town of Greenwood held great strategic significance "as the center for around five different counties." At a SNCC conference in April 1963, Moses explained SNCC's early thinking: "What we hope will happen is that we will get a drive in all these counties with Greenwood as a focus. And if you do that, then that will crack the heart of the Delta."[46] Now viewing the black masses as not only economically obsolete but also politically menacing, white planters and officials re-strategized, aiming to drive unemployed blacks out of the state by openly encouraging them to pursue better opportunities in northern cities like Detroit and Chicago or out west in the fertile lands of California. Many Mississippi blacks, of course, could not realistically entertain this possibility, as they had no savings, suffered poor health, headed large families, and possessed no marketable skills beyond the cotton fields.

In response to fairly isolated voting rights demonstrations and voter education and registration work in Greenwood during the summer of 1962, Leflore County officials made a brash move. After the usual tactics of intimidation and violence failed to discourage organizers, local administrators swiped the bottom out from under the local poor.[47] The Leflore County Board of Supervisors voted in July to eliminate from the budget the funds required to operate the surplus commodities program. Three months later, it formally shut down the winter commodities program, effectively cutting off thousands of poor Mississippians, black and white, from federal food relief.[48] Recalling the implications of this decision four years later, Delta organizers Lawrence Guyot and Mike Thelwell contended, "the State began a program which can best be characterized as one of gradual genocide, the goal of which was to effect the dispersal or extinction of the Negro population."[49] Following some initial opposition, the board held a public meeting on November 9 to hear testimony and reconsider the measure. Seventy people attended.[50] Board supervisor Lewis Poindexter stated that the winter commodity program cost the county $4,150 per month for six months each year, in addition to distribution costs of labor and transportation.[51] Poindexter insisted that the program would still serve those on welfare (families with dependent children, as well as the elderly, handicapped, and blind) but acknowledged that twenty-two thousand would no longer receive benefits as a result of the change. J. H. Peebles, president of the Bank of Commerce, motioned to support the board's decision. Forty of the sixty-nine people who voted agreed with the move.[52] The board's original decision would stand.

Many in town appeared content with the official explanation that the program had become too bloated and cumbersome to maintain. Aubrey Bell, attorney for the board of supervisors, insisted the "commodities were cut off purely for a financial reason and no other."[53] By way of evidence, Bell pointed out that twenty-six thousand of the county's forty-six thousand residents had previously received commodities. Rather than as an indication of widespread need, Bell and other opponents of the program framed these statistics as evidence of extensive abuse of the system.[54] The Mississippi Advisory Committee to the U.S. Commission on Civil Rights backed the county's decision, reporting it found "no concrete evidence" of civil rights violations as a result of the maneuver.[55] Thus, it appeared, business would continue as usual in Leflore.

Certain that the board had terminated federal food assistance as a reprisal against SNCC's work in Greenwood, organizers quickly recognized that their campaign—and their target constituency—faced immediate peril.[56] SNCC understood that the daily need to feed one's family took precedence over seemingly distant if no less pressing concerns about politics and elections. The organization thus immediately commenced a campaign to solicit food donations from movement supporters and altruistic citizens in the North, hoping this tactic would enable the project and its people to keep going. In addition to coordinating the enormous logistical task of gathering and distributing foodstuffs from such cities as Chicago, New York, and Boston, SNCC and COFO worked to politicize hunger, framing it as a result of institutional biases, systematic deprivation, racial cruelty, and political abuse rather than individual misfortune. By connecting hunger to politics in the minds of hungry Mississippians and other concerned Americans, SNCC hoped to convert a looming catastrophe into a coup. Ensuing food drives aimed to harness desperation wrought by hunger into widespread agitation in the Delta. The tactical miscalculation of Greenwood officials exemplified the life and death consequences of political dispossession across the rural South, bringing national attention to the daily injustices of Mississippi's racial caste system.[57]

The poor immediately felt the stinging loss of federal food aid. SNCC project director Bob Moses, a Harlem native widely remembered for his soft voice and understated yet unparalleled leadership style, wrote to a colleague in Ann Arbor, Michigan, in December 1962, relaying dismal conditions in the Delta. "I was sitting resting, having finished a bowl of stew," he explained, "and a silent hand reached over from behind, mumbling some words of apology and permission, and stumbled up with a neckbone from the plate under the bowl, which I had discarded, which had consequently some meat on it." Though the hungry stranger remained faceless to Moses, who did not want to embarrass him by looking, "the hand was back again, five seconds later, groping for the potatoes I had left in the bowl." In Moses's mind, the disembodied hand alone told a whole life's story, for it "was dark, dry and wind cracked, from cotton chopping and cotton picking." The broader ramifications of this scene for the prospects of the movement disheartened Moses. "What the hell are you going to do," he wondered, "when a man has to pick up a leftover potatoe [sic] from a bowl of stew?"[58]

To make matters worse, the winter of 1962–63 promised to be especially difficult. That year the picking season had ended around Thanksgiving, about a month sooner than usual.[59] Meanwhile, the price of cotton had fallen, squeezing the community's poorest during an unusually cold off-season. The vast majority of the black population would not likely find steady employment before cotton chopping began near the end of May. Moses's letter conveyed these dire circumstances to movement allies in the North. Several days earlier Moses and others had met to organize a food and clothing drive, headquartered in Clarksdale, to assist the hungry poor during the long months ahead.[60] He assured his colleagues in the North, "We *Do* need the actual food, I just hope you and others can gather it, and we can distribute it, so the people who need it can receive it." He concluded the letter with a single sentence about the ongoing voter registration drive and the need for a typewriter and mimeograph machine "if we are to get out the volume of material we need to contact people across the Delta." Though the letter addressed the voter registration campaign in Greenwood, Moses's message served on a more basic level to link the material needs of SNCC's target constituency to the project of political mobilization in a broader sense. About a week later SNCC's newsletter, the *Student Voice*, first published news of the emergency in Greenwood and emerging problems in the Sunflower County town of Ruleville, where local officials had begun aggressively to impede would-be voters from obtaining their monthly commodity allotment.[61]

In contrast to blatant measures in Greenwood to discontinue the commodity program outright, officials in Sunflower County quietly erected formidable obstacles to food access.[62] In response to movement activity, the county instituted newfangled policies and procedures regarding eligibility for federal food assistance, which had previously been accessible to nearly all who applied. By the end of 1962, officials required applicants to obtain proof of income from white employers not often willing to help, let alone acknowledge that their workers earned too little to feed themselves. In other cases, longtime commodity recipients encountered unannounced procedural changes regarding where and how to apply for or retrieve foodstuffs, most of which required great additional expenditures in time and cost of transportation. Field Secretaries Charlie Cobb of Springfield, Massachusetts, and Charles McLaurin, a Jackson native who established SNCC's Ruleville base, told of one woman who attempted to follow the new rules. When she went to apply for aid, the county official handed her a card. She soon heard Ruleville mayor C. M. Dorrough quip, "Most of them with cards ain't going to get any food," as he vowed to "mess up all of them" involved in voter activity.[63] In light of these new forms of harassment, COFO officials determined that food distribution efforts would focus on Greenwood in Leflore and Ruleville in Sunflower.[64] Cobb and McLaurin explained, "The success of our voter registration program depends on the protection we can offer the individual while he is waiting for his one small vote [to] mean something. It doesn't take much to tide ever [sic] the rural Mississippi Negro, but the commodities are vital."[65]

Sam Block, a skilled and fearless organizer from the Delta city of Cleveland, corroborated his colleagues' observations in early January 1963.[66] Having recently purchased a car to ease the enormous burden of traveling from plantation to plantation and town to town canvassing potential voters, Block noted that in addition to expediting registration efforts, motor transportation enabled organizers to familiarize themselves more intimately with the conditions and struggles of the people. Block reported to Executive Secretary James Forman, "We are now able to get around to these people who have been cut [off] from this surplus food deal, and man[,] some of them will make you cry to see the way they have been trying to live."[67] Enduring chilling temperatures in ramshackle housing "in little nasty alleys," mothers who had relied on commodity milk to feed their babies now had nothing to quiet their hungry cries, as they "had not received any food in a long time." Organizers scrambled to deliver aid, spending days at a time "running back and forth to Memphis, Clarksdale[,] and Jackson picking up food and clothing for the people"—and, Block believed, "seeing some results."[68] Certainly some of the same humanitarian and religious impulses that drew activists into the movement compelled them to act on behalf of the hungry. Many had experienced hunger and food insecurity as children, recognized the need and its physical and psychological ramifications, and did what they could to help.

The conditions of the Delta alone warranted shock and outrage, but the conscious and concerted efforts of local authorities to hold federal food aid hostage elevated the tragedies of hunger, starvation, and malnutrition in a country with unparalleled and costly agricultural harvests to the level of national scandal. Seizing the catastrophe, organizers highlighted the lengths to which the white power structure went to protect itself. Cobb, for one, had no doubt that the decision to end participation in the commodity program "was in clear reprisal for the voter registration—never mind that most of the people in the county had not tried to register to vote. All the Black people were made to pay the price for this."[69] Local officials surely expected the usual response to their tactics: cowering, perhaps some muted objections, but fear, resignation, and ultimate acquiescence. Rather than paralyze black residents with panic, however, the board of supervisors' decision incensed many, particularly in Greenwood, provoking them to act. They began flocking to the courthouse to register in greater numbers. Local officials' strategic blunder illustrated, in Cobb's estimation, the connection between political power and economic and physical well-being, a relationship innately understood, if not readily articulated, by the hungry poor. Cobb later approximated the sentiments of poor blacks emboldened to register by the food blockade: "If you're depending on this food, and it's not there . . . then you better do something about that."[70] As local people continued to react against the county's maneuver, SNCC worked to tend to their needs, implementing an intricate campaign among northern allies—the official offices of which the organization dubbed "Friends of SNCC"—to collect and distribute food to those struggling for their rights in the South. Infuriated by this policy of collective accountability and inspired by the determination of poor sharecroppers to stand their ground, SNCC and COFO launched what became known as the "Food for Freedom" campaign.[71] The simplicity of its message and the immediacy of its action plan compelled passionate responses far and wide.

Though many Mississippians scrapped and scraped to keep their neighbors from starving, the viability of SNCC's efforts in the Delta depended upon its capacity to inspire outsiders to take up the charge. On December 16, 1962, Aaron "Doc" Henry, a pharmacist from Clarksdale, made a national appeal as the titular head of COFO, and donations began arriving soon thereafter.[72] Located in Coahoma County, just north of Sunflower County and about sixty-five miles from the Tennessee border,

Clarksdale served as a convenient dropping point. Among the earliest to rally in support of the campaign, movement supporters in Michigan worked with Henry and others to facilitate a massive food drive in time for the holidays. Spearheading these efforts, Ivanhoe Donaldson of SNCC and his roommate Ben Taylor, both Michigan State University students, canvassed communities in East Lansing and Ann Arbor for food and clothing donations and then trucked the vital foodstuffs to the distribution headquarters in Clarksdale, some eight hundred miles away.[73]

Local authorities, of course, knew of Henry's movement activities and affiliations and of COFO's very public efforts to bring change to the Delta. Police therefore closely monitored Henry and his business in efforts to obstruct relief work. Donaldson and Taylor arrived at Henry's drugstore two days after Christmas with a load containing one thousand pounds of food and medicine from Louisville, Kentucky.[74] Unable to enter the building or get in touch with Henry upon their arrival in the early morning hours, they parked in front of the store and dozed off in the truck. Not long after, local police roused the exhausted men. Donaldson recalled, "We were harassed and juggled around and thrown in jail. The charges were that we were taking narcotics across state lines, but what we had were aspirins and bandages as parts of first aid kits for people who might need medical help."[75] Despite Donaldson's explanation (or possibly as a result of it), local authorities arrested them. Donaldson and Taylor spent five days in jail before getting word to Henry about their whereabouts and remained there until the NAACP Legal Defense Fund secured their release.[76] Perhaps emboldened to defy official tactics of coercion, Donaldson later estimated that he "made about thirty-odd round trips to Louisville, to Detroit, round trips from Clarksville and Greenwood, back and forth, and also to Chicago during that period. In fact, one of the interesting points about the food drive," he noted, "was that a prominent young black comedian named Dick Gregory got involved in the movement and it totally changed his life."[77]

Indeed, Gregory, who struggled with hunger and food insecurity from his childhood days in St. Louis into his early adulthood, famously and visibly responded to the crisis.[78] He wrote soon after, "There was a battle going on [in the South], there was a war shaping up, and somehow writing checks and giving speeches didn't seem enough. . . . I wanted a piece of the action now, I wanted to get in this thing. I got my chance sooner than I expected."[79] Gregory's call to become an active participant rather than a distant sponsor came from Greenwood. Informed of the situation by a SNCC ally in Chicago seeking the public support of a wealthy black celebrity, Gregory immediately answered calls from Leflore County, resolving, "If the government would not feed the people, then I would."[80] He launched additional relief efforts, appealing for donations from residents of his adopted hometown of Chicago. One letter signed by Gregory and Rev. Douglas M. Still of the National Council of Churches pronounced, "These people need food! They look to us in the North for help. . . . To secure the widest support possible we are asking prominent Chicago citizens in simple humanitarian, non-political terms, to endorse and support this effort."[81]

Chicagoans responded, and Gregory and a local disc jockey combined forces to collect fourteen thousand pounds of canned food, mostly fruits and vegetables.[82] In February 1963, Gregory chartered a plane to transport the goods to Memphis and then drove them 134 miles to Clarksdale. From there, SNCC trucked the supplies to Greenwood and Ruleville. "I was still afraid of the South," Gregory recalled, "and I wanted to leave that night." Reticent to venture beyond enemy lines but compelled to use his fame and fortune to support those at the front, Gregory felt prompted to act by the urgency of hunger, a condition he knew often begat shame, alienation, immobility, and numbness. Gregory and SNCC staff, including Stokely Carmichael and H. Rap Brown, passed out donations and planned a voting rights demonstration to dramatize the connection between food and politics. Feeling inspired, and perhaps somewhat cornered, Gregory wrote, "I promised the voter registration workers from SNCC . . . that I'd come back when the demonstrations began."[83]

The swarm of publicity and agitation stemming from Gregory's appearance and colorful comments succeeded in putting local white officials and residents on the defensive. Rather than assert that hungry people deserved to starve—a politically untenable message in almost any context—authorities sought to downplay the extent of local need while calling into question the motives of those opposing the commodity rollback. Shortly after Gregory's arrival, the local newspaper, the *Greenwood Commonwealth*, ran a front-page story based on the anonymous statements of a "concerned Negro citizen of Leflore County [who] said that local Negro citizens 'deplore[d] the adverse publicity the county is getting' around free food distribution." The unnamed source asserted "that food 'isn't really need[ed], nobody is destitute that we know of, but we will accept it [food] if it come with thanks.'"[84] Far from a blatant bid to silence political dissent, the article suggested that the "story" had been concocted by outsiders aiming to generate "bad publicity [for] Leflore County." The unidentified informant pointed to growing tensions in the North, suggesting that Gregory's energies would be better spent cleaning up his own backyard. "You won't find anybody being evicted from their homes here as you will in Chicago," the source falsely reported. "You won't find anybody's gas or lights being cut off." Suggesting that Greenwood authorities and community groups like the Negro Elk's Club met all needs of which they were aware, the witness avowed, "If anybody is destitute it is only because they haven't let their need be known." The *Commonwealth* expressed "[satisfaction] that [the anonymous source] speaks for a substantial group of Leflore County Negroes," pointing out that he "made the statement in the presence of several leading white citizens." Instead of calling into question the authenticity of the unattributed comments in light of this fact, the reporter implied that these circumstances actually bolstered the credibility of the account. The shadowy figure concluded, "If they've got free food, certainly let's take it with thanks. . . . Let's help them distribute it. Then let them be on their way." If hunger existed in Greenwood, the article implied, it would be remedied from within. Though local blacks might accept charity, the *Commonwealth* insisted that they nonetheless resented efforts to challenge or question those entrusted with protecting the public's interests, including their own.

On the contrary, Bob Moses of SNCC believed that beneficiaries of food aid would be more likely to stand up in support of those who delivered them from hunger. The population in Greenwood proved most receptive to the political implications of their food insecurity, as the food and clothing drives mobilized people there in new, sometimes astonishing, ways.[85] As a result, violence, tension, and repression gripped Greenwood throughout February and March. "Cars were wrecked, a Negro registration worker was shot in the back of the neck, the SNCC headquarters was set on fire," Gregory learned. "Bullets were fired into Negro homes. SNCC workers were beaten up. When Negroes marched in protest, the police put the dogs on them. They arrested the eleven top registration workers."[86] In the midst of the chaos, the food work continued. Given the scale of the anticipated need, SNCC required residents to apply for food aid, stipulating that "a person must be unemployed, have earned less than $500 last year (1962) and have two children of school age who are not attending school."[87] Block insisted that SNCC trusted applicants, "taking their word" about the extent of their need.[88] A day before one scheduled giveaway, Block reported receipt of nine hundred applications for food and clothing. Though twenty-two thousand people had been ousted from the commodity rolls in recent months, the *Commonwealth* reported that less than one thousand had signed up to receive SNCC food aid and that "Block and some of his co-workers had been going about the city and county seeking people to make application for the food." Rather than interpret this as evidence of the need to publicize the availability of free food or of widespread fear among local blacks that applying for and accepting aid might make them targets of retribution, the *Commonwealth* cited initial hesitance as proof that people who had been receiving federal aid had not actually needed it.[89]

Willie Peacock, a native of Charleston, Mississippi, who came to Greenwood to support Block's efforts, emerged as chairman of the "emergency relief committee."[90] On February 13, he oversaw food distribution at Greenwood's Wesley Methodist Church. The *Commonwealth* observed that two hundred to three hundred black residents received boxes marked "SNCC," which contained nonperishable foodstuffs like rice, flour, cereal, and canned goods, but "only about enough food for one or two meals." One woman with two children and a disabled husband at home acknowledged, "It's not much what they are giving, but it helps."[91] When the food ran out after four hours, an even greater number of people had to be turned away, while still seventy-five more waited to apply for help.[92] Despite their disappointment at leaving empty-handed, Peacock believed, "when [he] explained it to them they understood."[93] While the local paper and leading white citizens highlighted SNCC's inability to provide food for all who requested it, they curiously continued to downplay that a need actually existed. The paper emphasized, for example, that many of those seeking aid had arrived in cars, implying that people with private transportation could afford to buy their own food. This assumption infuriated organizers, who recognized that food expenses were more flexible than fixed costs like rent and car notes. "A car has nothing to do with it," Block insisted.[94] The following week, SNCC delivered more food, provisioning those previously turned away.[95]

Though Gregory had returned to Chicago after only a brief stay in Mississippi, the comedian still recalled feeling targeted by local white politicians and reporters who resented his intervention. "I knew they were laying for me down there," he remembered. State welfare commissioner Fred Ross tellingly characterized the "cheap publicity generated by Gregory and the gullibility of national news media who apparently relish the opportunity to disseminate half truths and outright lies" as "a distinct disservice to the Negro population of Mississippi."[96] Claiming that blacks composed 80 percent of the state's commodity recipients, Ross defended the extent of state relief efforts. "The white people of Mississippi are leaning over backwards and taxing themselves to the hilt to help the Negro race," he declared, warning that the "national ridicule and abuse" the state suffered as a result of the controversy "may well result in the surplus food commodity program in Mississippi being seriously curtailed or entirely wiped out."[97] First suggesting that Gregory and civil rights organizers had exaggerated the amount of food donated, white Mississippi leaders then implied, in Gregory's words, "if Dick Gregory was going to take care of their poor Negroes, let's send them all up to Chicago."[98]

An editorial from the *Clarksdale Press Register* echoed these sentiments in dramatic terms, dismissing Gregory and the "grocery situation" as "downright ridiculous."[99] Playing on Gregory's profession, the author stated that the "whole absurd spectacle" of his appeal "to the bleeding hearts of Chicago for food to bring down to the Southern hinterlands would be downright sidesplitting if it were not taken seriously by Mississippi's less knowledgeable Americans in the social wastelands of South Chicago, Gary, Harlem, and Hyannis Port."[100] This generalization of donors as bleeding-heart liberals overlooked the contributions of socially conservative organizations, including the Nation of Islam.[101] The suggestion that those sending food should focus on their own affairs in the North similarly ignored the likelihood that many who contributed maintained family ties in the South. Instead, the commentator attacked the "widespread and flagrant abuses by the [commodity program] participants, which have nothing whatsoever to do with voting, school integration, or what have you." Freedom from hunger, the author contended, was a privilege, not a right of citizenship.[102]

In attempting to belittle the need by characterizing "Gregory's Jet-Propelled Grocery Store" as an ill-advised, self-interested publicity stunt, opponents missed the point. The huge public response to the food drive stemmed less from the identity of the donor than from the extraordinary lengths to which he traveled to bring food to hungry people. By attacking Gregory's motives, white officials aimed to distract from the circumstances that necessitated outside intervention. Though white Mississippians understood, and often embraced, the state's customs and methods of operation, the peculiarities and injustices of southern social relations represented a source of embarrassment when illuminated by national media, evidence of the calculated measures deployed by the white power structure to keep black residents on the margins of life. The food blockade thus created a crucial opportunity for organizers to forge a human connection between the rural poor, regardless of race, and Americans beyond the Magnolia State. If interested citizens outside the South might be lulled into complacency or inaction by a shared sense that they as individuals could not do much to expedite desegregation, secure black voting rights, or overturn the plantation economy, they might—and apparently did—feel compelled to contribute food for the cause of freedom. Certainly widespread hunger stemmed from broader structures of political repression and economic exploitation, but it also offered a condition to which others might relate and a cause to which they could directly, and relatively easily, respond. In helping to meet the material needs of the poor, donors and movement friends demonstrated that everyone interested in justice had a role to play. As the days dragged on, local people finally began to move en masse.

The spark ignited on February 23, when police arrested Sam Block for "issuing a false statement designed to cause a breach of the peace."[103] The night before, four buildings near the SNCC office had burned. Block hypothesized to the United Press International that arsonists targeting SNCC had mistakenly torched the buildings in its vicinity in retaliation against recent food distribution efforts.[104] Though Block had been jailed numerous times in Greenwood by that point, on this occasion black residents responded in a decidedly different fashion. Charlie Cobb, who spent most of his time working in Ruleville, remarked, "People came from all over for Sam's trial. And they were doing stuff we had never seen in Ruleville or any other place . . . like deliberately drinking from the 'white' water fountains and talking back to white people. It was kind of a protest as well as an observation of Sam."[105] Such flagrant violations of one of the signposts of Jim Crow etiquette—segregated drinking fountains—indicated a striking refutation of social customs and political arrangements that marked black bodies as inferior and their physical needs and comfort insignificant. "With little to lose now," Bob Moses recalled, local residents "protested that Sam Block had done nothing wrong. Even we [SNCC staff] were surprised by their militancy."[106] This show of support represented a welcome change for Block, who had slept in his car for four months upon arriving in Greenwood because no one in the community dared to risk associating with him.[107] When city judge O. L. Kimbrough implied that the situation would improve for local blacks if Block left town, Block's defiant response further galvanized the crowd. "Well, judge, I ain't gonna do none of that," he reportedly retorted.[108] Mississippi-born and -educated, Block had literally been schooled in the system of white supremacy, and in the structures of black exploitation upon which it rested. He became a local hero that day not only for refusing to back down to a white man but also for openly defying an agent of the same local government that denied black voting rights and perpetuated black hunger.

Cobb and Moses viewed this sequence of events as a psychological turning point for the embattled community, as "for the first time people were making a connection between food on their table and political participation. . . . They recognized that the people who did this [withheld the commodities] were people who were elected to office."[109] Local blacks appeared to comprehend the implications of the judge's proposition—that is, that county leaders saw them, and the food they needed to survive, as pawns in a political battle. Judge Kimbrough showed his hand too soon, in effect acknowledging that officials squeezed the poor to squelch resistance. In Cobb's eyes, this episode cemented in the minds of both Greenwood blacks and SNCC organizers the vital connection between eating and voting. He recalled the new approach and mentality: "You're not only here to get food, but you're also here to fill out this registration form."[110] Moses meanwhile celebrated the manner in which SNCC food assistance facilitated communal autonomy, signified hopes for self-determination, and fostered self-respect. "The food is identified in the minds of everyone as food for those who want to be free," he believed, "and the minimum requirement for freedom is identified as registration to vote." Amidst rational fears of violence against those who joined or cooperated with the movement, local people might be moved to participate in the political process if they could see how their involvement might directly improve their quality of life. SNCC's relief work demonstrated the urgent need for compassionate community leaders, highlighting the link between political disfranchisement and destitution. "When a thousand people stand in line for a few cans of food," Moses contended, "then it is possible to tell a thousand people that they are poor, that they are trapped in poverty, that they must move if they are to escape."[111]

Several days after Block's arrest, Moses wrote to northern supporters, thanking them for their assistance and conveying the value of their efforts. In doing so, he directly reinforced the connection between food and the franchise. "The food drive you organized and publicized . . . has resulted in and served as the immediate catalyst for opening new dimensions in the voter registration movement in Mississippi," he assured them.[112] The logistics of direct aid distribution necessitated contact with community leaders, and, perhaps more importantly, encouraged rural blacks to come to SNCC for help. Moreover, while some liberal students and volunteers might cower from the violence and harassment that often accompanied registration drives, a campaign to feed the hungry held a philanthropic appeal that appeared, at the surface, apolitical in nature. Moses confidently informed supporters that the food drive had fueled the "development of a core of workers who come to help process the applications [for aid], packing and distribution of the food, and stay to help on the voter registration drive." In this way, SNCC's food work politicized staff and volunteers as well. Finally, and most critically to SNCC's broader political aims, the food drive fostered for the organization, philosophically and tactically dedicated to encouraging indigenous leadership, an "image in the Negro community of providing direct aid, not just 'agitation.'" This was no small matter in the Delta, where the threat of official or vigilante justice, firing, or eviction paralyzed the aspirations of many who otherwise might have been inclined to vote.[113]

As the days wore on, leading white citizens in Greenwood continued to endeavor to defuse the crisis by denying that a crisis existed. The mayor and city commissioners preached calm, blaming the upsurge in demonstrations on the work of outsiders "activated by motives other than the welfare of our people . . . [and] dedicated to creating disunity and discord among us."[114] Appealing to an imagined past of racial unity in which "the white and colored races of Greenwood and Leflore County have lived together in an atmosphere of harmony, understanding, and cooperation," the official statement, issued at the beginning of March, assured local residents that, if they refused to "permit [them]selves to become victimized by those whose sole purpose in being here is to bring about upheaval and unrest . . . they will move on; and we will continue, in the future as in the past, to manage our own affairs for the mutual benefit of all."¹¹⁵ As Greenwood officials couched objections to SNCC's work in terms of local autonomy rather than race or class conflict, they hinted at external pressures exerted by the USDA to ameliorate the situation. Finally, on March 19, the board of supervisors voted to reinstitute the commodity program. In a scathing editorial, a writer for the *Commonwealth* identified only as "T.W." characterized the vote as "surrender" to a USDA ultimatum that Leflore "furnish commodities to the masses of Welfare Cheats or 'we will do it for you.'" T.W. warned that, in allowing the federal government to intervene in "local" affairs, the board took the first step on a slippery slope. Considering the role of state welfare commissioner Fred Ross in the decision, T.W. ironically echoed Ross's threat that Mississippi should get "out of the welfare business altogether, because nowhere do the strings attached to federal money show up clearer than in that particular area which has become strictly an activity of the government, divorced entirely from the control of the people."¹¹⁶ Following the board's decision, SNCC leadership continued to collect and distribute food to dramatize its assertion that, even for those who received it, federal food assistance did not stave off hunger.

SNCC's decision reflected the utility of food as a tool to mobilize the dispossessed. In an organization committed to cultivating grassroots political movement, food aid provided something concrete and meaningful to the very people whose trust SNCC needed in order to make inroads in the "closed society." Food provided a relatively easy but absolutely vital entry point. People who at first shied away from organizers they feared would try to persuade them to register to vote might be more inclined to listen if they saw something to be gained in the here and now, not only for themselves but for their families. Long-term political organizing was hard and often dispiriting work. Food, however, not only helped to entice the poor to trust SNCC but also created an incentive for them to take greater risks with and for an organization that met their daily needs. More practically, SNCC's food aid made local people less reliant on often manipulative and unreliable government food aid, and it worked to reassure potential voters that, even if they lost their homes and jobs in retribution, at least they would not be left to starve. Reflecting upon the lessons of Greenwood, Moses explained, "We knew more about organizing now. A small dedicated band—even one person—could dig in, establish a beachhead, survive and perhaps get some kind of breakthrough, punch[ing] a small hole in the wall of white supremacy by linking everyday issues to political participation."[117]

Charles McLaurin, who at Moses's behest had recruited Fannie Lou Hamer to join SNCC's efforts, underscored this connection but described a more practical function of the food giveaways in February 1964. One day after a truck delivered twenty-four thousand pounds of food and clothing to Ruleville, seventy-five people signed up for aid, a third of whom then went to the county courthouse in Indianola to register.[118] On this occasion SNCC directly reinforced the continued imperative of voter registration by stating that those who attempted to register would be first to receive the free food distributed the following night. Of the three hundred people who came to the food giveaway the next day, more than half had attempted to register, some walking up to ten miles to do so. The following Monday morning, people began arriving at the SNCC freedom house before six o'clock, and by 7:30 about one thousand people stood in line while a queue of cars stretched ten blocks long. Within five days, the entire shipment of food had been distributed, and still many of the needy had been unable to collect provisions. Over the course of the week more than three hundred black Mississippians—about 30 percent of those who had come requesting food—tried to register to vote in Sunflower County. Most were illiterate and therefore certain to fail the test, but that, McLaurin noted, was not the point. "Now they could say that they had been to the courthouse to register to vote. The people who could not write or read may never become voters, but they had done what we asked—to register or to make an attempt to do so."[119] Forman agreed that the effort meant as much as the outcome. "We were interested in more than registering people. Going to the courthouse"—the seat of white power—"was a symbol of defiance. And the whites had recognized it as such."[120]

Initially SNCC had intended to continue the food campaign only through the start of cotton-picking season in mid-August, the lone phase of the cotton year not yet wholly automated. Though undoubtedly aware that hunger existed in depressed areas across the South (and, indeed, around the nation), SNCC maintained focus on providing relief to the Mississippi Delta.[121] In September 1963, as SNCC prepared to undertake a study of hunger conditions in Mississippi and South Carolina, James Forman explained to one prospective donor, "If there is a question of choosing states, we prefer to concentrate on Mississippi where we know of the needs, for the people are at our doors with their hungry children. This condition is not right and therefore we welcome whatever you might be able to do."¹²² To Forman's mind, SNCC organizers felt more enmeshed in Mississippi, and therefore more personally responsible for the worsening plight of many poor blacks since the organization's arrival. That day he also composed a revealing letter to Clarence B. Jones, advisor to Martin Luther King Jr., expressing frustration with the continued need for SNCC to feed hungry black southerners. With winter looming, Forman conveyed the "terrific need for food for the people with whom we are working," admitting, "sometimes we need it for ourselves. But that is incidental to the fact that thousands of Negroes in this country just do not have enough food." Focusing on the political dimensions and functions of hunger, Forman and SNCC sought to use the situation in Greenwood as an occasion "to wage a campaign that would force the issue of the government feeding people." By calling upon the conscience and resources of "volunteers to supply a governmental function," Forman hoped the Food for Freedom campaign would highlight the inadequacy of federal food aid, forcing donors and volunteers to question why the government did not provide for its needy citizens.

Despite this strategic rationale, Forman did not feign enthusiasm for the project. He instead expressed a reluctant acknowledgement of the food program's necessity to "meet the needs of the people insofar as we are capable of doing this." Eager to find another organization or agency willing to take on the task, Forman declared, "We are not at all happy with the fact that we must raise food for people in the South. It takes our attention from other work that we should be doing."¹²³ From his vantage as administrator of an organization incessantly in search of funds, a nationwide food aid program was entirely impractical, exacting immense costs in time, manpower, money, favors, and resources. Others shared Forman's sentiments. Despite their importance to SNCC's efforts to mobilize the poor, seemingly unending donation drives in truth aggravated many staff, particularly younger men who at times resented the tedium and monotony or disliked being responsible for meting out relief to people they occasionally felt took things they did not really need. Reporting on a largely successful distribution effort in Ruleville, McLaurin nonetheless lamented, "Yet there is always someone who did not[,] as they say[,] get a thing. You know how they act, someone got more meat than I did or two pairs of shoes and I only got one[,] things like that."¹²⁴ In their darker moments, staff and volunteers expressed disappointment with poor people who came for "hand outs" but still refused to participate in the voter registration drive. Thus, when the work did not yield immediate results, some questioned its efficacy as an organizing tool.

This survival mentality did, at times, neutralize the politicizing potential of food, as some destitute recipients conceptualized aid as an end in itself, a way to keep keeping on, rather than a spur for greater action. From the perspective of the hungry poor, this was not an irrational approach. Many needed and appreciated movement food aid, but its arrival did not immediately alter the reality of their dependency. In truth, SNCC handouts provided only meager sustenance. Despite the outpouring of support from around the country, thousands upon thousands of pounds of free food could not begin to address the dire conditions of the rural South. Those fortunate enough to obtain foodstuffs procured by SNCC had a few days' reprieve from hunger, but when the food ran out, as it always did, beneficiaries found themselves scarcely better off than before.

SNCC's food programs thus inherently raised a host of ethical issues that the organization did not directly or openly engage. Though inspired by evidently pure and noble intentions to organize and embolden destitute black Americans to assert themselves against abusive agents of authority, SNCC seemed unaware of—or perhaps unconcerned with—the ways in which this strategy and SNCC's system of food relief mirrored that of the white power structure the organization endeavored to dismantle. Whereas officials in Leflore and Sunflower had used food to reinforce white dominance, SNCC sought to use it to mobilize grassroots political power, channeling the material needs of the poor toward the causes of social justice and black freedom—as SNCC envisioned them.[125] In effect, then, rights organizers themselves played upon the physical hunger and desperation of often-terrified, broken sharecroppers to push them reluctantly to action. In both scenarios—that is, whether county officials or SNCC organizers retained control over food aid—people ensnared in systemic poverty remained beholden to and unduly influenced by those with the capacity and willingness to assuage their hunger. Subtly echoing opponents of social welfare programs who denounced recipients for "taking" without giving back, McLaurin and other organizers expressed frustration with those who came to SNCC for help but decided for themselves that the possible costs of voter registration outweighed the potential benefits SNCC touted. Though certainly SNCC sought vastly different ends than Mississippi officials, it utilized similar means to achieve them, means that pressured the needy to concede the right to exercise their own judgment in order to stave off imminent disaster. This significant imbalance of power between the black poor and those seeking to lead them perhaps helps to explain why the Food for Freedom project did not more effectively incite poor black Mississippians to advocate and act on their own behalf.

Indeed, it seemed that where the movement had already been failing—typically in areas paralyzed by the most repressive white violence—efforts to address the material needs of poor residents seldom sparked mass participation in larger campaigns. However, in areas characterized by more limited or subtle intimidation tactics or where organizers had moved in months or years earlier, feeding the hungry served to some extent to mobilize the local population. In many such cases, organizers had become part of the community, and therefore understood the obstacles facing local people. Government officials and plantation owners in these areas more often used economic reprisals than violence to discourage people from registering or otherwise aiding the movement; as a result, food and clothing drives elicited positive responses, if not always the desired outcomes. Seeing the direct connection between their own misery and the unchecked power of white leaders seemingly inspired some who might otherwise have been too afraid to join the movement or unconvinced that resistance could actually spark tangible change. In contexts where political action did not guarantee vigilante violence, localized issues of food access arguably offered a more compelling incentive for political participation than distant national concerns like a civil rights bill, as a single black vote in a county or state election held far more weight than one of millions in a presidential contest between candidates not likely to be seriously concerned with the hardships of rural southern life. In addition to wielding greater influence, black voters had more to gain by asserting themselves in a local context.

Hunger in the Delta rendered the importance of political action practical and concrete rather than idealistic and abstract. It created substantive political aims and targeted specific officials, policies, and practices responsible for the afflictions of the masses. SNCC's food activism continued for the duration of its work in the Delta, and in early 1964, the geographic center of the organization moved from Atlanta to Greenwood.[126] Though vastly overshadowed by the dramatic implications of the 1963 Freedom Vote and 1964 Summer Project, food aid and "welfare work" remained crucial to the movement's survival in Mississippi. Local schemes to drive or starve African Americans out of Mississippi threatened SNCC and COFO's strategy to bring change through electoral politics, a strategy that remained pragmatic only as long as blacks maintained a clear numerical advantage. The project of feeding the hungry not only spread SNCC's message and image of its "beloved community" but also helped to keep its voter registration drive viable. However, food welfare did not fundamentally challenge the shortcomings and biases of the existing system of food distribution or of resource allocation and property ownership in a broader sense. Though this fact did not escape the attention of leaders like Fannie Lou Hamer, who spearheaded the organization of a largely successful farm cooperative in 1969, SNCC continued to utilize food as an instrument to spawn local moral and political support, as well as vital national attention.[127] Despite the notable outcome in Greenwood and SNCC's success in reframing hunger in explicitly political terms, in the majority of cases food aid provided crucial assistance but little inspiration. SNCC, for the most part, conceptualized food as a means to the end of voting, a spark to get people interested in what politics could do for them, and a way of dramatizing the inhumanity of the southern system of white rule. By August 1964, it became clear to many black Mississippians, as well as many of the movement's most idealistic leaders, that while *politics*— movements to obtain and exercise power—might inspire and energize the oppressed, *politicians* and the Democratic Party that dominated the South until 1968 would in fact not do much good for them.[128] This quest for political responsiveness propelled the Mississippi Freedom Democratic Party challenge, which cruelly demonstrated the system's inability, if not outright refusal, to engage rights crusaders on equal terms.

In light of the Food for Freedom campaign, SNCC's inability to address widespread hunger in a lasting way reflected several realities. First, systems of emergency food relief work only to help the hungry endure brief periods of crisis. Because SNCC food programs and projects relied on human generosity rather than systemic reform, they did not—and could not—forestall future emergencies. Moreover, efforts to transport massive amounts of food to aid a regional catastrophe required intricate coordination and great expense. Food sent from distant places like California, for example, reflected meaningful sentiments, but served only temporarily to ameliorate the daily suffering of the hungry poor. Moreover, in addition to collecting food, organizers had to raise funds to cover the costs of delivery. Thus the actual value of donated assistance diminished in transit. Nationwide food drives helped to feed people in limited ways but did not address the underlying sources of racialized poverty and hunger.

Though an important tactic for organizing, SNCC's food programs and its emphasis on food security and nutrition were always secondary to the organization's chief ideological and strategic concern of political enfranchisement during the early years of the Mississippi movement. Moreover, the daily work of food distribution exhausted the time, energy, and occasionally the patience of staff and volunteers concerned with supposedly loftier aims. The promise of the 1963 Freedom Vote, the frustrations and ambiguous reverberations of the 1964 Freedom Summer, and the unceremonious, heartbreaking defeat of the Mississippi Freedom Democratic Party at the Democratic National Convention that August monopolized the focus and energies of SNCC and COFO. Many key leaders—Bob Moses, John Lewis, and Stokely Carmichael among them—felt disillusioned by the year's setbacks, and though the passage of the Voting Rights Act the following summer represented a landmark triumph for civil rights, those remaining on the ground in Mississippi increasingly realized that political power in theory without economic power in reality could not advance the goals of racial equality or social transformation in any enduring way.

Passage of the Voting Rights Act in ways signaled a decline of national interest in the affairs of Mississippi and the Deep South, as media coverage, as well as the efforts and attention of many movement leaders, turned to conditions in Northern cities like Chicago. Poor blacks in Mississippi emerged from the 1960s with federal protection of voting rights, but little else. Years later, Stokely Carmichael reflected on the impact of SNCC's work in the Delta. "In black Mississippi certainly, some oppressive—carefully constructed and brutally enforced—psychological barriers had been breached forever," he concluded. "But in hard political and economic terms, conditions were, of course, still as grim as they ever were. That work remained (and much unfortunately still does) to be done."[129] James Forman offered a similar assessment, suggesting, "The work SNCC had done was, in its time and place, revolutionary. We were not struggling for the vote as an end in itself, but to attain human dignity. And any struggle for dignity is revolutionary. SNCC was a pacesetter, a vanguard, in the early 1960s, and would continue to be one." Despite this, Forman admitted, "it is possible to do revolutionary work in certain situations without being a revolutionary. This was what SNCC as a whole had done until then, and we had reached the point where it was necessary to become a revolutionary organization in every sense."[130] From a strategic standpoint, the persistence of hunger and malnutrition in Mississippi after SNCC's departure suggested the impossibility of utilizing liberal means to achieve radical ends—that is, to work through the electoral system to redress biases and injustices built into the system itself. Quite simply, the U.S. government had not been designed to protect the interests of the poor or powerless. Though food aid did encourage many black Mississippians to register to vote—or at least to entertain the idea of doing so—the two-party system in which they cast their ballots continued to exclude them from positions of leadership, severely diminishing the power promised by legal protection of the franchise.

Indeed, after James Meredith's 1966 March Against Fear, Forman and other key SNCC leaders followed newly elected SNCC chairman Stokely Carmichael's increasingly radical approach to black liberation, encapsulated by his famous call for "black power," first publicly articulated during that trek at a rally in Greenwood. In doing so, many of SNCC's leading voices began to assert the need for and possibility of revolutionizing not only race relations but class relations as well. Their vision would be tested in the San Francisco Bay region of California, where the Black Panther Party, named after the political mechanism guided by Carmichael in Alabama the previous year, strived to mobilize the black poor, transforming urban hunger into a rallying cry "to feed the revolution."

Notes

The title of this chapter is a phrase from Fannie Lou Hamer. During a speech at Berkeley in 1969, Hamer acknowledged that many people disillusioned with the system were ready to give up on politics. "But, baby," she reminded her audience, "what we eat is politics." See "To Make Democracy a Reality," speech delivered at the Vietnam War Moratorium rally, Berkeley, California, Oct. 15, 1969, in *To Tell It Like It Is: The Speeches of Fannie Lou Hamer*, ed. Megan Parker Brooks and Davis W. Houck (Jackson: University Press of Mississippi, 2010), 101.

1. Initially formed during the 1961 Freedom Rides, COFO reestablished itself in February 1962 to coordinate work among the NAACP, CORE, and SNCC. SNCC provided most of the ground troops and spearheaded civil rights work across most of the state. Aaron Henry, a black pharmacist from the Delta town of Clarksdale who led the state NAACP, officially directed COFO, but historian John Dittmer, among others, contends that SNCC project director Bob Moses and assistant director Dave Dennis more significantly influenced COFO's work. See John Dittmer, *Local People: The Struggle for Civil*

Rights in Mississippi (Champaign: University of Illinois Press, 1994), 118–19; and Charles M. Payne, *I've Got the Light of Freedom: The Organizing Tradition and the Mississippi Freedom Struggle* (Berkeley: University of California Press, 1995), 62, 130–31.

2. James C. Cobb, *The Most Southern Place on Earth: The Mississippi Delta and the Roots of Regional Identity* (New York: Oxford University Press, 1994), 154–56, 176–78; Jack Temple Kirby, *Rural Worlds Lost* (Baton Rouge: Louisiana State University Press, 1987); Pete Daniel, *Breaking the Land: The Transformation of Cotton, Tobacco, and Rice Cultures since 1880* (Champaign: University of Illinois Press, 1985).

3. See, for example, Cobb, *The Most Southern Place on Earth*, 253–76. Contemporary works on this topic include the Citizens' Board of Inquiry into Hunger and Malnutrition in the United States (hereafter CBIHMUS), *Hunger USA* (Boston: Beacon Press, 1968); and Nick Kotz, *Let Them Eat Promises: The Politics of Hunger in America* (Reprint, Garden City, NY: Doubleday, 1971).

4. SNCC executive secretary James Forman, who spent much of his childhood living with his grandmother in Mississippi poverty, recalled that for want of food he had often eaten dirt. He used the term "dirt poor" to emphasize both the squalor of his surroundings and the utter desperation of his family and community, who ate the earth when they had nothing else. This term also points to the irony of hunger among farmers, people who worked the soil but rarely benefited from its harvest. See James Forman, *The Making of Black Revolutionaries* (Seattle: University of Washington, 1972), 12.

5. Council of Federated Organizations (COFO), "Mississippi: Structure of the Movement, Present Operations, and Prospectus for the Summer," 1964, Civil Rights Movement Veterans website, http://www.crmvet.org/docs/64_cofo.pdf.

6. Bob Moses referred to efforts to provide immediate aid as "holding actions" that threatened to thwart the coming revolution. Stokely Carmichael similarly emphasized the need for SNCC "to see the difference between social work and social change." See SNCC, "Minutes of the Meeting of the SNCC Executive Committee (27–31 Dec 1963)," Civil Rights Movement Veterans website, http://www.crmvet.org/docs/6312_sncc_excom_min.pdf, 5–6.

7. Stokely Carmichael was one of several staff members who voiced such concerns. See SNCC, "Minutes of the Meeting of the SNCC Executive Committee (27–31 Dec 1963)."

8. The generations-old interplay between black economic oppression and political marginalization has been well documented by historians of agriculture, economics, and race relations. See, for example, Kirby, *Rural Worlds Lost*; and Pete Daniel, *Breaking the Land*, and *Dispossession: Discrimination against African American Farmers in the Age of Civil Rights* (Chapel Hill: University of North Carolina Press, 2013).

9. Charles Cobb and Charles McLaurin (of SNCC), "The Economy of Ruleville, Mississippi," Nov. 1962, Civil Rights Movement Veterans website, http://www.crmvet.org/docs/rulevill.htm. See also Kirby, *Rural Worlds Lost*, 27; and R. Douglas Hurt, *Problems of Plenty: The American Farmer in the Twentieth Century* (Chicago: Ivan R. Dee, 2002), 5–6.

10. Chris Myers Asch, *The Senator and the Sharecropper: The Freedom Struggles of James O. Eastland and Fannie Lou Hamer* (New York: New Press, 2008), 69.

11. Kirby, *Rural Worlds Lost*, 145; Cobb and McLaurin, "The Economy of Ruleville, Mississippi."

12. In contrast, only a third of white southern farmers were tenants or sharecroppers. See Hurt, *Problems of Plenty*, 6.

13. Hamer recalled the rhythmic demands of sharecropping in 1971: "Now sharecroppers is really something; it's out of sight. Number one, what I found since I been old enough, it always had too many 'its' in it. Number one, you had to plow it. Number two, you had to break it up. Number three, you had to chop it. Number four, you had to pick it. And the last, number five, the landowner took it. So, this left us with nowhere to go; it left us hungry. . . . We never had so many days in my life that we had cornbread and we had milk and sometimes bread and onions. So, I know what the pain of hunger is about." See "Until I Am Free, You Are Not Free Either," speech delivered at the University of Wisconsin, Madison (Jan. 1971), quoted in Brooks and Houck, *To Tell It Like It Is*, 123.

14. Black children typically attended schools far inferior to those of their white counterparts, their educational prospects handicapped by unqualified or underpaid teachers, overcrowded classrooms, and a lack of basic supplies and facilities like libraries. SNCC's newspaper, *The Student Voice*, charged, "Whites who control Mississippi have little respect for education, but use it unscrupulously to prevent Negroes from obtaining the basic democratic right, the right to vote." To address these conditions, SNCC established Freedom Schools during the summer of 1964 as part of "a war against this academic poverty [sic]." See "FREEDOM SCHOOLS[:] MISSISSIPPI," *Student Voice*, Aug. 5, 1964.

15. Eric Foner, *A Short History of Reconstruction* (New York: Harper and Row, 1990), 191–93.

16. Though this provision applied to all voters, regardless of race, at least one convention delegate articulated its racist intent, stating, "The very idea of a poll qualification is tantamount to the State of Mississippi, saying to the Negro, 'We will give you two dollars not to vote.'" Quoted in U. S. Commission on Civil Rights, *Voting in Mississippi: A Report* (1965), 4.

17. As the report of the U.S. Commission on Civil Rights noted in 1965, this remained true even years after the 1954 *Brown* decision deemed racially segregated public school facilities unconstitutional. Bob Moses lambasted the insult and injustice of imposing a literacy test under such conditions, arguing, "You can't deny people an educational opportunity and then say the reason people can't vote is because they can't read." See Robert P. Moses and Charles E. Cobb Jr., *Radical Equations: Math Literacy and Civil Rights* (Boston: Beacon Press, 2001), 69.

18. U.S. Commission on Civil Rights, *Voting in Mississippi*, 10.

19. For the foundational study of the Delta as place, see Cobb, *The Most Southern Place on Earth*. See also Kim Lacy Rogers, *Life and Death in the Delta: African American Narratives of Violence, Resilience, and Social Change* (New York: Palgrave Macmillan, 2006).

20. Asch, *The Senator and the Sharecropper*, 12.

21. The social, political, and economic circumstances of life in the South served as "push" factors during the Great Migration, the implications of which have been widely studied. See, for example, Nicholas Lemann, *The Promised Land: The Great Black*

Migration and How It Changed America (New York: Knopf, 1991); Isabel Wilkerson, *The Warmth of Other Suns: The Epic Story of America's Great Migration* (New York: Random House, 2010). Lemann's journalistic account focuses on the lives of migrants between Clarksdale in the Mississippi Delta and the south and west sides of Chicago.

22. Lawrence Guyot and Mike Thelwell, "The Politics of Necessity and Survival in Mississippi," *Freedomways* 6, no. 2 (1966), Civil Rights Movement Veterans website, http://www.crmvet.org/info/lg-mt66.pdf, 124, 127.

23. For a detailed rendering of the interplay between politics and economics in Mississippi agriculture, see Kotz, *Let Them Eat Promises*.

24. Asch, *The Senator and the Sharecropper*, 151.

25. Cobb, *The Most Southern Place on Earth*.

26. For more on Carmichael's organizing efforts in Greenwood, see Peniel E. Joseph, *Stokely: A Life* (New York: Basic Civitas, 2014), 47–50, 55–58.

27. Stokely Carmichael with Ekwueme Michael Thelwell, *Ready for Revolution: The Life and Struggles of Stokely Carmichael (Kwame Ture)* (New York: Scribner, 2003), 281.

28. Asch, *The Senator and the Sharecropper*.

29. Carmichael with Thelwell, *Ready for Revolution*, 278.

30. Forman, *The Making of Black Revolutionaries*, 278.

31. This reality quickly became apparent to organizers. Bob Moses later remarked upon Mississippi's "use of law as an instrument of outright oppression. Mississippi stood out as the state most completely organized in terms of its state apparatus to foster apartheid." See Moses and Cobb, *Radical Equations*, 58.

32. Herbert C. Covey and Dwight Eisnach, *What the Slaves Ate: Recollections of African American Foods and Foodways from the Slave Narratives* (Santa Barbara: Greenwood Press, 2009), 1–2.

33. Kirby, *Rural Worlds Lost*, 56; Daniel, *Dispossession*, 9; Hurt, *Problems of Plenty*, 67–96.

34. CBIHMUS, *Hunger USA*, 5.

35. Cobb and McLaurin, "The Economy of Ruleville, Mississippi" (Nov. 1962).

36. *Hunger in America*, CBS Reports (CBS, May 21, 1968).

37. Testifying in April 1967 before the Senate Subcommittee on Employment, Manpower, and Poverty about the efficacy of the Economic Opportunity Act and the overall progress of the War on Poverty, Marian Wright, a twenty-seven-year-old African American lawyer with the NAACP Legal Defense Fund, denounced the daily administration of Mississippi state welfare offices: "Welfare practices . . . in Mississippi are terrible. . . . People are not treated with dignity when they go into the welfare office, and they are not allowed to be people, and they are threatened, and this is a terrible kind of thing that has to be stopped." See *Examination of the War on Poverty: Hearings before the Senate Subcommittee on Unemployment, Manpower, and Poverty of the Committee on Labor and Public Welfare*, 90th Cong. (1967), part 2 (Jackson, MS: Apr 10, 1967), 654.

38. U.S. Commission on Civil Rights, *Voting in Mississippi*, 21.

39. Mary Oliver Welsh, quoted in U.S. Commission on Civil Rights, *Voting in Mississippi*, 22. The report does not specify when this incident occurred. G. H. Hood took

office in 1960. See Timothy J. Minchin and John A. Salmond, *After the Dream: Black and White Southerners since 1965* (Lexington: University Press of Kentucky, 2011), 165.

40. Established in July 1967, the Citizens' Board of Inquiry on Hunger and Malnutrition in the United States set out to study "within the nexus of the problems of poverty . . . those absolutely elemental ones of food." Though its subsequent publication, *Hunger USA* (1968), offered a survey of the nationwide hunger crisis, it tellingly dedicated an entire chapter to a "case history of bureaucratic non-response" in Mississippi. See CBI-HMUS, *Hunger USA*, 4, 11–15, 38, 94–96, 49–76. See also Kotz, *Let Them Eat Promises*, 1–18.

41. James C. Cobb, "'Somebody Done Nailed Us on the Cross': Federal Farm and Welfare Policy and the Civil Rights Movement in the Mississippi Delta," *Journal of American History* 77, no. 3 (Dec. 1990): 912–36.

42. For more on the rise of the mechanical cotton picker, see Daniel, *Breaking the Land*, 246–48.

43. James Forman wrote that Hamer's story "would in the next two years be told from one end of the United States to another[,] . . . a worldwide symbol of black heroism, or revolutionary black womanhood, a warm and always human symbol of the power of people to struggle against hardship, adversity, terror—the living realities of the Mississippi Delta" (*The Making of Black Revolutionaries*, 290–91).

44. Chana Kai Lee, *For Freedom's Sake: The Life of Fannie Lou Hamer* (Urbana: University of Illinois Press, 2000), 25.

45. In comparing the two locations, Moses explained, "McComb was isolated where Greenwood essentially is not. People from [nearby] Clarksdale, Ruleville, Tallahatchie, [and] Cleveland have been continually moving in and out of Greenwood in leadership capacity. . . . You didn't have that in McComb, [as] there were no other cities around there" (Moses, quoted in Forman, *The Making of Black Revolutionaries*, 306).

46. Forman, *The Making of Black Revolutionaries*, 306.

47. For background on SNCC's move into the Delta, see Dittmer, *Local People*, 125, 129, 134.

48. "Leflore Won't Have Commodity Program," *Greenwood Commonwealth*, Nov. 9, 1962. See also Dittmer, *Local People*, 143–44.

49. Guyot and Thelwell, "The Politics of Necessity and Survival in Mississippi" (1966).

50. "Leflore Won't Have Commodity Program."

51. The United Press International (UPI) later cited the estimate of political scientist Charles Hamilton, who calculated the combined annual costs of administering the commodity program in Leflore and Sunflower counties to be about five thousand dollars. See UPI, "Negroes Say Thousands 'Starving,'" *Clarksdale Press Register*, Feb. 1, 1963.

52. "Leflore Won't Have Commodity Program."

53. Associated Press, "C-R Committee Backs County on Free Food: No Racial Issue Involved, Report Justice Advisors," *Greenwood Commonwealth*, Feb. 7, 1963.

54. Associated Press, "C-R Committee Backs County on Free Food." Four years later, USDA secretary Orville Freedom assured the Senate Subcommittee on Employment, Manpower, and Poverty, "Every county in the state has one of the two distribution

programs. . . . The Mississippi distribution is the largest in the nation" (quoted in "The Mississippi Story: A Case History in Bureaucratic Non-response," in CBIHMUS, *Hunger USA*, 11).

55. Quoted in "More Turned Away: Food Distribution Here Ends As Groceries Trickle Out," *Greenwood Commonwealth*, Feb. 13, 1963.

56. James Forman, for one, refused to believe the board's decision was unrelated to civil rights activity (*The Making of Black Revolutionaries*, 296).

57. Historian Charles Payne notes, "It was an awkward reprisal in several ways. It was non-selective, punishing the innocent as well as the guilty. It put some people in a position where they no longer had anything to lose by trying to register. It made plain a point COFO workers always wanted to put across, that there was a connection between exclusion from the political process and poverty. It also gave COFO a chance to show that they were more than the bunch of rag-tail kids they might appear to be" (Payne, *I've Got the Light of Freedom*, 158).

58. Letter from Bob Moses to Martha Prescod, Dec. 11, 1962, Civil Rights Movement Veterans website, http://www.crmvet.org/lets/6212_moses-prescod-letter.pdf.

59. The local *Greenwood Commonwealth* regularly covered these stories during late fall and early winter 1962. See, for example, "Cotton Harvesting Season Now Underway over Most of the State," Aug. 31, 1962; "Machine and Hand Harvest Is Pushed," Sept. 14, 1962; Associated Press, "Area Shivers through Early Cold Spell with Rest of the Nation," Dec. 12, 1962; "Area Residents Shiver, Firemen Busy," Dec. 13, 1962; and "Cold and Wet Is 30-Day Outlook," Dec. 19, 1962, 12.

60. Clarksdale, home to many legendary blues musicians, was an agricultural depot. Its large rail station served as the point of departure for many blacks leaving the South during the Great Migrations. See Francoise Hamlin, *Crossroads at Clarksdale: The Black Freedom Struggle in the Mississippi Delta after World War II* (Chapel Hill: University of North Carolina Press, 2012).

61. In its first story about the commodity crisis, SNCC's paper, the *Student Voice*, explained, "Many sharecroppers now have to fill out new registration papers showing how much they earned from each employer, many of whom keep no records. . . . Due to the voter registration drive . . . in Ruleville, the 'responsible people' are not particularly inclined to favors for the Negro." See "In Ruleville, Miss.: Surplus Food Denied to Registrants," *Student Voice*, Dec. 19, 1962.

62. "In Ruleville, Miss.: Surplus Food Denied to Registrants."

63. Quoted in Cobb and McLaurin, "The Economy of Ruleville, Mississippi," Nov. 1962. Italics removed from original text.

64. "Comic to Make Deliveries: Food For Delta's 'Starving' Expected to Arrive Today," *Clarksdale Press Register*, Feb. 11, 1963.

65. "Comic to Make Deliveries"; Clayborne Carson, *In Struggle: SNCC and the Black Awakening of the 1960s* (Cambridge: Harvard University Press, 1981), 78.

66. Forman described Block as "tall, lean, dark-skinned, with a deep voice and a dry sense of humor" and "a kind of courage that defies imagination" (*The Making of Black Revolutionaries*, 283).

67. Letter from Sam Block to Jim [Forman], Jan. 9, 1963, Civil Rights Movement Veterans website, http://www.crmvet.org/lets/6301_block-let.pdf.

68. Letter from Sam Block to Jim [Forman], Jan. 9, 1963.

69. "Oral History/Interview, Charlie Cobb, February, 2009," Civil Rights Movement Veterans website, http://www.crmvet.org/nars/cobb1.htm#cobbruleville.

70. "Oral History/Interview, Charlie Cobb, February, 2009."

71. An official campaign by this name began in New York in March 1963.

72. "Comic to Make Deliveries."

73. Kenneth Fairly, "Two Accused of Violating Narcotics Act: Negroes Say Drugs Were for Needy," *Clarksdale Press Register,* Dec. 28, 1962.

74. This was Donaldson and Taylor's second trip in three days ("Two Accused of Violating Narcotics Act").

75. Donaldson quoted in Henry Hampton, Steve Fayer, and Sarah Flynn, eds., *Voices of Freedom: An Oral History of the Civil Rights Movement from the 1950s through the 1980s* (New York: Bantam Books, 1990), 149.

76. Hampton, Fayer, and Flynn, *Voices of Freedom,* 149.

77. Hampton, Fayer, and Flynn, *Voices of Freedom,* 150.

78. Dick Gregory with Robert Lipsyte, *Nigger: An Autobiography* (New York: Washington Square Press, 1964).

79. Gregory with Lipsyte, *Nigger,* 160.

80. Dick Gregory with Shelia P. Moses, *Callus on My Soul: A Memoir* (Atlanta: Longstreet Press, 2000), 62.

81. Form letter from Rev. Douglas M. Still and Dick Gregory, Jan. 31, 1963, reel 29, SNCC Papers (Sanford, NC: Microfilming Corp. of America, 1982).

82. The *Clarksdale Press Register* reported the amount to be equal to "three truck loads and a U-Haul trailer load"; see B. J. Skelton, "Negro Comic Visits City: Brings Food For 'Starving,'" *Clarksdale Press Register,* Feb. 12, 1963.

83. Gregory with Lipsyte, *Nigger,* 160–61.

84. Thatcher Walt, "Negro Here Hits 'Food Publicity,'" *Greenwood Commonwealth,* Feb. 9, 1963.

85. "Oral History/Interview, Charlie Cobb, February, 2009."

86. Gregory with Lipsyte, *Nigger,* 161.

87. "Negroes Sign for Free Food at Church," *Greenwood Commonwealth,* Feb. 12, 1963.

88. "Negroes Sign for Free Food at Church."

89. "Negroes Sign for Free Food at Church."

90. In Moses's view, the trials of Greenwood fortified "SNCC organizers like Willie Peacock from neighboring Tallahatchie County [who] had come through the fires of Greenwood annealed like steel" (Moses and Cobb, *Radical Equations,* 66).

91. Quoted in "More Turned Away: Food Distribution Here Ends As Groceries Trickle Out," *Greenwood Commonwealth,* Feb. 13, 1963.

92. "More Turned Away."

93. "More Turned Away."

94. "Negroes Sign for Free Food at Church."

95. "More Food Is Distributed," *Greenwood Commonwealth*, Feb. 20, 1963.

96. Quoted in Associated Press, "State Welfare Boss Blasts Food Hoopla," *Greenwood Commonwealth*, Feb. 14, 1963.

97. "State Welfare Boss Blasts Food Hoopla."

98. Gregory with Lipsyte, *Nigger*, 161.

99. The local Greenwood paper reprinted this editorial. See "Gregory's Groceries," *Greenwood Commonwealth*, Feb. 14, 1963.

100. "Gregory's Groceries."

101. See the following articles from *Muhammad Speaks*: "A Time of Terror and Torment: Chill Wind of Horror, Hunger, Rakes Negroes in Mississippi" (Mar. 18, 1963), 18; "Fallacy of the Free World: Grim History of Greenwood, Miss." (Apr. 29, 1963), 10; "Shabazz: Market of the Midwest" (Sept. 11, 1964), 19.

102. "Gregory's Groceries."

103. "SNCC Staff Jailed as Greenwood Negroes Register in 'First Breakthrough' in Mississippi," *Student Voice*, Apr. 1963.

104. "'No Evidence at Scene': Negro Arrested for Charging Arson Was Committed Here," *Greenwood Commonwealth*, Feb. 23, 1963.

105. "Oral History/Interview, Charlie Cobb, February, 2009."

106. Moses and Cobb, *Radical Equations*, 63.

107. Block quoted in Forman, *The Making of Black Revolutionaries*, 283. See also Douglas Martin, "Samuel Block, 60, Civil Rights Battler, Dies," *New York Times*, Apr. 22, 2000.

108. "Block Convicted," *Greenwood Commonwealth*, Feb. 25, 1963.

109. "Oral History/Interview, Charlie Cobb, February, 2009."

110. "Oral History/Interview, Charlie Cobb, February, 2009."

111. Bob Moses, "Letter to Northern Supporters," Greenville, MS, Feb. 27, 1963, Civil Rights Movement Veterans website, http://www.crmvet.org/lets/moses63.htm.

112. Bob Moses, "Letter to Northern Supporters."

113. SNCC fastidiously documented instances of official and vigilante intimidation. See SNCC, "MISSISSIPPI: A Chronology of Violence and Intimidation in Mississippi since 1961" (pamphlet, 1963), Civil Rights Movement Veterans website, http://www.crmvet.org/docs/sncc_ms_violence.pdf; and "Miss. Workers Face Police Harassment," *Student Voice*, Jun. 2, 1964. The 1963 Freedom Vote, a mock election, successfully demonstrated that in the absence of threats of violence or reprisal, tens of thousands of unregistered blacks in Mississippi would exercise their voting rights. See Dittmer, *Local People*, 200–207.

114. "Ignore Groups in Greenwood, Urges Council," *Greenwood Commonwealth*, Mar. 5, 1963.

115. Quoted in "Ignore Groups in Greenwood, Urges Council."

116. T.W., "Pressured Supervisors Vote for Commodities," *Greenwood Commonwealth*, Mar. 20, 1963.

117. Moses and Cobb, *Radical Equations*, 67.

118. Charles McLaurin, "Report from Sunflower County," Feb. 19, 1964, Civil Rights Movement Veterans website, http://www.crmvet.org/lets/6402_sncc_sunflower.pdf.

119. McLaurin, "Report from Sunflower County."

120. Forman, *The Making of Black Revolutionaries*, 296; Moses and Cobb, *Radical Equations*, 62.

121. In a letter to the SNCC Chicago office, Block minced no words: "Things are going bad here," he admitted. His thoughts centered on malnourished children in need of medical attention, too hungry to concentrate at school. His personal inability to help them deepened his anxiety and melancholy. Block described having watched a ten-year-old boy shoo away a dog digging in a trashcan so that he himself could scavenge some "potato peelings and some hard white bread." When the boy asked "Mr. Freedom man" for "a nickel to buy me something to eat," Block started to cry because he "didn't have not one penny to give the little boy and he had to go on to school hungry" (Samuel Block to Ralph Rapoport, Sept. 25, 1963, SNCC Papers, reel 29).

122. James Forman to Eddie Albert, Delmonico's Hotel, Sept. 23, 1963, SNCC Papers, reel 49.

123. James Forman to Clarence B. Jones (23 Sep 1963), SNCC Papers, reel 49. Forman had experience organizing food relief as part of the Emergency Relief Committee, a subcommittee of Chicago CORE established in 1961 to support destitute blacks evicted for voter activity in Fayette County, Tennessee. Working to build a "support movement," the committee solicited food and cash donations in front of Chicago grocery stores before moving on to organize local churches. Los Angeles CORE assisted by sending support to neighboring Hayward County. In Forman's view, "A movement developed in Chicago around the plight of people in Fayette County." The United Packinghouse Workers and, later, the AFL-CIO Industrial Union Council of Cook County supported the committee's efforts (Forman, *The Making of Black Revolutionaries*, 131–36).

124. McLaurin, "Report from Sunflower County."

125. Anne Moody of CORE described her disheartening experiences distributing food and clothing in the Madison County town of Canton, near Jackson, in September 1963. Needy people barraged the Freedom House seeking clothes but exhibited a strong aversion to voting, as well as an open suspicion of rights workers; see Anne Moody, *Coming of Age in Mississippi: An Autobiography* (New York: Random House, 1968), 344, 356.

126. The national headquarters of SNCC moved from Atlanta to Greenwood in preparation for the 1964 Freedom Summer project. Moses had lobbied for this move since late 1963. See Forman, *The Making of Black Revolutionaries*, 378.

127. Hamer outlined this venture during a 1971 speech ("Until I Am Free, You Are Not Free Either"). See also Lee, "Poverty Politics and Freedom Farm," *For Freedom's Sake*, 136–62; and Kay Mills, *This Little Light of Mine: The Life of Fannie Lou Hamer* (Penguin Group, 1993), 258–60.

128. Much has been written about the 1964 DNC and the challenge posed by the Mississippi Freedom Democratic Party. See, for example, John C. Skipper, *Showdown at the 1964 Democratic Convention: Lyndon Johnson, Mississippi and Civil Rights* (Jefferson: McFarland, 2012); and Dittmer, *Local People*, 272–302.

129. Carmichael with Thelwell, *Ready for Revolution*, 425.

130. Forman, *The Making of Black Revolutionaries*, 412.

6

Riot, Revolution, or Rebellion?

Civil Rights and the Politics of Memory

ROSIE JAYDE UYOLA

> This drug thing, this ain't police work. No, it ain't. I mean, I can send any fool with a badge and a gun up on them corners and jack a crew and grab vials. But policing? I mean, you call something a war and pretty soon everybody gonna be running around acting like warriors. They gonna be running around on a damn crusade, storming corners, slapping on cuffs, racking up body counts. And when you at war, you need a fucking enemy. And pretty soon, damn near everybody on every corner is your fucking enemy. And soon the neighborhood that you're supposed to be policing, that's just occupied territory.
>
> Bunny Colvin, The Wire

Why would anyone have wanted to open old wounds by publicly commemorating the civil disorders that decimated over 125 of America's cities a generation ago? Although some physical signs remain of that turbulence—such as deteriorating and worn-out housing and abandoned lots—for the most part, the areas most affected have been reconstructed; those who witnessed or participated in the riots have largely moved on with their lives or are no longer with us; and the underlying social issues that animated the late 1960s—police brutality, systemic urban poverty, local opposition to war, and lack of political representation for communities of color—had been relegated to the periphery of contemporary public discourse.

That is, until the events in Ferguson, Missouri, in 2014 and Baltimore in 2015, when excessive use of force by police led to the deaths of two unarmed young black men, Michael Brown and Freddie Gray, respectively, and ultimately produced another round of uprising. In the immediate aftermath, many politically engaged citizens took to Twitter, blogs, and news aggregator sites to contextualize the protests—what some have called "riots"—within a larger arc of the black freedom struggle.

Today, diverse political camps take up nationwide public discussions about the punitive policies that exacerbate racial disparities and criminalize blackness. From protesters to policymakers, from the attorney general to the FBI director to, begrudgingly, the president of the United States, there has been a sea change in the way in which Americans think and talk about race. Referencing the "simmering distrust" between police departments and minority communities, Barack Obama said, "This is not a problem just of Ferguson, Missouri. This is a national problem." Locating Ferguson and Baltimore within the long civil rights narrative, Attorney General Eric Holder used Dr. King's words to close his remarks during the interfaith service and community forum at Ebenezer Baptist Church: "It was Dr. King who reminded us—in his very last speech, on the night before his life was taken—that it's only when it is dark enough that the stars can be seen. Tonight, once again, it is dark enough." On March 7, 2015, the Koch brothers and the American Civil Liberties Union—strange bedfellows indeed—announced a three-year bipartisan effort to reduce our nation's bursting prison system by launching the Coalition for Public Safety. In July, Senators Cory Booker (D-NJ) and Rand Paul (R-KY) proposed the REDEEM Act to assist nonviolent drug offenders, especially juvenile offenders, seal their records, making it easier for those former offenders to secure a job. Yet the policy implications in the aftermath of Ferguson and Baltimore, and in the wake of the Black Lives Matter protest, remain unclear.

Beyond the blogosphere and twenty-four-hour media circuits, conversations about the causes and effects of social unrest are exploding in local public forums. And this is not a wholly brand new phenomenon. In 2007 and 2008, for example, Newark, New Jersey, and Baltimore, Maryland, observed the fortieth anniversaries of their civil uprisings through a series of commemorative events. Rutgers University-Newark and the University of Baltimore, serving as anchor institutions in Legacy Cities (older industrial cities that have experienced steady job and population loss over the past few decades) led unprecedented remembrance efforts by collecting oral histories of those whose lives were affected by the riots. Their efforts marked a large part of the *Remembering Newark's Summer of Discontent: Forty Years Later* and the *Baltimore '68: Riots and Rebirth* projects.[1]

A polyphony of voices also emerged in the oral history interviews that professors and students collected for both civic engagement projects. Anyone who wanted to participate was given an opportunity to tell her or his story. As a result, commemoration participants learned of memories that are not often shared in public spaces. Jewish shop owners, whose stores were looted, recounted events often too painful to discuss; police officers and National Guardsmen shared that they feared being painted as racist villains; and black residents admitted to having cheered white police officers arresting black looters. Understandably, such stories are typically not shared out of fear of what neighbors would say.[2]

These voices—culled from more than one hundred oral history interviews recorded in Newark and Baltimore—formed the backbone of both *Remembering Newark's Summer of Discontent: Forty Years Later* and the *Baltimore '68: Riots and Rebirth* commemorative projects. Moving into new realms of civic engagement and urban leadership, project organizers partnered with community stakeholders to act as agents of change in the public sphere. For Newark, that meant asking the public to acknowledge that the disturbances and legacies of the summer of 1967 should be remembered and should inform the new Newark that was now taking shape. For Baltimore, the project's public mandate was "to help the people of Baltimore learn how to live together." While it is clear from the testimonies of those who played an active role in creating the commemorative activities that participation was transformative, we must ask, how can we measure the impact either commemoration had on its city's citizenry or on the nation writ large in the long term?

This chapter suggests that deeply creative public programs like *Riots and Rebirth* enable us to ask challenging questions about the role of memory in urban development. What *is* the role of commemoration in not just remembering a city's past but shaping its future? What are the possibilities for institutions to engage with the past in ways that are meaningful to current social issues? What are the potential consequences of creating a public forum in which all first-person accounts have a legitimate claim on, or stake in, the history of the riots? And finally, what philosophical and ethical dilemmas emerge when the commemoration is framed as therapeutic, healing, or reconciliatory? The sections that follow grapple with these questions by providing an overview of the cultural and political processes that shaped the planning of each project, by conducting a close reading of one of the cultural texts produced by each commemoration, and by offering suggestions for future commemorative initiatives that seek to engage with contested memories.

Baltimore '68: Riots and Rebirth in an American City

For an East Coast port city, Baltimore was surprisingly under-researched in the late twentieth century. In the rich array of published manuscripts on Baltimore's past—ranging in topics from biographical accounts of Jewish and Irish immigration to photo essays of the city's famous cast-iron buildings, through visitor guides to recreational trails on the Chesapeake Bay and recipe books on local culinary offerings—surprisingly absent is the historiographical account of the city's 1968 civil disturbances, during which five thousand soldiers from Fort Bragg were deployed to the city to suppress civil unrest in the wake of the assassination of Dr. Martin Luther King Jr.

While the availability of primary source documents is ample, there are no books, articles, or chapters that explain *why* Baltimore erupted in fire, murder, and chaos in the days following the assassination. With the upcoming fortieth anniversary of the disturbances in sight, urban historian (then a graduate student) Jessica I. Elfenbein sought to fill this gap in the literature.

To remedy the omission, Elfenbein and Tom Hollowak, Special Collections archivist at the University of Baltimore's Langsdale Library, developed a conference series that aimed to add to the scholarly understanding of the events of the Baltimore riots. In 1996, and again in 1999, Elfenbein and Hollowak organized two conferences entitled *From Mobtown to Charm City* in order to provide a much-needed historical context to contemporary civic issues. To document the making of modern Baltimore, the commemorative programs touched upon varied facets of everyday life. Conference topics included the histories of early murder trials, alley houses, volunteer fire companies, slums, secession, the city's post–civil war racial accommodation, World War II aircraft workers, public housing, and the school system.[3] Hundreds of Baltimoreans attended both events, and the programs received high praise from leaders across diverse segments of the community.

Still, while innovative in scope and methodology, ultimately, neither conference engaged with the events of 1968. This lack of public dialogue about the causes of the riots and their effects on the development of the city over the past forty years both reflected and propagated a fissure in the civic fabric of the community. Current and former residents who lived through the civil disturbances were left to grapple with contested memories of that time without the opportunity to air their grievances or to learn about the experiences of others. In Baltimore, as in scores of other American cities, memories of the disturbances still prompted visceral reactions and resentment: "If it hadn't been for the riots our family would have stayed in the city." "After the riots, we never went downtown anymore." "Baltimore was wonderful before the riots, but it's been downhill since then."[4]

Operating under the belief that an examination of the social forces that led up to the riots could improve the quality of life in Baltimore, Elfenbein began orchestrating a campaign that would allow the city to finally document and publicly commemorate the 1968 riots/revolution/rebellion, since, after all, it was an event that she and others believed had profoundly and permanently altered the city.[5] Five years later, in the fall of 2005, Elfenbein's efforts gained traction among her university colleagues. Elfenbein reached out to faculty and students on the University of Baltimore (UB) campus, asking whether they were in Baltimore in 1968 and if so what they were doing during the unrest. Responses ranged. Some reported memories of hateful remarks overheard in white working-class neighborhoods while others provided witness accounts of looting. Nearly everyone on campus had a story to tell about '68. Encouraged by the overwhelming response to her inquiry, Elfenbein invited public historian Elizabeth M. Nix to create an undergraduate seminar, "The New South and Civil Rights," in order to train students to conduct and transcribe interviews so that they could systematically collect stories about the disturbances from local residents.

In response to the project's first initiative in 2006, the steering committee of *Baltimore '68* put forth an ambitious and progressive "truth and reconciliation" agenda. They aimed to spark community dialogue about a controversial topic, to explore the meaning of anchor institutions in urban spaces, and to "heal wounds that festered even after forty years."[6] To achieve these goals, the committee brought together a remarkably diverse group of stakeholders composed of archivists, law professors, labor economists, community artists, playwrights, oral historians, high school teachers and students, museum professionals, members of the chamber of commerce, public radio hosts, UB students, and AmeriCorps volunteers.

Together, they created a platform for scholarship, civic engagement, and community-building by exploring not only the causes of the riots but also the efforts at reconciliation and healing that followed and continue still to take place in the city of Baltimore.

There are several reasons why the University of Baltimore would prove itself a rich repository of local memories. UB is a commuter school; the majority of its students are older than traditional college students and are from the surrounding neighborhoods. Furthermore, most students remain local after graduation. Given this unique set of circumstances, the interviewers were part of two discourse communities—the university itself (the project initiators) and the community at large (the project participants). These lines were largely blurred as many participants identified as part of both groups. Students interviewed each other, their parents, extended family members, neighbors, and parishioners at local churches. The level of community access available to UB students would have been challenging, if not impossible, for most academics to establish. This set of circumstances, coupled with UB's commitment to creating an inclusive community in which diversity is respected and celebrated, generated an intensely fertile space for civic dialogue about race relations in a city that remained segregated for forty years after the 1968 unrest.[7]

From this space a series of commemorative activities sprouted that drew on the testimonies of those who bore witness. Commemorative activities were presented via a rich array of media through the work of local artists, civic activists, students, and scholars. For example, UB sponsored a three-day public history conference to place the events of '68 within a larger historical context and to spark further conversations about what happened and why. Viewing their work as a means by which to bridge the past and the future, the conference organizers aimed to "allow [their] community a deeper, more comprehensive understanding of where we have been and where we are going."

In order to understand the scope of the damage caused in Baltimore by the riots of 1968, UB also developed a driving tour of many of the affected areas. This self-directed driving tour, playfully titled "Best Tour for Visiting In-Laws" by the *Baltimore City Paper*, was limited mostly to business districts where the destruction was most concentrated. While the streetscape of the city has changed significantly over forty years, many scars of the episode—leveled, vacant lots, abandoned structures, whole neighborhoods with their natural centers left neglected or gutted by poorly planned developments—remain. The tour acted as a time portal, superimposing the history of 1968 onto the geography of the twenty-first-century city and offered participants the opportunity to use all of their senses and faculties in order to physically "move through" the riot's disorderly mobs' looting, rock-throwing, window-smashing, and fires.

Another component of the commemoration, *One Particular Saturday*, was a powerful full-length play performed by local high school students that transformed the language and memories of six witnesses of the disturbances, recalling the uncertainty of those days while also encouraging discussion about race and history. "I knew that to hear their words on a stage, spoken by others, would have a power," said playwright and director Kimberley Lynne. "It would bring these explosive events into the present, and allow all of us to consider what happened and how we—and they—must work together to make sure that it never happens again. These were the worst times during a very bad time in our nation's history, but good can come out of it."[8]

Arguably, the success of these fortieth-anniversary memorials, remembrances, and tributes lies in a deeply held belief, or at least a yearning to believe, that such "good" can come out of suffering and that the tragedy that the city endured does not have to be in vain. Through this therapeutic framework, conference organizers and participants alike were able to commemorate the urban unrest of the late 1960s, because, by doing so, they were able to mark a turning point of healing in their cities. The overarching theme of these commemorative narratives was one of progress and reconciliation; from the ashes of the riots, a new, more tolerant city was born, as witnessed by the civic maturity that allowed urban residents to come together to commemorate the deeply contested history of their city. A most interesting outcome of this process, and one that I will discuss in my next section, is the creation of the Baltimore '68 Mosaic Monument, which brought together a dozen eyewitnesses of the riots to create a memorial mural.

One Mosaic, Many Voices: The Baltimore '68 Mosaic Monument

As part of the fortieth-anniversary commemoration, every Saturday morning (from January through March of 2008) twelve eyewitnesses of the 1968 Baltimore riots came together to create a mosaic in a community art workshop sponsored by the University of Baltimore. The participants told their stories using colorful acrylic paints on a six-feet-by-six-feet white ceramic tile with the longer-term goal of later creating one united piece with all of the tiles—a mosaic that would represent the various experiences of those who witnessed the unrest. In the final stages of the project, the individual story tiles were affixed into a mosaic on a wall surface, the design of which came about through multiple workshop discussions. Collectively, these mosaic tiles tell a complex humanistic narrative of what happened in Baltimore forty years ago and in the decades that followed. Ultimately, the mosaic monument was part of a broader public history effort to bring Baltimoreans together in an open dialogue about the racial, economic, and political issues that galvanized the civil unrest in 1968 and continue to perpetuate segregation in the city today.

The monument and the process by which it was created embody the educational value of oral history; it makes use of primary sources in order to shift the voice of authority from scholar to narrator. A deceptively simple precept of oral history, shared authority is a movement in cultural institutions that aims to create spaces for subaltern groups—social groups who are socially, politically, and geographically outside of the hegemonic power structure—to contribute to a body of knowledge that is then shared with the public.[9] Similar instances of shared authority also took place between interviewees as they came to learn of each other's very different perspectives, shaped by each of their varied social positions. In assessment surveys following the last session, all contributors reported that they had reached a new level of understanding with regard to the 1968 unrest as an outcome of their listening to the memories of their workshop colleagues. "I went in the door realizing I didn't know the whole story," said participant Terry White, whose tile depicted a scene of military vehicles swarming a block of row houses in what he described as a neighborhood under martial law. "I brought in one story from one guy, and I left with the heartfelt stories of 12 people."

Christina Ralls, the workshop organizer and a graduate student at the Maryland Institute College of Art, learned of her own family's history for the first time by conducting oral history interviews with her parents, both workshop participants. Ralls's maternal grandmother, a white single mother of ten who was nearly sixty years old at the time of the riots, reported that she was terrorized out of her home during the riots. The family lost everything "down to the wallpaper," she said; the neighbors even tore up family photos, Ralls's mother told the workshop members.

Responding to Ralls's story, other participants empathetically shifted their own perspectives. "As I looked at the riots while they happened in my neighborhood," reflected a soft-spoken educator, Robert Birt, who grew up in a public housing project in East Baltimore and identified the events of 1968 as a "rebellion" in response to the "murder" of Dr. King, "I knew the stores of white merchants were burned. But to be frank, after King was killed, I didn't give a damn. That was my attitude. But when you hear the story of Christina's mother getting burned out of her home—somebody's family—come on. And she was my neighbor, too, I realized." Birt's testimony shows a shift in perspective as marked by his realization that the devastation caused by the riots affected white children and families—not just business owners or landlords—who were part of the same community as those who participated in the protest.

Another shift in perspective came during a moment of discord when one of the attendees described the riots as a "carnival." Immediately, the artist facilitator Christina Ralls thought moderation was necessary. "I got nervous about the response his comment would generate and tried to set ground rules," she explained. "But the group immediately dismissed my suggestion, believing such rules unnecessary." Later that day, another group member approached the man who had described his experience as fun, recreational, or "carnival-like" and said, "Sorry that I misinterpreted you. I'm sure if I were in your position at the time I would see it in that light also. I respect that."

Another white participant admitted his ignorance of race relations after a black participant described his experience with segregated hospitals, saying, "I had no idea that hospitals refused patients based on the color of their skin; I always thought they were to treat everyone who needed help and care. I understand now why anyone would riot if they were treated like that." These multidirectional shifts in perspective illustrate the efficacy of community art in fostering civic dialogue and cultural empathy among participants who would otherwise not have the opportunity to hear the experiences of others, those that often served to counter their own memories of the event.

The Baltimore '68 Mosaic Monument, which was created by the workshop participants and pictured below, embodies these shifts in perspectives by featuring diverse eyewitness accounts embedded within a larger narrative of destruction and rebirth.

Reminiscent of allegorical Byzantine icons, the monument features a

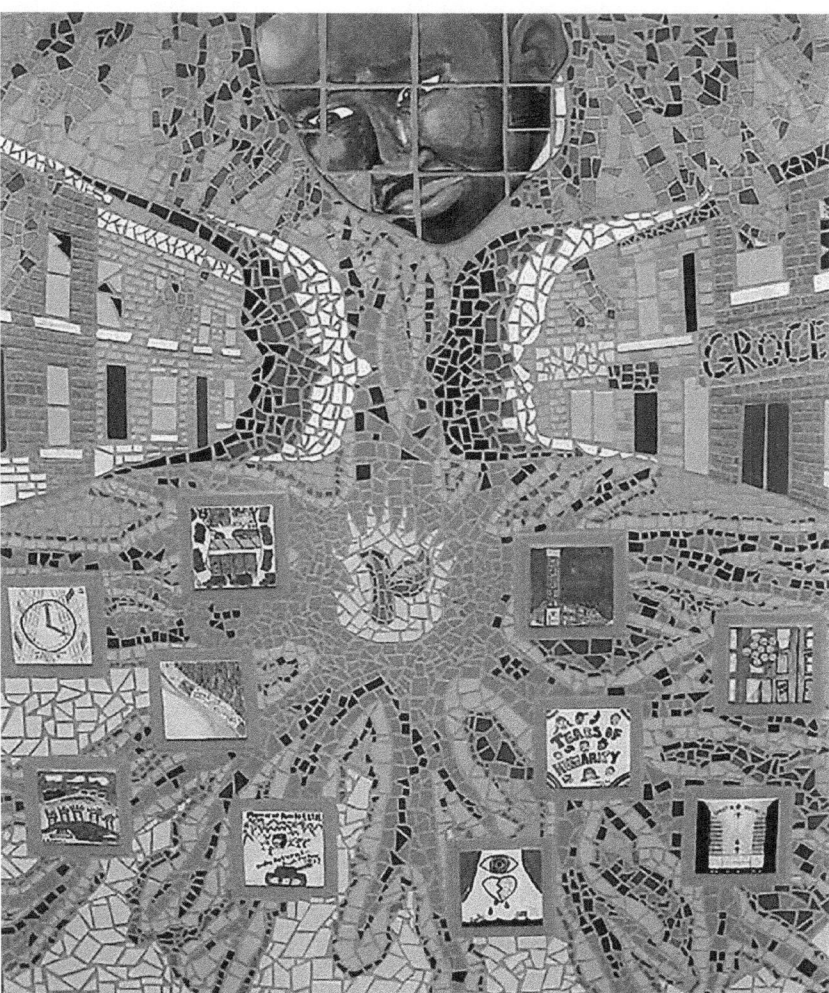

Figure 6.1. Baltimore '68: Riots and Rebirth Mosaic Monument, installed in the lobby of the Harry and Jeanette Weinberg Family Center Y at Stadium Place, 900 East 33rd Street, Baltimore, Maryland.

central figure, in this case a Christlike Dr. Martin Luther King Jr. who watches over a scene of destruction below with his eyes simultaneously engaged with, and turned away from, the viewer. The mosaic is composed of two overlapping sections: a larger mosaic and ten individual ceramic story tiles encompassed therein. At the center of the image we see a seedling breaking through the asphalt, ensconced in a halo-like glow, which is reverberating in what could be interpreted as tree roots (or bolts of energy) that connect all of the individual story tiles to each other; to the burning row houses; and to Dr. Martin Luther King Jr. This composition suggests the interconnectedness of residents' individual experiences within an overarching narrative of the Civil Rights Movement and the decline of America's inner cities, all as one story.

Anchoring the individual images together is the tree, a symbol of life that aims to chart the process of the city flourishing after decline. In memorials, the arboreal imagery is often symbolic of resilience, life, and revival. For example, the National September 11 Memorial in New York and the Oklahoma City National Memorial both feature "survivor trees" that represent "a spirit that cannot be broken." The trees serve as living tributes that grow stronger year after year; they offer visitors a space to reflect on a tragedy through a narrative that transcends decline and suggests life and rebirth.

Trees also occupy a special place in Judeo-Christian liturgy, which closely relates to humanity's relationship with the natural environment. For example, a broken branch or tree stump motif on a gravestone often signifies someone who has died young. In both the Hebrew Bible and the Qur'an, Noah is instructed by God to build a ship, which allows a few members of humankind and two specimens of each species of animals to survive the great flood. A small branch, carried by a dove, signified the end of the disaster (an image used widely to represent peace).[10]

In turn, by placing a seedling at the heart of the Baltimore '68 Mosaic, Ralls and workshop participants both honored the victims of the riots and laid claim to a renaissance for the city of Baltimore. The scene's juxtaposition of a sapling breaking through the concrete amidst a burning downtown backdrop suggests a reawakening and regrowth of the neighborhood after a destructive event. In turn, perhaps the piece represents Baltimoreans' participation in the commemorative activities as a chance for growth amidst resentment, disaster, and tragedy.

While the center of the Baltimore '68 mosaic monument depicts an optimistic narrative of progress, the rest of the mosaic gestures toward the difficult process of reconciliation in a neighborhood marred by violence and loss. In the top portion of the mosaic, a troubled Dr. King looks down from heavenly clouds, shedding a single tear. Both sides of the mosaic depict a string of row houses—some with broken windows, others engulfed in flames—drawn in perspective and disappearing toward the horizon. At the vanishing point, the buildings morph into a series of facial profiles—black, grey, and white—that are posed as mirror images, facing each other. The ceramic tiles used to compose these buildings are shaped like bricks, evenly spaced and equal in size, archetypically urban. Yet as the buildings turn into faces, the ceramic tiles become jagged with rough, sharp protruding points, suggesting that the human element of the scene has become unraveled, irregular, and fragmented. The individual experience cannot be reduced to "one size fits all" narratives; people's identities are not regularly shaped like buildings made of evenly sized bricks.

The tile composition is reflective of what many historians have identified as the single most important cause of the widespread phenomenon of rioting: the "system of apartheid in America's major cities," as it was described by the National Advisory Commission on Civil Disorders in 1968. In what was informally known as the Kerner Report, the commission declared that the nation was "moving toward two societies, one black, one white—separate and unequal." The commission's famous—and highly contested—claim about the unrelieved pattern of racism across the country and the city is echoed in the mosaic's disjointed faces that literally materialize from the destruction of the built environment.[11]

This lack of coherent sequence or cohesion in the composition of the faces also alludes to the fragmentation of public memory in the city. Nearly five decades after the riots of 1968, Baltimoreans' memories of what caused the breakdown of civil order in their city continue to exist as splintered and wide-ranging, not unlike the tiles of the mosaic that serve to represent it. The individual tiles of the mosaic monument, as pictured below, capture this diversity of public memory.

The smaller individual story tiles float in the foreground, fastened to the outermost layer of the mural and appear physically closer to the viewer in perspective than the rest of the mosaic. This composition privileges the individual stories of the ten eyewitnesses who participated in co-creating the monument by placing them in the foreground of the piece. Yet because of the relatively small size of the images on these tiles, their memories fade to the background. To understand what is happening in each of the eyewitness tiles, the viewer is forced to "zoom in" or to stand so close to the mosaic that the overall larger narrative scene is no longer discernible. The constraint in viewership gives the feeling of sitting too close to the stage at the ballet; if one is close enough to see the principal dancer emoting, one can no longer see the choreography performed by

Figure 6.2. Individual story tiles created by mosaic participants who were profoundly affected by the riots and their aftermath, Baltimore '68: Riots and Rebirth Mosaic Monument.

the company. The mosaic's layout represents how memories are interpreted, suggesting that we lose sight of individual memories of the riots when we try to understand them as a singular historic narrative.

In turn, the limited focus created by the mosaic's organization evokes a sense of dissonance. Like most mosaics, the Baltimore Monument is rooted in pointillism, a painting technique for which small, distinct dots of pure color are applied in patterns to form an image. However, *unlike* most mosaics, this piece is composed of several different smaller murals in seclusion, giving the overall narrative a texture of "many views" that compete for the viewer's attention. Texturally, the mosaic pieces vary in size, gesturing to the importance of some images over others. For example, the tiles that form Dr. Martin Luther King Jr.'s face are the same six-inch-by-six-inch tiles that eyewitnesses used to record their memories, thus indicating a sense of equivalence between the memories of everyday people on the streets of Baltimore and the legacy of one of the Civil Rights Movement's great leaders.

One reading of this composition suggests that diverse memories of everyday people collectively represent the vision of Dr. King called "Our America." Accepting the Man of the Decade prize from the Baltimore Community Relations Commission a year and a half before his assassination, King shared his hope for a nation that would be "inhabited by millions of the fortunate whose dreams of life, liberty, and the pursuit of happiness are poured out in glorious fulfillment," where "little boys and little girls grow up in the sunshine of opportunity."[12] Given the overall focus of the Baltimore '68 project on identifying King's assassination as the cause of the riots, it is plausible that the artists sought to visually connect King and the eyewitness memories of the riots as "cut from the same cloth" by rendering both from the same ceramic tiles.[13]

The symmetrical positioning, orientation, and balance among these elements echoes back to the shared authority embedded in the mosaic's design. As a heuristic device, the Baltimore '68 Mosaic Monument serves as a window into the historiography of the black freedom struggle.[14] This project clearly shows the practice of shared authority in action. The creation process, which was executed through the collaboration of both academic scholars and community members (those typically underrepresented in historical narratives and commemorative art-making), created a space for co-generated production of knowledge. The use of a mosaic as the project's presentation medium, which locates memories of regular citizens alongside—but not secondary to—the legacy of Dr. King, has the potential to disrupt a top-down view of history by exploring human agency. Through its process and medium, the Baltimore Mosaic Monument moved beyond the charisma of a single personality in order to recover the experiences of previously unknown women and men in a spectrum of political roles and perspectives.

While the monument created opportunity for shared authority and civic engagement, it also presents a problematic view of the black freedom struggle. As the largest single image of the mosaic, a postmodern portraiture of Dr. King hovers in the top center of the main scene. The artists offer subtle hints of the subject's identity: small white tiles around the neck are reminiscent of a clerical collar, and the face is adorned by a prominent mustache—a look that King donned most of his adult life.

It's also hard to miss that the subject's facial expression connotes stoicism and sorrow as a single tear slides toward the nose, assumedly in response to the destruction of the urban neighborhood below his panoptical gaze. The shedding of a single tear will likely remind viewers of the iconic 1971 public service campaign "Keep America Beautiful." In the original television ad—which sitcoms and cartoons have reintroduced into contemporary popular culture through parodies of the clip—an actor playing an American Indian, replete with a long black braid, single feather, and dark complexion deepened with makeup, paddles his canoe down a pristine river to booming drumbeats.[15] Reaching the city harbor, he gazes upon a highway when someone flings a bag of trash from a passing car. The camera deadpans and zooms in as the Indian looks directly at the viewer; a single tear rolls down his cheek. Drums swell to frenzy just as the narrator declares, "People start pollution. People can stop it."

The problematic nature of this advertisement parallels the similarly problematic messages of the mosaic monument, which exist despite the artists' efforts to include diverse voices in its creation. Regardless of the stereotypes associated with this image—the stoic Indian is rendered a nostalgic caricature in this campaign, a type of "noble savage" that atones for the iniquities of a consumer-driven society—King is presented as a parallel in a way intended to honor him. As a sentimental, misty-eyed prophet in the Baltimore '68 mosaic monument, his image serves as a symbol of his sacrifice and atonement for America's racist sins. The message of both representations yields a powerful emotional response because the figures are symbolic of national ideals: sacrifice, nobility, and honor.[16] They also offer a tale of redemption, the great American comeback story. Both figures wept for our collective transgressions—those against the natural world and people of color—and hence, from their tears, sprang forth a new age based on a hope for a green and colorblind America.

The imagery is also, of course, reminiscent of the sacrificial Jesus figure, the archetypal martyr who, according to Christianity's central doctrine, atoned for the sins of mankind and brought peace and restoration to a broken world.[17] In Christian iconography, Jesus is represented as the innocent Lamb of God, He who looks down at a world that has disappointed him but that he himself worked so hard for. The religious undertones of the Baltimore '68 mosaic suggest that King's sacrifice paved the way for the city's reclamation—its salvation even—an ultimate price paid for the city's deliverance from harm, ruin, or loss.

The portrayal of King as a romantically tragic figure rather than as a confrontational freedom fighter—once decried by FBI director J. Edgar Hoover as "the most dangerous man in America"—functions to deradicalize the civil rights struggle in contemporary public memory. Moreover, by locating a passive, almost sacred King at the center of the '68 story (instead of crowds of protestors), the monument delegitimizes "rioting" (more accurately described as revolutionary acts, insurrections or rebellions by people of color in response to highly aggressive policing) as valid acts of political action in democracy. Such depictions reflect—and, arguably, *promote*—an individualistic view of activism by suggesting that social change lies in personal choice rather than government regulation.[18]

In this way, the commemoration implicitly argues for a worldview that is problematic in two ways. First, the Baltimore Mosaic obscures the important role of Black Power political action—forceful advocacy of self-defense, physical retaliation in the face of violence, and proactive revolutionary violence—by revealing the limited impact that legal and political legislation had on democracy's ability to challenge economic inequality and social injustice. The mosaic frames the late 1960s as a high-tide period of nonviolent social unrest in the postwar era.[19] Its familiar cast of characters is led by the ubiquitous King and largely precludes the appearance of black militants.

The exception is a single reference to Black Power on the monument. One of the individual story tiles portrays two stick figures who hold small flames in their hands, a likely reference to Molotov cocktails. However, without historical context to accompany this image and the individual tiles' low-profile positioning (in contrast to King's face) within the whole mosaic design, any reference to the civil rights struggle beyond the rhetoric of the nonviolence movement is largely illegible.

Secondly, the monument fails to address issues of police brutality, which would have been an opportunity for UB, as an anchor institution in a Legacy City, to engage with the past in ways that are meaningful to social issues in the present. While the anniversary organizers stated that their mission was to "empower participants to pursue informed, *responsible* civic action of their own," the commemoration failed to engage with challenging questions surrounding political action without the neutralizing rhetoric of respectability politics. Arguably, the mosaic does not encourage viewers to think about some of the most difficult issues arising from reflection on memories of the city's civil disturbances: How can underserved communities of color peaceably assemble or address grievances toward government without being criminalized in mainstream media outlets as animals, looters, and snipers? When an overwhelmingly white occupying army is deployed to suppress the First and Eighth Amendments rights of black and brown citizens, what recourse do they have to make their voices heard?[20] How can heavily armed paramilitary units dressed not as police officers but as soldiers quell the anxieties of a community outraged by allegations regarding the excessive use of force?

I contend that wrestling with questions such as these would have given commemoration participants an opportunity to tune into the lower frequencies of the postwar era in order to show glimpses of a panoramic black freedom struggle in which Black Power militancy paralleled and, at times, overlapped with the "heroic period" of the civil rights era. It also would have brought the past into the present. The public memory of these events is important, because it frames how we understand eerily similar occupations of poor black and brown communities that take place today in response to protest, like the one in Ferguson, fostered by a militaristic and racialized mindset.[21]

Regardless of whether the commemoration asked the right questions about the riots—those deeply problematized by police brutality and rioting as political action—the truth arguably remains, as Martin Luther King Jr. declared in 1966, that "whether we like it or not, the riots are the voice of the unheard," an opinion reiterated by Congresswoman Maxine Waters in 1992 shortly following the Rodney King riots in Los Angeles.[22] Twenty-two years later, in Ferguson, Missouri, these protesting voices continue to be met by a militarized police force; flash grenades, automatic rifles, army fatigues, heavy armored vehicles, and tear gas transformed a small suburban town of twenty-one thousand with zero murders in 2014 (prior to the police slaying of Michael Brown) into a war zone. This is also what happened in Newark, New Jersey, in 1967.

Newark

One of the nation's oldest cities, Newark, New Jersey, has been said to be on the verge of revitalization since the 1950s. In 1958, Mayor Leo P. Carlin told residents, "Our city has embarked on a program of renewing itself with the initial objectives of eliminating existing slums and blight and preventing the recurrence of such conditions." During his term, the city witnessed an upsurge in development. Towering public housing, new schools, and building projects by local insurance giants Prudential and Mutual Benefit Life transformed the city's skyline. Carlin promised that construction initiatives would usher in the city's revival. Failure to invest in the physical conditions of the community, he warned, would "doom older American cities like Newark to residential and slum status." Almost half a century later in 2006, continuing in the footsteps of his city hall predecessors, Mayor Cory A. Booker pledged that through new development "Newark [would] set a national standard for urban transformation."

In between these administrations, the city exploded in violence over a five-day period in the summer of 1967. Twenty-six people were killed, another 725 were injured, 889 stores were looted, and close to 1,500 people were arrested.[23] Looting alone led to over $10 million dollars in damage (about $62 million in 2007 dollars). The sniper fire, on which many of the 26 riot deaths were blamed, was gunfire from authorities (not mythological black "outside agitator" snipers), who unwittingly shot at each other as a result of a communication breakdown.[24] In local and national news media, the events of 1967 were scapegoated for the city's decline in the late 1960s. In reality, Newark was already in the midst of a steady downward spiral that had begun with the Great Depression.[25]

Remembering Newark's Summer of Discontent: Forty Years Later

In 2007, for the first time, the city of Newark publicly commemorated its 1967 riots. The participation in the fortieth anniversary commemoration was prodigious. Thousands of Newarkers and residents from neighboring towns attended one or more of the activities marking the commemoration, and tens of thousands more read newspaper articles, viewed a documentary film broadcast on public television, and explored the resources posted online. From July through November of 2007, commemoration participants explored intersections of race, memory, social class, and urban development through a rich array of public-oriented activities: guided walking tours, brown bag lunch lectures, family programs, photography and oral history exhibitions, academic discussions, video installations, professional development workshops for middle and high school teachers, documentary film screenings, call-in radio broadcasts, and a memorial service.

The fortieth anniversary comprised activities sponsored by two dozen local not-for-profit organizations, corporations, cultural institutions, advocacy associations, universities, and government officials who would commemorate Newark's most difficult historical moments—the riots—with the collective recognition that the summer of 1967, still a painful memory to some, is "a part of history that will never be repeated."[26] A year later, the city of Baltimore followed suit, and, as I write, smaller-scale collective remembrance efforts are currently under way in Milwaukee, Buffalo, St. Louis, Cleveland, Watts, and Detroit.[27]

The commemoration came about through the efforts of a group of Newark's leaders, those who viewed the anniversary as an "opportunity and obligation for civic institutions to help the city and indeed, the nation, to better understand what happened in the city and the complicated legacies of that era." The 40th Anniversary Commemorative Committee, affectionately referred to as the Big Bad Committee (in reference of James Brown's linguistic appropriation of the term "bad" in the songs "Say It Loud—I'm Black and I'm Proud" and "Super Bad"), came about as a collaborative effort between the New Jersey Historical Society (NJHS) and the Rutgers University Institute on Ethnicity, Culture, and the Modern Experience (IECME).

Beginning in 2002, the organizations signed a pact to work together in the five years leading up to the fortieth anniversary "through the promotion of public scholarship" and by "enhancing the statewide presence of both institutions while forging deeper links with local communities in Newark." The NJHS and IECME served as anchors by hosting informal planning meetings and offering financial support to groups who were interested in participating in the fortieth anniversary. Most importantly, the partnership spurred collaboration among other city stakeholders.

As a result of programs sponsored by local stakeholders, including not only the universities but also multiple local nonprofits galvanized by the spirit of collaboration, preparations for a dozen commemorations that paid tribute to the events of 1967 dotted the Newark landscape as the anniversary approached, including an oral history archive of witness testimonies (the first of its kind), a state-of-the-art multimedia exhibit, and the thirty-fifth anniversary conference. These commemorations underscored Newarkers' urgent desire to take control of the narrative around its riots and to reconcile segregated memories of the issues that animated the late 1960s in visibly public contexts.

Encouraged by these successes, the Big Bad Committee was created to more formally coordinate events for the summer of 2007 and held its first meeting on May 2, 2007, at the offices of the New Jersey Historical Society. In their first executive action, anniversary organizers designed a schedule of events to be published as a master calendar that would be distributed around the city.[28] The committee's mission statement illuminated the importance of remembering the past in Newark's present and future development: "We hope these commemorative events will enrich Newark's civic culture, acknowledge the emotional impact of 1967, and shed light on Newark's progress beyond 1967." By its second meeting, organizers decided to petition city hall to place a commemorative plaque on the Fourth Police Precinct building. It would become its most ambitious project to date.

Fourth Police Precinct Plaque

The morning began with a dedication ceremony at the Fourth Police Precinct, the ground zero of the Newark '67 riots. Mayor Cory Booker stood on the steps of the building and unveiled a cardboard prototype of a plaque before a cheering crowd of community members, elected officials, and visitors. "On this site on July 12, 1967, there began a civil disturbance that took the lives of twenty-six people and forever changed our city," it read. "May this plaque serve as a symbol of our shared humanity and our commitment to seek justice and equality. Dedicated July 12, 2007, by the People of Newark."

Notably, the plaque reads not unlike a monument honoring those perished in a natural disaster. Unlike the narratives provided by those interviewed, the Fourth Precinct plaque suggests a "blameless" narrative devoid of race, class, gender—or anything "human" at all, for that matter. According to the plaque's wording, the event *itself*—not the people involved (police, military, politicians, rioters, bystanders)—"took" victims' lives. In what could be read as a deliberate act of deradicalization, the

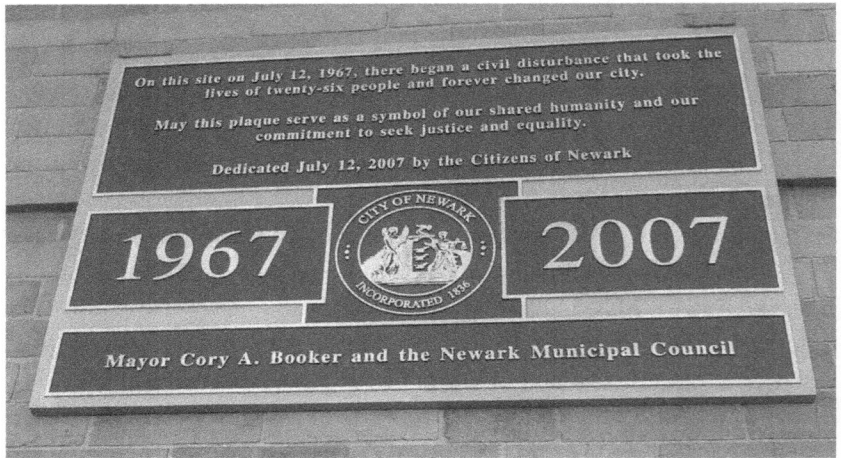

Figure 6.3. Nearly a year after the fortieth anniversary of the Newark riots, Newark mayor Cory Booker unveiled a commemorative plaque that was placed on the front of the Fourth Precinct, on 17th Ave., the origin of the uprising in 1967.

language takes away the agency of the people involved. It personifies an act, as if the act itself—and not those who committed the acts—is the agent. In turn, the content—with regard to "blame" specifically—is purposely nebulous.

So, the question becomes: Who *is* to blame? Who took the lives? Whose lives were lost? Why make this nebulous? Who's in charge of this language and what's to gain from their rhetoric? In the absence of historical consciousness, the average viewer would never know that all but two of the casualties were poor black men and women who were shot by police or National Guard troops. Or that several victims, including Eloise Spellman, a mother of eleven children, and Elizabeth Artis, a sixty-eight-year-old woman, were fatally wounded in their own homes when soldiers fired indiscriminately into the city's public housing projects.

Nor is there mention of the local Black Power and interracial political activism that gained traction among Newark's citizens in response to the disorders, which led to the appointment of African Americans and Latinos to city council and ushered in a three-decade era of black mayors. In turn, the plaque condenses public memory, dislodging the events of 1967 from their civil rights context. In doing so, it allows for a remembrance of the tragedy without political affiliation; the Booker administration is able to draw on the community acceptance acquired through the commemoration without risking political backlash for addressing the deeply entrenched economic and institutional inequality and ongoing police brutality in Newark.

In analyzing the rhetorical choices reflected on the plaque's face, it is important to note that the first planning sessions for the Fourth Police Precinct Building Plaque began with a battle over the words which would be used to document public memory. Was it a *rebellion* by a black community against police brutality and long-standing discrimination in employment, housing and civic empowerment? Were the events a *police riot* waged against poor black residents by ill-prepared, overwhelmingly white male officers of the New Jersey National Guard, New Jersey State Troopers, and local police? When asked about the debate over language, Linda Epps, director of the New Jersey Historical Society and member of the fortieth anniversary committee explained, "The term 'riot' was contested. Some called it a revolution."[29]

"The plaque obviously tells a story and a lot of the word choices in that plaque are deliberate and were not done without great thought and great consideration," reflected Brad Parks, a commemoration committee member and reporter for the local newspaper the *Star-Ledger*. "I think even the word choices say a lot. . . . We don't call it a riot; we call it a civil disturbance. That word choice is very meaningful when we talk about the lives of 26 people."[30] In response to this debate, the organizing committee eschewed both "riot" and "rebellion" and instead designated the event a "civil disturbance." Notably, the term "civil disturbance" is kaleidoscopic; its meaning spirals off into millions of interpretive frameworks. It can infer action of an unruly mob or convey a political schism. According to the U.S. Department of Defense, a civil disturbance is defined as "any incident that disrupts a community where intervention is required to maintain public safety." Black's Law Dictionary, the definitive legal resource for the U.S. judicial system, defines it as a "public disturbance involving three or more people who commit violent acts that cause immediate danger or injury to people or property." According to the Pentagon, "civil unrest may range from simple, nonviolent protests that address specific issues, to events that turn into full-scale riots," and, in the case of the latter, the military believes it is legally permitted to use lethal force. Yet the first search result in Google (and, algorithmically speaking, the most frequently clicked-on definition by users performing a similar Google search) displays a more progressive take via Wikipedia, which defines civil disturbance as "typically a symptom of, and a form of protest against, major socio-political problems."

By framing the '67 unrest as a civil disturbance, and not as a riot or rebellion as was emblematic of the Baltimore and Detroit anniversary commemorations, respectively, the Big Bad Committee forged a "livable past."[31] The Fourth Police Precinct plaque shifted public memory away from a "culture of entitlement" (based on exclusionary understandings of victimhood) and toward a "culture of reconciliation" (based on the notion of "shared humanity"). Yet cultures of entitlement and reconciliation have always been with us and often overlap, as demonstrated in the dedication ceremony of the Fourth Police Precinct plaque.

During his impassioned speech about the past, present, and future at the closing of the dedication, Mayor Booker argued that, moving forward, the city's focus would be on continuing to improve Newark by learning from past lessons. "My generation needs to pick up the baton, sword, plows and let us declare a new day in Newark," Booker said, "to declare that in our city we will make a difference." The mayor and his senior advisor, Bari Mattes, promised that the bronze plaque would soon be mounted to the building, the place where the riots were sparked. In the closing of the ceremony Booker promised, "We will never forget what happened here 40 years ago."

Yet, the plaque itself was seemingly forgotten by city hall for an entire year, as it was not unveiled until the forty-first anniversary, and only after much prodding by concerned citizens. I suggest that Booker's desire to claim the memory of 1967, followed by his delay to mount the commemorative plaque—which was, perhaps, an attempt to avoid drawing renewed attention to difficult issues in a context where he was pursuing broader political ambitions—underscores the political nature of commemoration. Because representations of the past are shaped by political debates in the present, the administration may have been hesitant to lay claim to such a contested memory. Actually mounting the bronze plaque would be an indelible public acknowledgment of Newark's riots for generations to come. Booker's vision of the future—"let us declare a new day in Newark; to declare that in our city we will make a difference"—depended on Newark's ability to break free from this past in the twenty-first century. For city hall, "progress" was arguably bound up with Newark's ability to embody a new post-riot identity.

Interestingly, just a year earlier, the administration drafted plans to demolish the Fourth District Police Precinct Building altogether until Newark's statesman and historian Clement Alexander Price convinced Booker that doing so would be reprehensible. "San Antonio wouldn't tear down the Alamo," Price explained. "Newark shouldn't tear down the 4th Precinct."[32] Other community leaders echoed Price's sentiments. "Having a plaque in the place where the riots were sparked will give future generations a sense of place when they reflect on the city's past," agreed community activist Roger Smith, who attended the dedication ceremony at the Fourth Precinct in 2007. He was only fifteen years old when he witnessed his neighborhood burn. "It *is* history and no different than George Washington's march or the Civil Rights Movement. History is history and we should never forget it," stated Smith.[33] Price and Smith's comparisons indicate that for many Newarkers, the events of 1967 are pivotal revolutionary moments in the nation's history. Their statements also suggest that, for those who lived through 1967, the riots were a deep-rooted part of the American experience, one of equal importance to the master narratives of presidential and military histories.

The juxtaposition of the need to remember with the desire to forget as indicated by the proclamations of Smith, Price, and Booker highlights the "messiness" of commemoration by uncovering the political work of public memory. By concretizing the memory of the '67 disturbances in a bronze plaque, is the city's public commemoration a mode of forgetting? Public memory is constructed. Our understanding of the past is shaped by society's needs in the present.[34] If societies manipulate the past in order to mold the present, what can be distilled from the twenty-first-century commemorations of the 1967 and 1978 Newark and Baltimore riots? This chapter suggests that the legacies of the Newark and Baltimore riots are anything *but* remote historical events, those that can be commemorated from any safe vantage point created by time.

Notes

1. Alan Mallach and Lavea Brachman, *Regenerating America's Legacy Cities* (Cambridge, MA: Lincoln Institute of Land Policy, 2013). In their 2013 report, *Regenerating America's Legacy Cities*, Mallach and Brachman examine the historic legacy and current conditions of U.S. cities that were once the very backbone of the American economy, and some of the most desirable places to live and work. Today, these same cities are

symbols of American deindustrialization, coping with high levels of urban decay, racial segregation, and poverty. They wrote, "American legacy cities were once industrial powerhouses and hubs of business, retail, and services scattered across New England, the Mid-Atlantic, and the Midwest. Their factories provided jobs, and downtown areas contained department stores, professional offices, and financial institutions that served large regions. Since the mid-twentieth century, however, these cities have seen sustained loss of jobs and population, and now face daunting economic, social, physical, and operational challenges" ("Reinventing America's Legacy Cities: Strategies for Cities Losing Population," 110th American Assembly, April 14–17, 2011, *Regenerating America's Legacy Cities*, Lincoln Institute of Land Policy, Policy Focus Report/Code PF034, 2013).

2. For an excellent retrospective on the memories of Newark '67 seldom shared in the public sphere, see Brad Parks's award-winning four-part series "Crossroads: A Neighborhood's View of Despair, Riot and Recovery in Newark," *Star-Ledger*, July 9, 2007. For examples of divergent memories of the Baltimore 1968 riots, captured within three edited oral histories, see Jessica I. Elfenbein, Thomas L. Hollowak, and Elizabeth M. Nix, eds., *Baltimore '68: Riots and Rebirth in an American City* (Philadelphia: Temple University Press, 2011).

3. In Jessica I. Elfenbein, John R. Breihan, and Thomas L. Hollowak, *From Mobtown to Charm City: New Perspectives on Baltimore's Past* (Baltimore: Maryland Historical Society, 2002), a collection of thirteen original and illuminating essays representing the scholarship drawn from the Baltimore History Conference of 1996 and 1999 through the Maryland Historical Society.

4. Oral history statements quoted in the preface to Elfenbein, Hollowak, and Nix, *Baltimore '68*.

5. Interview by the author, Oct. 26, 2012, Urban History Association Conference.

6. Linda Caldwell Epps, *From Zion to Brick City: What's Going On? Newark and the Legacy of the Sixties* (LittD thesis, Drew University, 2010).

7. The school defines cultural diversity as the inclusion of those racial and ethnic groups and individuals who are or have been underrepresented in higher education. See University of Baltimore Office of the Provost, "Cultural Diversity Plan 2009–2014," University of Baltimore website, February 26, 2009, http://www.ubalt.edu/downloads/2009-02-26_UB%20Diversity%20Plan%20for%202009-2014.pdf.

8. Phone interview by the author, Sept. 2, 2014.

9. Michael H. Frisch, *A Shared Authority: Essays on the Craft and Meaning of Oral and Public History* (Albany: State University of New York Press, 1990).

10. In the Qur'an, surah 17 is named after Noah, but he also figures in other surahs. The Biblical story of Noah is found in Genesis 8:6,8,11; For an interesting comparison of passages in both texts, see: Marlies ter Borg, *Sharing Mary: Bible and Qur'an Side by Side*, 2nd ed. (CreateSpace Independent Publishing Platform, 2010).

11. The Kerner report delivered an indictment of "white society" for isolating and neglecting African Americans and urged legislation to promote racial integration and to enrich slums—primarily through the creation of jobs, job training programs, and decent housing. President Johnson, however, rejected the recommendations. In April 1968, one month after the release of the Kerner report, rioting broke out in more than one hundred

cities following the assassination of civil rights leader Martin Luther King Jr. In the following excerpts from the Kerner Report summary, the commission analyzed patterns in the riots and offered explanations for the disturbances. In 1998, thirty years after the issuance of the report, former senator and commission member Fred R. Harris coauthored a study that found the racial divide had grown in the ensuing years with inner-city unemployment at crisis levels. Opposing voices argued that the commission's prediction of separate societies had failed to materialize due to a marked increase in the number of African Americans living in suburbs. See *The Kerner Report: The 1968 Report of the National Advisory Commission on Civil Disorders* (New York: Pantheon Books, 1988).

12. For an excellent discussion of Dr. Martin Luther King Jr.'s prescient speech, see Peter Levy, "The Dream Deferred," in Elfenbein, Hollowak, and Nix, *Baltimore '68*.

13. The University of Baltimore hosted the commemorative program on the anniversary of the assassination of Dr. Martin Luther King Jr. in 2008.

14. Evelyn Brooks Higginbotham's analysis of the 1963 March on Washington shapes my understanding of new civil rights historiography, in Jeanne Theoharis and Komozi Woodard, eds., *Freedom North: Black Freedom Struggles outside the South, 1940–1980* (New York: Palgrave Macmillan, 2001). For more, see Patricia Sullivan, *Days of Hope: Race and Democracy in the New Deal Era* (Chapel Hill: University of North Carolina Press, 1996); Kevin K. Gaines, *American Africans in Ghana: Black Expatriates and the Civil Rights Era* (Chapel Hill: University of North Carolina Press, 2006); Thomas J. Sugrue, "Affirmative Action from Below: Civil Rights, the Building Trades, and the Politics of Racial Equality in the Urban North, 1945–1969," *Journal of American History* 91, no. 1 (June 2004): 145–73, and *Sweet Land of Liberty: The Forgotten Struggle for Civil Rights in the North* (New York: Random House, 2008); Robin D. G. Kelley, "'We Are Not What We Seem': Rethinking Black Working Class Opposition in the Jim Crow South," *Journal of American History* 80, no. 1 (June 1984): 75–112; Glenda Elizabeth Gilmore, *Defying Dixie: The Radical Roots of Civil Rights, 1919–1950* (New York: W.W. Norton, 2009); Barbara Ransby, *Ella Baker and the Black Freedom Movement: A Radical Democratic Vision* (Chapel Hill: University of North Carolina Press, 2003); Mary L. Dudziak, *Cold War Civil Rights: Race and the Image of American Democracy* (Princeton, NJ: Princeton University Press, 2000); Lizabeth Cohen, *Making a New Deal: Industrial Workers in Chicago, 1919–1939* (Cambridge: Cambridge University Press, 1990); Nancy MacLean, *Freedom Is Not Enough: The Opening of the American Workplace* (New York: R. Sage, 2006); Robert R. Korstad, *Civil Rights Unionism: Tobacco Workers and the Struggle for Democracy in the Mid-Twentieth-Century South* (Chapel Hill: University of North Carolina Press, 2003); Komozi Woodard, "Amiri Baraka, the Congress of African People, and Black Power Politics from the 1961 United Nations Protest to the 1972 Gary Convention" in *The Black Panther Movement: Rethinking the Civil Rights–Black Power Era*, ed. Peniel Joseph (New York: Routledge, 2006), 55–78; Peniel E. Joseph, *Waiting 'til the Midnight Hour: A Narrative History of Black Power in America* (New York: Henry Holt, 2006); Komozi Woodard, *A Nation within a Nation: Amiri Baraka (LeRoi Jones) and Black Power Politics* (Chapel Hill: University of North Carolina Press, 1999); Timothy B. Tyson, *Radio Free Dixie: Robert F. Williams and the Roots of Black Power* (Chapel Hill: University of North Carolina Press, 1999); James Edward Smethurst, *The African American Roots of Modernism: From*

Reconstruction to the Harlem Renaissance (Chapel Hill: University of North Carolina Press, 2011); Matthew Countryman, *Up South: Civil Rights and Black Power in Philadelphia* (Philadelphia: University of Pennsylvania Press, 2006); Robert O. Self, *American Babylon: Race and the Struggle for Postwar Oakland* (Princeton, NJ: Princeton University Press, 2003); and Yohuru R. Williams, *Black Politics, White Power: Civil Rights, Black Power, and the Black Panthers in New Haven* (Malden, MA: Blackwell, 2008).

15. The "Crying Indian" ad has been parodied on *Married . . . with Children*, *Wayne's World 2*, *The Simpsons* episode "Trash of the Titans," the Farrelly brothers movie *Kingpin*, and the *South Park* episode "Go Fund Yourself."

16. Liam Kennedy and Scott Lucas, "Enduring Freedom: Public Diplomacy and US Foreign Policy," *American Quarterly* 57, no. 2 (2005): 309–33.

17. "The next day he saw Jesus coming toward him, and said, 'Behold, the Lamb of God, who takes away the sin of the world!'" (John 1:29 [English Standard Version]).

18. For an interesting analysis of the lasting impact of the campaign ad see Ginger Stand's "The Crying Indian: How an Environmental Icon Helped Sell Cans—and Sell Out Environmentalism," *Orion*, Nov./Dec. 2008.

19. On the Black Panther Party, see Kathleen Cleaver and George Katsiaficas, *Liberation, Imagination, and the Black Panther Party: A New Look at the Black Panthers and Their Legacy* (Florence: Taylor and Francis, 2014); William L. Van Deburg, *New Day in Babylon: The Black Power Movement and American Culture, 1965–1975* (Chicago: University of Chicago Press, 1992); Curtis J. Austin, *Up against the Wall: Violence in the Making and Unmaking of the Black Panther Party* (Fayetteville: University of Arkansas Press, 2008); Jama Lazerow, *In Search of the Black Panther Party: New Perspectives on a Revolutionary Movement* (Durham, NC: Duke University Press, 2007); Yohuru R. Williams and Jama Lazerow, *Liberated Territory: Untold Local Perspectives on the Black Panther Party* (Durham, NC: Duke University Press, 2009); Paul Alkebulan, *Survival Pending Revolution: The History of the Black Panther Party* (Tuscaloosa: University of Alabama Press, 2012); Jane Rhodes, *Framing the Black Panthers: The Spectacular Rise of a Black Power Icon* (Urbana: University of Illinois Press, 2007); Kimberly Springer, *Living for the Revolution: Black Feminist Organizations, 1968–1980* (Durham, NC: Duke University Press, 2005); Kimberly Springer, *Still Lifting, Still Climbing: Contemporary African American Women's Activism* (New York: New York University Press, 1999); Bettye Collier-Thomas and V. P. Franklin, *Sisters in the Struggle: African American Women in the Civil Rights–Black Power Movement* (New York: New York University Press, 2001); and Stephen Ward, "The Third World Women's Alliance: Black Feminist Radicalism and Black Power Politics," in Joseph, *The Black Power Movement*, 119–44.

20. Amendment 1: "Congress shall make no law respecting an establishment of religion, or prohibiting the free exercise thereof; or abridging the freedom of speech, or of the press; or the right of the people peaceably to assemble, and to petition the government for a redress of grievances." Amendment 8: "Excessive bail shall not be required, nor excessive fines imposed, nor cruel and unusual punishments inflicted" (U.S. Constitution).

21. For compelling scholarship that does draw connections between the militarized police response to protests in the late 1960s and today, see Robert Stephens II, "In Defense

of the Ferguson Riots," *Jacobin Magazine*, Aug. 14, 2014; and Peniel E. Joseph, "After Michael Brown's Killing, Echoes of the '65 Watts Rebellion," *The Root*, Aug. 13, 2014.

22. In 1966, in an interview with Mike Wallace, Dr. King continued to stress the path of nonviolence: "I contend that the cry of 'black power' is, at bottom, a reaction to the reluctance of white power to make the kind of changes necessary to make justice a reality for the Negro. I think that we've got to see that a riot is the language of the unheard" (CBS Reports, Sept. 27, 1966), transcript available online at http://www.cbsnews.com/news/mlk-a-riot-is-the-language-of-the-unheard/.

23. Brad Parks, "Crossroads: A Neighborhood's View of Despair, Riot and Recovery in Newark," *Star-Ledger*, July 9, 2007.

24. Max Arthur Herman, *Summer of Rage: An Oral History of the 1967 Newark and Detroit Riots* (New York: Peter Lang, 2013); Paul J. Scheips "Violence in Newark," in *The Role of Federal Military Forces in Domestic Disorders, 1945–1992* (Washington, DC, Center of Military History, 2005), 173–77; Tom Hayden "The Occupation of Newark," *New York Review of Books* 9, no. 3 (Aug. 24, 1967): 14–24; Ron Porambo, *No Cause for Indictment: An Autopsy of Newark* (Hoboken, NJ: Melville House, 2007); Albert Bergesen "Race Riots of 1967: An Analysis of Police Violence in Detroit and Newark," *Journal of Black Studies* 12, no. 3 (Mar. 1982): 261–74; James Ridgeway and Jean Casella, "Newark to New Orleans: The Myth of the Black Sniper," *Mother Jones*, July 16, 2007; Epps, *From Zion to Brick City*; Jeffrey M. Paige, "Political Orientation and Riot Participation," *American Sociological Review* 36, no. 5 (Oct. 1971): 810–20.

25. Historian Paul Stellhorn has shown that in much of urban America in the 1930s the critical focus of decision-making was firmly centered at city hall, not in Roosevelt's White House. New Deal policies also had an effect. Like hundreds of America's cities, Newark suffered from disinvestment caused by the Federal Housing Administration's National Housing Act of 1934 and the Federal Aid Highway Act of 1956, the racial barring of African Americans and Latinos from collection of the GI Bill and Social Security disbursements, and the inability of Newark to annex its municipalities at a time of exorbitant taxes and aging housing stock.

26. Clement Alexander Price (city historian), "Newark's Nadir," *NJ Voices*, Aug. 8, 2007.

27. To learn more about the commemoration of the 1968 riots in Baltimore, see Elfenbein, Hollowak, and Nix, *Baltimore '68*. Kristin M. Simonetti's "Mediated Memory: Framing and Sustaining Collective Memory of the 1967 Milwaukee Race Riots in Contemporary and Retrospective Newspaper Coverage" (MA diss., University of North Carolina at Chapel Hill, 2008, https://cdr.lib.unc.edu/indexablecontent/uuid:da690c14–05ec-4f47-a03f-3b1ed2eaa2d0), particularly chapter 5, "Retrospective and Commemorative Coverage of the Milwaukee Race Riots," is a fascinating study that explores how local newspapers treated the riots in coverage published on the ten-, twenty-, twenty-five-, thirty-, and forty-year anniversaries of the riots. For a comparative analysis of commemorative activities in Newark and Detroit, see Max Herman, "The Stigmatized City: Addressing the Legacy of the 1967 Riots/Rebellion in Newark and Detroit," paper presented at the American Sociological Association Annual Meeting, New York, NY, Aug. 9, 2013. Amy Goodman conducted an incredible retrospective interview for *Democracy*

Now! with renowned poet, playwright, activist, and Newark native Amiri Baraka and Larry Hamm, a Newark community organizer and chair of the People's Organization for Progress, who organizes a commemoration of the Newark rebellion every year. The interview was titled "On 40th Anniversary of Newark Rebellion, a Look Back at Historic Unrest that Changed the Nation."

28. "The importance of this meeting cannot be overemphasized. Newark is not a coalition-forming kind of city," elaborated Linda Epps. "It is my contention that because funding for not-for-profit, non-service organizations is so scarce, the battle to secure those resources is all that much more intense" (Interview, 40th Anniversary Oral History Archive, New Jersey Historical Society, Newark, NJ). Minutes from the Big Bad Committee meetings are housed at the New Jersey Historical Society in Newark, NJ.

29. Interview by the author, July 25, 2012.

30. Interview by the author, Sept. 24, 2012.

31. Kristin Kopp and Joanna Nizynska, eds., *Germany, Poland, and Postmemorial Relations: In Search of a Livable Past*, Europe in Transition: The NYU European Studies Series (New York: Palgrave Macmillan, 2012).

32. Interview by the author, July 7, 2007.

33. K. Kasi Addison, "Plaque Commemoration 1967 Newark Riots Unveiled," *Star-Ledger*, July 23, 2008.

34. Michael Kammen, *Mystic Chords of Memory: The Transformation of Tradition in American Culture* (New York: Vintage Books, 1991).

7

Ferguson, USA

A Scholar's Unforeseen Connection and Collision with History

STEFAN M. BRADLEY

Some years back, I read an important biography of a civil rights legend who desegregated a predominantly white institution. In the epilogue, the esteemed scholar who wrote the book mentioned a controversy over whether the institution (where incidentally the scholar worked) that the freedom fighter desegregated should create a monument to the civil rights legend. The biographer explained that it was the place of scholars to remain disinterested on contemporary controversial matters and that it was best for scholars to observe and record for the sake of posterity. I could not understand that sentiment. Three of my scholarly heroes are the late John Hope Franklin, Derrick Bell, and Vincent Harding; they made sure to use their talents to benefit what Harding termed the Black Freedom Struggle. With no disrespect to the venerated biographer, I say thank goodness some scholars committed to planting and cultivating the seeds of righteousness and justice. In the recent campaigns and events surrounding the Ferguson crisis, I have consciously chosen to use what few abilities I have to help the community address issues of justice.

"Now do you understand how we felt?!" asked a participant in the now famous 1968 rebellion at Columbia University in New York City on November 24, 2014, the night that St. Louis County prosecuting attorney Robert McCulloch announced that he would not be indicting Officer Darren Wilson for the shooting death of Ferguson teenager Michael Brown Jr. After short-stopping an interview with MSNBC's Chris Hayes and crawling under the fence of a locked-down compound to race to my car that was twenty feet from the Public Storage building on W. Florissant Ave. that had gone up in flames, pulling on the hot handles and entering the smoke-filled vehicle, driving through the red light, driving on the wrong side of the road to avoid the burning garbage cans on the right side of the road, seeing police and National Guards everywhere, and hearing the moans of mothers and the threats of young hopeless people, I had finally felt what I had written about for so many years. Before I ended the interview with Hayes, I explained that, more than angry or shocked, I was saddened because the narrative of that night would be that the lawless, ungrateful, black youth delighted in destroying other people's property. The narrative I understood from my interactions with the people on the ground was that of hopelessness because of the poverty-stricken circumstances in which they lived and powerlessness in the relationship with the justice and political systems.

In terms of scholarship, I thought I had done a decent job researching material for the *Harlem vs. Columbia University* book; I mean I spoke with many of the right people and read the documents and papers, but I could only imagine the frenzy of the moment and try to write about it the best I could. The night of the non-indictment, when the Columbia alumnus called, I felt the anxiety and fear and anger that so many others felt a half-century ago when demonstrations and rebellions were more commonplace—when if young people had a problem with a system or a president or a war, they took to the streets or took over a building or just made noise to voice their displeasure. The Columbia alumnus told me to be careful but more importantly to not expend all my energy because there will be plenty more nights to demonstrate and many more issues to protest. He said that I should prepare for a protracted struggle for freedom and justice in addition to the emotionally charged battles that the people were waging. That was sage advice.

On Saturday, August 9, 2014, I got a text from a former student telling me a young black man in the Canfield Green apartment complex in Ferguson had been shot and people were starting to get rowdy. I hoped it would not get out of hand, but it seemed like the boy's body lay in the street for an eternity. To understand the tragedy in this, one must spend some time in St. Louis during the month of August to experience the combination of heat and humidity that leads some residents to refer to their home city and state as St. Louis, *Misery*.

It just so happened that my father, Command Sergeant Major (retired)

Alphonso Bradley, had come to visit, so I gathered him from the airport, which is quite near Ferguson. The next day I was supposed to deliver a lecture at Washington Tabernacle Baptist Church (a St. Louis city landmark where both Martin Luther King Jr. and Angela Davis had spent time) on the "History of Education in the Black Community." I started off by wishing my father a happy birthday and asking for a moment of silence for Michael Brown Jr., yet another young black man who had been shot dead.

That Sunday night my phone went abuzz as a current student of mine notified me that the QuickTrip on W. Florissant Ave. was burning. I knew people had to be out of their rational minds because it seemed no one thought through setting fire to a gas station. I received a phone call from the same student just after midnight; he said he was afraid for another one of my current students, who had been in a confrontation with the police near W. Florissant Ave. The police had pepper-sprayed and teargassed my student and shot him with rubber pellets. All I heard was "shot," so I started getting dressed and reached for my knife. The student who called said his friend had just made it to another mentor's home, where he was trying to wash the pepper spray off of his skin and out of his eyes.

I heard from my students later Monday morning (August 11), and they had, prayerfully, lived through it all. They said they were headed back out that evening; I told them not to and that I did not need any martyrs to know that they cared about justice. They were, however, "turned up" and not listening to my dissuasion. Even though I had personally taught them about the Black Freedom Struggle, my students had seen something that changed them forever; inasmuch, they were resolute about hitting the streets again. I knew then that if I could not stop them, I would have to join them.

I have written about black revolutionaries like H. Rap Brown (Jamil Abdullah Al-Amin) and Stokely Carmichael (Kwame Ture), but I am no revolutionary—I vote and wear ties to go to work at a predominantly white institution. I am not easily given to marching in the streets or fist-pumping for causes. There was, however, the issue of my students, so I knew I had to be where they were. With that in mind, I parked my car at the auto parts store on W. Florissant Ave. and called my wife to let her know where it was in case I got arrested or worse. As I walked up on the burnt-out QuickTrip, I saw two young black women writing on the asphalt with chalk. When I approached them, I read three of the most profound and unforgettable words ever. They wrote, "Black Men Matter."

(this was before the phrase "Black Lives Matter" became prevalent). It was so simple but so crucial for the moment.

As I took that statement to heart, I met up with my students. Then, representatives of Chris Hayes's MSNBC show called to interview me. I told them that I would be glad to do the interview as long as my students could be there too. I stood on this position because the portrayal of young black people in the national media to that point was of the "young black thug" who was not following instructions and making life hard on the police by refusing to be quiet when their friend was shot and laid out in the street. The news was not showing young black men who did not have tattoos or who were in college or who could coherently communicate their rage to an audience that stopped listening to black men when they saw the dreads. I did not believe that college students were any better or more respectable than other youth, but I brought my students (one of whom happened to live in Ferguson) to provide some diversity to the portrayals of black youth.

We told our stories of why something was waiting to happen—that black people had been mistreated in North County since they had begun to move out there forty years ago. I listened while a Missouri state senator tried to explain to Hayes that race had nothing to do with the crisis that was unfurling. I disagreed, knowing that decades ago black people who could afford it moved to the county. Then when the public housing that city planners and architects in the postwar era thought would save the city closed, a large portion of those residents moved to places like Ferguson and the Canfield Green complex. Black people in the St. Louis Metropolitan Area also implicitly know that it is risky to drive a car in the county because police are frequently looming to write tickets that provide revenue for the small municipal governments. Furthermore, black residents know that the court systems of the municipalities are nearly impossible to navigate. For anyone who has ever been to one of the courts, it is clear that, yes, race had something to do with it.

As people took to the streets, they were exercising maybe the last piece of power they had—their constitutional rights. It was an electric feeling to be among the people because the people believed they were right. I saw old people carrying signs and young people squaring off against the police because they believed righteousness would protect them. Later in the week, while out one night, I encountered a friend I had not seen in twelve years and we stopped to catch up and talk about what we were witnessing.

At that moment, an officer with a rifle approached us and said that we had to keep moving—that we could not stand in one spot for more than five seconds. There was, of course, no law against talking on a public sidewalk when not obstructing anyone, and I challenge anyone to show me a line in the Constitution where it reads that we did not have the right to "be." In spite of my clear knowledge of this, the officer's rifle was persuasive. I chuckled because, again, I hardly fathomed myself as a threat in the spectacles and tie I wore. Apparently, my outfit of respectability did not convince the police that I was not dangerous. With each minute I spent on the street, I realized the situation was deteriorating. Later that night, my students and I tried to outrun the police clad in riot gear, who rode atop the armored personnel vehicles that belched teargas canisters.

After eating my share of teargas that particular night, I made it home safely to find my father still awake. He asked, "How did the CN gas taste?" He told stories about how during training he would have a good laugh at the soldiers who were exposed to the gas; I did not find the story funny that night. The previous day, we had driven through Ferguson, and when he heard the thumping of helicopters and saw the heavy police presence, the combat veteran of the Korean and Vietnam conflicts said, "This place is occupied!" He told me to be careful and that he was proud that I was taking a stand.

I watched the news to see that police were deeply concerned that some of the people protesting had firearms. I thought that was silly—because of course some people had firearms; Missouri is proudly a concealed carry state, and guns are everywhere. There is even a constitutional right to bear arms for citizens, and the members of the Tea Party have been known to exercise that right in near proximity to the president of the United States without police donning riot gear. The threat of members of the mostly black protesting crowd having firearms, however, must have been quite frightening to the police and the rest of the nation. Part of this has to do with how some people envision citizenship. Rather than looking to the Fourteenth Amendment of the U.S. Constitution, many have bought into the concocted narrative that citizenship requires waving a flag or not ever criticizing the state. I realize it is hard for some to believe, but even loud, tattooed "thugs" are U.S. citizens deserving of freedom rights. I made the comment once that if U.S. citizens were abroad and treated the way some of the citizens in Ferguson had been those nights, the United States would have sent drones to ensure their freedom.

Things during those days and nights moved quickly. A group of young black and progressive professionals who had access to resources and young people met to discuss strategy. The group included a leader of a nonprofit college readiness service, a city treasurer, two state representatives, a college president, two college professors, a teacher placement administrator, an aeronautical company executive, a psychologist, diversity trainers, artists, activists, and others. We called ourselves the Young Citizens Council of St. Louis, and our purpose was to ensure that young people were being heard. Regarding the rebellion, we met with faith leaders in North County and with the Missouri governor; some of us met several times with a U.S. senator; others spoke with the U.S. attorney general and the senior advisor to the president. Members organized events for the youth to share their experiences. We met constantly, but all the while our nights were spent in the streets. Sometimes, feet aching from walking up and down W. Florissant Ave., we stopped for a bite to eat at the Ferguson Burger Bar. We provided commentary to nearly every major (and seemingly minor) international and national news network, demanding the following: that the mayor and police chief of Ferguson step down; that the police wear body cameras; that the Ferguson police force increase the number of black officers; that a community policing model be implemented throughout the county that would include residency requirements; and that a civilian review board with subpoena powers be instituted. We always tried to have young people flanking us if we were on television; if not, we instructed the interviewers to speak with specific young people. We spoke with the representatives from the Department of Justice and U.S. Civil Rights Commission and met with the U.S. secretary of education when they came to town. Members went to the United Nations to discuss the crisis in the St. Louis Metropolitan area. Eventually one of our members was even chosen to serve on the Ferguson Commission and the White House Task Force on Policing.

Indeed, life continued as we spent sleepless nights with the people. On August 25, at the funeral of Michael Brown Jr. that was held at Friendly Temple Missionary Baptist Church, I sat directly behind his friend Dorian Johnson, who shed tears but remained strong; he sat next to the first black mayor of St. Louis, who was acting as his attorney. It is a bit of a sad blur, but I also remember three rows in front of me sat leaders such as Jesse Jackson and T. D. Jakes and other figures. I do recall there being a small controversy about who got to sit where. In those days, I constantly fielded requests for lectures and interviews. When speaking in the fall as part of the Harris-Stowe State University symposium on the sixtieth anniversary of *Brown v. Board of Education*, I remarked that perhaps the Missouri homeboy, Mark Twain, was right: "History doesn't repeat itself, but it does rhyme." I made note of the fact that we were again waiting on a Brown decision—actually a decision regarding the indictment of Officer Wilson. I commented that everyone had a role to play in the 1954 Supreme Court case that was supposed to lead to the racial desegregation of public schools. Attorneys like Charles Hamilton Houston and Thurgood Marshall, scholars like John Hope Franklin and Kenneth Clark, parents like Gardner Bishop, and students like Barbara Johns were necessary participants in the movement toward black freedom. I made the point that it would again take people from every walk of life to achieve justice. At Washington University in St. Louis, I talked with young people about historic and current representations of black and Latino youth in the media as well as the relationship between law enforcement and communities of color. At Clark University in Massachusetts, I spoke to the need for young people to be aware of life outside of campus—aware of what life was like for people their age who could never attend a private university. I spoke to the collateral effects of the War on Drugs and War on Terrorism when I testified to the U.S. Civil Rights Commission about the events in Ferguson. At a California Western Law school, I challenged the aspiring attorneys to value justice as much as they did the law, to never put policy before people, and to make righteousness not right their ultimate goal. I spoke with an organization of Missouri social workers about what could be learned from the Kerner Commission report and how poverty, policing, institutional racism, and a dearth of quality education make for a dangerous mix. I spoke with an educational policy group about how the crisis traumatized schoolchildren who could not breathe at night because of the teargas or could not sleep because of the noise of the helicopters, protesters, flash bombs, and sirens. I told of how mothers were afraid to let their children play outside because there were always strangers in the neighborhood. At the First Unitarian Church in St. Louis, I gave a speech titled "The Democracy Experiment: Black Youth in America" and explained that, historically, the nation has used black youth as test models to find out the limits of policing and justice. And, of course, I carried on with my professorial duties, which included interacting with many more university affiliates than is typical for a fall semester.

In the midst of all of this, St. Louis City police shot dead the son (VonDerrit Meyers Jr.) of a Saint Louis University employee. The incident took place just blocks from the campus. On October 14, a night that scholar/activist Cornell West had come to a campus arena as part of an event that the university and a local ministerial alliance put together, young people rebelled against the decidedly older religious leadership and the politics of respectability that some wielded. After commandeering the microphone from their elders, some protesters lambasted the event and eventually left. When marching down Grand Ave. they decided that they were taking the protest onto SLU's campus. That was the onset of what became known in the media as #OccupySLU; the demonstration lasted for six days. During that period, mostly black demonstrators camped out in the center of campus, at the clock tower. I could not help but think of the campus demonstrations of the 1960s. The administration was frantic in trying to figure a solution to the occupation. Some parents called in with the most racially vitriolic messages imaginable, while students reacted in different ways. Some students joined the effort of the demonstrators, some observed, while others were noticeably annoyed that someone was disturbing their midterm study time. In addition to me, several other faculty members from the African American Studies Program were in constant contact with the contingent of protesters who identified themselves as Tribe X. After some effort, I was able to get some Tribe X members (some of whom were students), their community advisors, and the president of the university in the same room, which was an incredible sight. When taking in the scene of SLU president Fred Pestello and the activists, I thought of college and university presidents S. I. Hayakawa (San Francisco State College), Grayson Kirk (Columbia University), and Kingman Brewster (Yale University) and their meetings with black militants in the 1960s and early 1970s. Back at SLU, after some tense hours and days, the occupation ended with a thirteen-point agreement (referred to as the Clock Tower Accords) that addressed issues of diversity on campus and SLU's role in the surrounding black community.

On March 11, 2015, the night that the Ferguson police chief announced his intention to step down, I was with the people at the police station. As an aside, the night I remember most at the Ferguson police station on S. Florissant Ave. was when McCulloch made his announcement (November 24, 2014). Back then, I saw people standing on a car, not realizing that one of them was Brown's mother. When I heard her and the other mothers' wails of grief, frustration, and pain, I shuddered. Soon after, I heard screeching tires and piercing declarations of anger. In contrast to the character of that night, the tone of the demonstrations was celebratory and relatively light (there were people even grilling in a parking lot) on March 11. Believing that all was well, I left forty-five minutes before two police officers were shot. I felt terrible for the officers, but I was also fearful that the narrative would again shift to lawlessness, with the actions of one representing the behavior of the many. My fears were realized on some cable news networks, but I was reassured that the progress that demonstrators had made regarding reform was not lost on news organs like the *St. Louis American*.

As I reflect, it is clear to me that my students have provided the impetus for my participation in this moment in history. Two of them have agreed to share reasons for joining the Black Freedom Struggle. Jonathan Pulphus is an African American Studies and women's and gender studies major at SLU. He is secretary of Tribe X and a resident of St. Louis, Missouri. Joshua Jones received an MSW from SLU in 2016. He was the graduate assistant for the African American Male Scholars (AAMS) Initiative. Jones is a lifetime resident of Ferguson, Missouri.

> SMB: What on earth possessed you to leave your safe homes to go to Ferguson on Aug. 9–10?
>
> Jonathan: It was emotion. After seeing a picture of Mike's stepfather with a sign stating "they shot my son," I was not only angry and confused but had friends with cars that felt similarly. Angry because young Mike had a family that felt wronged—but police only use force when they have no other choice. Confused because I kept hearing news that the police and community were in tension because Mike's body was laid out in the street for 4.5 hours in the sun—that image can cause trauma.
>
> Joshua: On August 9th I was actually in ATL [Atlanta] with my family for my sister's birthday and we came back home the night of the 10th. I'm a Ferguson resident, so I was in Ferguson all along. I didn't make it to West Florissant until later in that week when I heard that one of our African American Male Scholars (AAMS) members had been pepper sprayed while peacefully protesting. It was but a 3-minute drive/20-minute walk for me to get to the area. Similarly, in November when the non-indictment announcement

happened, my brother and I walked from my house to downtown Ferguson in front of the police department. What "possessed" me to be there was that I had an obligation to demand that my voice as a born and raised EDUCATED & CONSCIOUS Black male resident of Ferguson be heard. Also since my initial observations were from another part of the country, it was important for me to be there for myself to gain an accurate and personal experience of what was taking place in my own city/neighborhood.

SMB: What was your reaction to what you saw in Ferguson? Were you fearful, angry, sad, etc.?

Jonathan: I felt good. Two things caught my attention: the police and the people. Organized in formation, stone-faced, and emotionally controlled, they stood by quarantining part of West Florissant while people vented. Some vandalized the nearby QuickTrip; many more screamed their hearts out at the frontline, smoked, drank, fought, cried, argued, mourned, laughed, and sang. This commotion was not all within the law—yet the law enforcers were just watching the crowd like tourists at a zoo.

Joshua: Again my initial reactions were based on what I saw via social media at dinner with my family in ATL. I saw the pictures and initially thought it was one of those spams from unreliable resources that people get a hold of and run with on social media. Then I got a text confirming it from my brother who was still in STL (St. Louis). And, immediately, my heart sank. I read closer into it and found out that Mike Brown's body had been lying in the street for several hours. Then I pictured myself in Mike Brown's shoes. Knowing the location in comparison to my home, it became very personal even from ATL because Mike Brown very easily could have been me.

SMB: Why did you keep protesting even though it was unsafe?

Jonathan: The reason is that it's bigger than me or the next protester—unfortunately, we (the protesters) are not the anomaly when it comes to state violence. While we do not hope to be harmed, we often accept that arrogance (of the State) and agitation (of the people) do not make the best formula for safety. I did not hope to [be] harmed the first time I was pepper sprayed for engaging an officer, all I had was a sign and my voice. I did accept that anything can happen so—luckily, my partner Alisha Sonnier, agreed to come with me because after the assault, she transported me away and helped me to health. As months go by, the police remain unpredictable—they know how to bend the rules while controlling the narrative in order to harass or instigate us with impunity. We accept their position and move forward in the most strategic way possible.

Joshua: I continued to protest because my main safety concerns weren't with the protesters around me, but with those who were being paid to assure my safety (i.e.[,] the police). The police made me the most concerned for my safety and I knew that should not be. I continued to protest because my community and I needed this all too common fearful perspective of the police force to change immediately. I continue(d) to protest because I want(ed) to be a part of the modern Civil Rights Movement that was happening, inevitably, right in my backyard.

SMB: What did it mean for the movement to come closer to SLU (Shaw Neighborhood)?

Jonathan: Opportunity and relevance. For one, students and residents are likelier to go to areas closer to where they live—VonDerrit's dad is an employee at SLU. When VonDerrit was shot in early October, it happened to be around the time for Ferguson October—a massive call bringing activists in and out of St. Louis to designated local areas. SLU agreed to host Cornel West. Without this and several main factors, Occupy SLU would not have happened.

Joshua: It meant Ferguson was/is not just a Ferguson issue. It meant the beginning of some crucial progress on SLU's campus through the raising of the students' consciousness and administrative involvement through the Clock Tower Accords (CTA).

SMB: What were you hoping to accomplish with Occupy SLU and how did your peers react to you? What about professors and administrators?

Jonathan: To pop the SLU bubble and get the Clock Tower Accords. From Tribe X's perspective, this meant educating, empowering, and organizing. We educated by hosting teach-ins about student-activism, the Black Lives Matter movement, and policing. We organized by helping galvanize many liberal students through education alongside direct action such as the Grand-street shutdown and occupation. We empowered by creating an atmosphere where the university was willing to negotiate. Peer reactions varied—some against it, for it, and indifferent. Protestors, particularly non-students, were insulted (called "thugs" or "unpatriotic") by people with negative extreme views, harassed by DPS (Department of Public Safety) by way of being stalked around campus / or selectively asked for their I.D., and denied access to bathrooms in university buildings recently made inaccessible to non-students. A lot of snide comments and threats were made towards me or passed along—but none to my face. Professors also varied; some letters of support for the occupation bore some faculty signatures but there are many more faculty at SLU than signatures on the letters. I had more positive experiences with my professor in African American studies who took her students to the occupation to better inform the class. Administration—those that mattered—were welcoming. Pestello (President Fred Pestello), as a representative voice of administration, even added clarifying line items to the demands for CTA.

Joshua: Being an MSW student, my academic experiences were different than what I know happened for many undergrad students. Social workers (i.e.[,] my peers and professors) tend to be very socially conscious and active people, so they were very passionate about the actions taking place as well. And many spent late nights at the Clock Tower dialogues along with me. From a professional standpoint as a graduate assistant in the CCC (Cross Cultural Center) under the Student Development Division, I was hoping to assure to [sic] the students that I serve that they have a powerful voice and that I could not be more proud of them for their work and diligence in this movement on campus. I wanted to actively listen, so that I could accurately present the perspective of the students and occupiers to those who were watching from afar with a dangerously skewed perspective (i.e.[,] parents, alumni, co-workers, community members, etc.)

SMB: What did you learn from all of this about yourself and your peers?

Jonathan: That we've got to continue to press forward. Reverend and activist Traci Blackmon once stated that the CTA (Clock Tower Accords) is the only tangible institutional change made since the movement began. With CTA, we need a timetable for each line item. With the Ferguson movement, we need more gains.

Joshua: [I] learned/reconfirmed that everything that happened in my life leading up to August 9th happened for a reason that's so much bigger than me alone. Becoming the AAMS graduate assistant on SLU's campus as a born and raised Ferguson resident who is studying to be [a] social worker, I have been placed exactly where I need to be for the betterment and empowerment of my people and community[,] which means the betterment/empowerment of self. Prior to this situation I knew that my various mediums of privilege gave me obligations to serve those who may not have the same privileges. After all of this, it became very clear that while my privileges and gifts have been given to me for the benefit of all in need, I have an obligation to represent, serve, and grind for Black communities in a unique and special way. As for my peers, let's just say my true friends and family are still around.

The young people may not know it, but they have been effecting change in the region and all over the nation. In the St. Louis Metropolitan area, the city established a new civilian review board. Then, several of the smaller county municipalities revised or began revising their court procedures and fining systems, and some are even combining police departments. The Ferguson police chief stepped down and the Ferguson city council now has two new black members. There are several more progressive steps that have been made possible only because young people took action. My students motivated me to move beyond the archives, classrooms, and lectures to demonstrate for freedom. Their courage was infectious. I owed them my support. Before August 9, I tried to correct the injustices that affected the community quietly as an individual, but my students helped me to realize that there is a time to be loud and for seemingly disparate groups of people to act as one. In that way, they taught the teacher. By risking their lives and access to socioeconomic security and status, these young people are rescuing American democracy by challenging the nation to reconsider how it polices black bodies.

Conclusion

To answer the Columbia alumnus who called on the night of the non-indictment announcement, I *feel* at least some of what the demonstrators at Columbia and in Harlem felt in 1968. Perhaps some may feel that it is not appropriate for me to play a part in the Ferguson and Occupy SLU crises, but I argue that history collided with me. As a historian, I know that there were those who felt that people like me should have never had the opportunity to read, or should not have been admitted to college, or should not have had access to a program in black studies. When, however, the people I have most admired in life paved the road by choosing to act when they observed injustice, then the least I could do was represent the voices of those who may not have the opportunity to be heard. I doubt that anyone will ever remember me as an esteemed scholar, but someone will remember me as a person who used whatever little talent and influence I had to help others toward freedom and justice. In that way, I hope I am living in the spirit of Franklin, Bell, and Harding, who like others before them sacrificed their status and lives for the Black Freedom Struggle. They, the elders, planted the seeds of struggle and did the work of resistance so that my students and I could reap the harvest of opportunity. Although the work of racial justice remains unfinished, I am proud to have been in fellowship with those willing to labor for freedom and human rights.

8

Religion and the Black Freedom Struggle for Sandra Bland

PHILLIP LUKE SINITIERE

> I want to hear Sandra Bland say well done.
> Reverend Sekou and the Holy Ghost, "Heaven"

> It's time for me to do God's work. . . . I know everybody don't believe in God, which is fine, but I want you to know on Sandy Speaks, I'm gonna talk about God, because he has truly opened my eyes and shown me that there is something out there that we can do.
> Sandra Bland, "Sandy Speaks"

> [Women] build movements one by one, in tens, hundreds, thousands, and eventually millions.
> Mumia Abu-Jamal, "Rosa Parks, Claudette Colvin and Jo Ann Robinson"

On the afternoon on Friday, July 10, 2015, just outside of Prairie View A&M University (PVAMU) in Waller County, a Texas Department of Public Safety (DPS) officer named Brian Encinia pulled over twenty-eight-year-old Chicago native Sandra Bland for failure to signal a lane change. Dashcam footage documented how Encinia escalated tensions by stoking Bland's irritation to the point of pulling a taser and shouting, "I will light you up!" Forcibly pulling Bland from the car, he subsequently arrested her. Ironically, Encinia apprehended Bland directly in front of Good Hope AME Church; not only was Bland a member of DuPage AME Church in Chicago, but Good Hope also became a central protest site in the Sandra Bland movement. Three days later, and about seven miles from where Encinia handcuffed, arrested, and detained her, Bland died inside of the Waller County Jail, located in the small town of Hempstead about fifty miles northwest of Houston. Officials ruled Bland's death a suicide; family and friends contested this conclusion.

Twelve months later on Sunday, July 10, 2016, activists and organizers from the Sandra Bland movement gathered at her arrest site to memorialize her life. Along the newly named Sandra Bland Parkway—formerly known as Farm Road 1098—in poetry and performance art, attendees at the "She Speaks" event prayed, spoke, and sang insurgently about police brutality and state violence. Artists also exhibited calls for hope and justice through a vigorous commitment to self-determination. This signature event took place in front of Good Hope AME. To commemorate the movement that Bland's death galvanized, the "She Speaks" event inaugurated a sixty-four-hour sit-in at Waller County Jail, which included prayer walks and communion services.

The juxtaposition of these opening anecdotes—the life and death in police custody of one black woman in Waller County, Texas, and the quest for meaning, solace, and resolve, activists, allies, and organizers enacted at the sites of her apprehension and death—invites fuller comprehension of the Sandra Bland movement's historical significance and cultural meaning. This chapter chronicles the Sandra Bland movement's first year to ponder religion's place within contemporary forms of black protest. Throughout, it also comments on the ways that social media shaped and formed the movement's work that pressed for social and political change. By documenting how Protestant Christianity, much of it related to the Methodist tradition, inspired and informed the Sandra Bland movement's freedom work, both on the ground in Waller County and across the digital universe, it argues that the recent genesis of the Sandra Bland movement underscores the enduring role that religion plays in some expressions of the Black Lives Matter (BLM)-era freedom struggle.

While BLM has overtly advocated for and welcomed broad-based constituencies whom religious institutions have historically resisted, religion has been neither absent nor excluded from the movement's activities. In fact, BLM cofounder Patrisse Cullors practices Ifà, a West African Yoruba tradition. She has found the tradition's spirituality a source of existential strength in black freedom work. "When you are working with people who have been directly impacted by state violence and heavy policing in our communities, it is really important that there is a connection to the spirit world," Cullors explained in 2015. Spirituality, she maintained, helped Cullors to make sense of the everyday material and political circumstances

Figure 8.1. Good Hope AME Church, Prairie View, Texas, 2015. Photo by author.

within which she found herself; she also observed similar sensibilities in others with whom she worked. "People's resilience, I think, is tied to their will to live, our will to survive, which is deeply spiritual," she said. "I don't believe spirit is this thing that lives outside of us dictating our lives, but rather our ability to be deeply connected to something that is bigger than us. I think that is what makes our work powerful." Cullors's comments suggest that BLM is not a wholly secular, materialist movement, and indicate that scholars of the black freedom struggle should account for the place of religion in BLM-era activism.[1]

Using religion as the primary lens through which to observe the first year of the Sandra Bland movement's history while also paying attention to the role of digital protest and local activism, this chapter strands together several threads of civil rights historiography. Most obviously, it converses with the work on religion and the black freedom struggle, a subject scholars have documented in a number of important studies, especially in recent years. On the one hand, important work explains how religious ideas, beliefs, and practices fostered political commitments to justice; on the other hand, the ways that racialization undergirds religion in the United States also means that religion serviced the arguments and actions of white supremacists and segregationists. The religious shape of Sandra Bland protests, based on the discourse and practice of Protestant Christian activists, connects most specifically to Martin Luther King's conception of the beloved community. Attention to religion and the Sandra Bland movement also ties to a burgeoning scholarship on religion and BLM. In Missouri, for example, as Leah Gunning Francis's book *Ferguson & Faith* details, black and white and male and female Christian clergypersons linked spiritual prayer with robust protest work that involved placing their bodies on the front lines of confrontation. Christianity-based activism in Ferguson inspired similar actions in Waller County a year later.[2]

A focus on the locality of Sandra Bland freedom work between Houston and Waller County orients it as a rural, southern civil rights story, while it also reflects a particular kind of civil rights groundwork. Scholarship on the black freedom struggle's local and regional history points to the particularities of place and illuminates connections to wider national and international freedom work. Although centered in a rural Texas community outside of Houston, the Sandra Bland movement's story connects to networks outside of the region, thus linking it to wider, historical trends.[3]

The centrality of social media in the Sandra Bland movement documents its BLM-era genesis. Twitter, Instagram, and Facebook, along with blogs, are modalities within the digital landscape on which its history has played out. While social media is specific to the contemporary age, scholarship highlights technology's history in civil rights struggles, from photography and print media to television and the Internet. As in previous eras of black freedom work, the convergence between technology and civil rights struggles provides new opportunities and also imposes severe limitations. Social media registers the immediacy of black resistance and can thus enter news streams in real time to effect political change, while technology also gives the state new surveillance capabilities and provides it with tools for repression. At present, such contemporary history lacks a fuller, longitudinal analysis; however, social media's role in the Sandra

Bland movement illustrates technology's vital impact on contemporary black protest.[4]

A disclaimer is helpful here: it is important to note that I wrote this chapter both as a historian of American religion and African American studies and as an active participant-observer in the Sandra Bland movement. A former resident of Waller County, I presently reside in northwest Houston, about thirty miles east of the towns of Hempstead and Prairie View, where the majority of Sandra Bland movement activity has taken place. While I live in Harris County, I have remained politically active in Waller County, particularly with environmental justice concerns and, most recently, actions related to the Sandra Bland movement. While I did not participate in Sandra Bland movement actions with the intent of producing scholarship about them, my decision to write about the 2015 Waller County Jail vigil on the African American Intellectual History Society's blog *Black Perspectives* led to a request to reproduce that blog post for this volume. As I continued to participate in Sandra Bland movement activities throughout 2015 and the first half of 2016, my activist work and scholarship began to converge more intentionally, which ultimately produced the research featured in this essay. My rendering of what I call *history in the present tense*, the attempt to document and interpret contemporary events as they happen, builds on established black freedom struggle scholarship while it also invokes the late Manning Marable's ideas about a "multidisciplinary methodology" to include the use of oral history and digital data in the production of "living black history."[5]

Locating an analysis of the Sandra Bland movement within its first year allows for a close exploration of critical details necessary for grasping its larger historical importance. Understanding how the Sandra Bland movement illustrates historic practices within the black freedom struggle—the role of religion in protest politics, the locality of its work in light of wider activist networks, and the use of technology in activism—presents ways to consider its cultural significance. In what follows I first explain the relationship between religion, social media, and black freedom in the Sandra Bland movement by telling the stories of several female activists, people I call Sandra Bland's sister comrades. Second, I highlight aspects of the "She Speaks" event and the following sixty-four-hour sit-in at Waller County Jail that concluded the Sandra Bland movement's first year.

Year One of the Black Freedom Struggle for Sandra Bland: A Brief Overview

As reports surfaced about Sandra Bland's death and as dashcam footage of her arrest circulated on the Internet, Houston-area friends who knew her as a PVAMU student joined with activists on the evening of July 15, 2015, to pray in front of Waller County Jail, the site of Bland's death. As they made the sixty-minute drive from Houston to Hempstead, black and white participants used the Anglican *Book of Common Prayer*, anointed each other with oil to symbolize protection and empowerment, and voiced silent petitions. Methodist pastor Reverend Hannah Bonner, a white radical clergywoman who became a key leader in the Sandra Bland movement, and Houston LGBTQ faith activist Rhys Caraway, lit a tall, slender votive candle on the steps of Waller County Jail to mark the solemn moment. The side of the candle read "What Happened to Sandra Bland?" The votive's flame—the same votive Bonner used several weeks earlier to honor the Charleston Nine from Emanuel AME Church in South Carolina—announced an emerging movement and signaled a committed agitation to demand answers and find justice for Sandra Bland.[6]

The July 15 evening action turned into an eighty-day vigil outside of Waller County Jail. For nearly three months local activists as well as allies from across the country sat with protest signs and sometimes spoke with local officials about what happened to Sandra Bland. Veteran activists joined hands with student protestors. Rural farmers stood in solidarity with university professors. LGBTQ persons linked arms with cisgender people, who collaborated with transgender or gender-nonconforming allies, while atheists fellowshipped with Christians. Members of the Nation of Islam stood with representatives from the National Black United Front, and leaders in the New Black Panther Party supported the voices of millennial revolutionaries. Methodists, Lutherans, Presbyterians, and Pentecostals put faith into action through clergy solidarity by praying, preaching, and tapping ministerial networks to get the word out about Sandra Bland. Eventually, hundreds of people participated in the vigil, brought water or food for protestors, lent their voices of concern, or otherwise supported the quest for justice. While the physical presence of allies spurred the spirits of vigil participants, technology also drove part of the vigil's power as blogs, tweets, and Facebook posts not only

Figure 8.2. Protestors from the Unitarian Universalist congregations of Houston gather at the Day of Remembrance and Response, August 15, 2015, Waller County Jail. Photo by author.

documented the protest but also kept the image, name, and cause of Sandra Bland alive.[7]

In early August, organizers held a Day of Remembrance and Response to mark the momentum of the Sandra Bland movement and engage in continued work for justice and equality. August 9, the day of the action, marked the one-year anniversary of Michael Brown's death, another theme of the event. Presenters at the rally represented the racial, religious, and ethnic diversity of those assembled. Chants of "Sandy Still Speaks" echoed messages like "We Want Justice Now" and "Sandra's Life Mattered" on protest signs. A Sandy Speaks video segment, played from a cell phone, concluded the peaceful, nonviolent event, after which the National Black United Front led a solidarity march around Waller County Jail. As the day ended, Waller County sheriffs and DPS officers suited in riot gear emerged in front of Waller County jail to stage provocative gestures designed to incite reaction, and to silence and intimidate protestors. Local news media seized on this particular moment to delegitimize the day's planned and organized agenda of remembrance and action. The next day, and in the weeks that followed, Waller County sheriff R. Glenn Smith

Figure 8.3. At the same event, Houston activist and Nation of Islam member Deric Muhammad speaks on a boycott of Waller County, while a National Black United Front flag flutters proudly. Photo by author.

sought to intimidate vigil-keepers. He postured with verbal threats and pushed activists away from Waller County Jail's main entrance by placing concrete and wooden barriers along with "No Loitering" signs in front of the building. He also engaged in environmental destruction by felling a large oak tree under whose shade protesters had begun to assemble.[8]

As summer turned to fall, the Sandra Bland movement remained active. A GoFundMe site sought to galvanize support for Sandra Bland and raise funds for legal fees associated with the wrongful death lawsuit Bland's family had filed against Waller County Jail and the DPS. The Department of Justice received petitions to open an investigation into the case of Sandra Bland. Protesters, led by a Lutheran pastor named Carolyn Albert Donovan, began holding weekly vigils outside of DPS headquarters in Austin to demand that it fire Brian Encinia. After much debate and rancorous discussion, the Prairie View City Council passed a resolution to rename University Drive—the road that leads into PVAMU and the road on which Sandra Bland was apprehended—Sandra Bland Memorial Parkway. Several weeks later, in a chance encounter at a Washington, DC, restaurant with 2016 Democratic presidential candidate Bernie Sanders, Geneva Reed-Veal, Sandra Bland's mother, spoke with the Vermont senator about the death of her daughter and the movement her passing had incited. Only days later, in a debate with other Democratic presidential candidates, Sanders invoked the name of Sandra Bland. In mid-October, Sandra Bland's family, along with the Reverend Hannah Bonner, participated in the "Justice or Else" anniversary event in recognition of the Million Man March. Reed-Veal, along with others impacted by police brutality and death of loved ones in police custody, spoke in Washington, DC.[9]

Important developments associated with the Sandra Bland movement took place in the middle of winter. Houston federal judge David Hittner held a second hearing on the wrongful death lawsuit filed against Waller County and the DPS by Sandra Bland's family and set a date for the civil trial. Just before Christmas, on December 22, a Waller County grand jury returned no indictments against Waller County Jail officials in Sandra Bland's death. In response, chants of "No Justice! No Fear! Sandra Bland is marching here!" and "No justice! No peace! Sandy still speaks!" thundered near downtown Houston the following day. Waller County grand jury deliberations continued in early January to consider DPS officer Encinia's actions in Bland's arrest. On January 6, 2016, special prosecutors announced an indictment of perjury against Encinia for falsification of a police report. DPS then indicated that it had initiated termination proceedings against the state trooper. Encinia turned himself in to Texas Rangers on January 7 but posted bond at Waller County Jail shortly after booking. (As I completed this chapter in June of 2017, Waller County state district judge Albert McCaig dropped Encinia's perjury charge; as a result, he surrendered his police license and will never again seek law enforcement employment.) After grand jury deliberations, Houston congresswoman Shelia Jackson Lee renewed calls for federal intervention in Bland's case by sending a letter to U.S. Attorney General Loretta Lynch on behalf of the Congressional Black Caucus to investigate Bland's death. Finally, in early January, friends, scholars, and supporters of Sandra Bland launched a website, SandySpeaksOn.com. It named the Sandra Bland movement through hashtag activism, local organizing events in Texas, and educational projects such as the Sandra Bland Social Justice Scholarship at PVAMU. "The goal is to let people know that while Sandy is no longer here, nonetheless she has sparked a positive and powerful movement," the site read, "a movement that focuses on #BlackLivesMatter, discusses difficult topics like white privilege and police brutality, and encourages people to step up and change the world."[10]

Increasing attention to Bland during the winter expanded into broader national and international exposure throughout the spring and summer. For example, U.S. journalists produced major pieces on Bland. In *Chicago Magazine* reporter Bryan Smith published a substantial biographical profile of Bland titled "An American Tragedy." The story covered Bland's visit to Waller County in anticipation of working at her alma mater, and it offered rich and stirring details of her life and family history in Chicago. "Fully understanding the depth of [the Bland family's] pain—and of the tragedy itself—requires far more than digesting a few sound bites on CNN," Smith wrote. "It requires a nuanced look at the real woman behind the headlines and at how a heartbreaking combination of factors years in the making—racial, cultural, intimately personal—collided devastatingly in the waning light of a late afternoon on what was once an unremarkable stretch of road in Texas." While the well-known Sandy Speaks videos humanize Bland and keep her voice alive, Smith's story added an equally compelling human portrait of Bland.[11]

Veteran reporter Debbie Nathan published two articles on Sandra Bland in the *Nation*. Her first piece, "The Real Reason Sandra Bland Got Locked Up," documented the vicious and unfortunate ways that Texas rakes in money from traffic tickets and court costs and fees, not unlike the over-policed municipalities that surround Ferguson, Missouri, a subject the film "Ferguson: A Report from Occupied Territory" documented. "The worst place in Waller County to be driving is probably where Bland was stopped—the little town of Prairie View, with its 6,000 overwhelmingly black residents and 8,000 overwhelmingly black students," observed Nathan. "When it comes to local revenue, the place is a cash cow—a cow of color." Nathan's article connected the dots between law enforcement, the policing of black bodies, and state and county budgets. Nathan's second *Nation* article, "What Happened to Sandra Bland?" like Smith's *Chicago Magazine* essay, humanized Bland with new details about her life growing up in Illinois. However, it presented a far less flattering portrait that focused on run-ins with law enforcement, drug use, self-harm, and depression, factors that Nathan suggested in part ultimately led to Bland's death.[12]

On the international scene, in early 2016 the Human Rights division of the United Nations, under the auspices of the UN Working Group of Experts on People of African Descent, visited the United States on a fact-finding mission that included testimony from victims and survivors of police brutality and racism. Bland's sister Shante Needham spoke before the working group to share her family's experience of dealing with state-sanctioned violence against black women. In its statement about its U.S. visit, the working group related cases like that of Sandra Bland to historic patterns of legal and extralegal discrimination:

> The colonial history, the legacy of enslavement, racial subordination and segregation, racial terrorism, and racial inequality in the US remains a serious challenge as there has been no real commitment to reparations and to truth and reconciliation for people of African descent. Despite substantial changes since the end of the enforcement of Jim Crow and the fight for civil rights, ideology ensuring the domination of one group over another, continues to negatively impact the civil, political, economic, social and cultural rights of African Americans today. The dangerous ideology of white supremacy inhibits social cohesion amongst the US population. Lynching was a form of racial terrorism that has contributed to a legacy of racial inequality that the US must address. Thousands of people of African descent were killed in violent public acts of racial control and domination and the perpetrators were never held accountable. Contemporary police killings and the trauma it creates are reminiscent of the racial terror lynching of the past. Impunity for state violence has resulted in the current human rights crisis and must be addressed as a matter of urgency. . . . The Working Group is concerned about the alarming levels of police brutality and excessive use of lethal force by law enforcement officials committed with impunity . . . [and] the Working Group is deeply concerned about the low number of cases

where police officers have been held accountable.... Racial profiling is a rampant practice and seriously damages the trust which African Americans have in relation to law enforcement officials.

Needham's testimony about her sister's unlawful arrest, and death, conformed to a long-standing historical practice of internationalizing the black freedom struggle with appeal to global institutions to adjudicate justice or exact international pressure on the United States. In addition, the UN working group's statement on state-sanctioned violence against black people and racialized mistreatment put into sharp historical context the sequence of events that precipitated Sandra Bland's arrest, incarceration, and eventual death. Broader attention to Bland's case from both domestic journalists and international actors resulted in part from the consistent presence of local activists and allies on-site and online in Houston and in Waller County.[13]

International attention to Bland's case and the increasing national prominence of Bland's family and their consistent calls for black human rights in the United States resulted in several moments of celebration as the first year of the Sandra Bland movement ended. A Waller County ceremony on April 15, 2016, unveiled the Sandra Bland Parkway sign along the route that leads into PVAMU. Another of the singular achievements of the Sandra Bland movement to date, the symbolic power of Sandra Bland Parkway, according to Bland's mother Geneva Reed-Veal, provided cultural leverage that further pressed the U.S. justice system for law enforcement accountability and transparency. "It's not about just Sandy," stated Reed-Veal at the ceremony. "It's about other women and men who've died at the hands of officers who've sworn to protect them."[14]

Three months after the unveiling of Sandra Bland Parkway, activists and allies gathered at the same site to host a "She Speaks" event to honor Bland's life, mark a year of action and struggle, and inaugurate year two in the battle for justice. "She Speaks" hosted poets and performers who used art as a creative form of protest. Houston poet Arrow, for example, in a spoken word performance echoed Sandy Speaks videos and presented a message of resolve to continue Sandra Bland's black freedom struggle. She stated, "Good morning my beautiful kings and queens / and suddenly her body begins to bleed," and finished with, "I'm here to let the whole world know / that even though she is dead Sandra still speaks." The conclusion of "She Speaks" even launched a sixty-four-hour sit-in at Waller County

Figure 8.4. Sandra Bland Parkway sign, April 2016. Photo by author.

Jail to symbolize the amount of time Bland spent incarcerated before officials pronounced her dead. The sit-in simultaneously ended the first year of the Sandra Bland movement and commissioned year two of Sandra Bland's black freedom struggle.[15]

The first year of the Sandra Bland movement enacted protest strategies with historical precedent such as sit-ins and marches while it capitalized on new media technologies to link local work in rural Waller County to a national and global audience. Local activists kept pressure on law enforcement officials, the federal government, and the state of Texas to spark political, legal, and cultural responses to the issues surfaced by Sandra Bland's arrest, incarceration, and death. In response, local and national media reported on Bland's case, and the United Nations spotlighted the legal, criminological, and cultural concerns her story represented. The contemporary context of Bland's death in 2015 and the ways in which her Sandy Speaks videos embodied current practices of twenty-first-century activism, along with the digital archive that activists created in the name of resistance to state violence against people of color, unquestionably connect the first year of the Sandra Bland movement to the era of BLM. BLM has voiced powerful demands for black liberation that continue to confront a society that has yet to recognize fully the humanity, dignity, and beauty of black people.

Commentary by veteran activist and scholar Angela Davis added historical relevance to these contemporary events by providing illuminating political perspective. Her *Guardian* essay in late 2014 cogently exposited the historical underpinnings of the BLM era. "Although racist state violence has been a consistent theme in the history of people of African descent in North America, it has become especially noteworthy during the administration of the first African American president, whose very election was widely interpreted as heralding the advent of a new postracial era," wrote Davis in "From Michael Brown to Assata Shakur, the Racist State of America Persists." She continued, "The sheer persistence of police killing of Black youths contradicts the assumption that these are isolated aberrations." Davis echoed this observation in a June 2015 speech in Ferguson, Missouri, just days before Sandra Bland's arrest, incarceration, and death. "It is quite interesting that in the very last period of Obama's presidency, the Pandora's box of racism has been unbolted," Davis remarked to her Ferguson audience. "Your movement announced that we do not now need the traditional, recognizable Black male charismatic leadership. We definitely love Martin and Malcolm and deeply appreciate their historical contributions, but we need not replicate the past. Besides, this is the twenty-first century and by now we should have learned that leadership is not a male prerogative." While Davis historicized BLM, in hindsight she also foretold the advancing power of the Sandra Bland movement. "Women have always done the work of organizing Black radical movements, so women should also be in the leadership.... When Black women stand up—as they did during the Montgomery Bus Boycott—as they did during the Black liberation era, earth-shaking changes occur."[16]

Religion and the Black Freedom Struggle for Sandra Bland

As the first section of the essay detailed, it is significant to observe that the first year of the Sandra Bland movement began and ended with a prayer vigil at Waller County Jail. This fact registers religion's role in contemporary BLM protest actions while it also calls to mind the intensely local dimension to Sandra Bland groundwork in Waller County. The votive "What Happened to Sandra Bland?" lit on the evening of July 15, 2015, on the steps of Waller County Jail sparked a political movement both steeped in and deeply inspired by Protestant Christianity, much of it connected to the Methodist tradition. The substantial presence of clergy—most of whom were black and white Methodist female pastors—along with faithful allies (not all of whom identify as Christian or even as religious at all) places the story in the longer narrative of how religion has historically informed black freedom struggles. The final section of this essay unpacks the religious history between the prayer vigils that bookended the first twelve months of the Sandra Bland movement. It explains how the day-to-day rhetoric and spiritual expressions of Christian women whom I call Sandra Bland's sister comrades spearheaded, supported, and sustained the activities and actions during the first months and closing weeks in the Sandra Bland movement's inaugural year.

Methodist clergywoman Hannah Bonner was one of Sandra Bland's sister comrades whose religious faith fueled her embodied commitment to racial justice. Bonner, originally from Pennsylvania, undertook a seminary education at Duke Divinity School that not only ushered her into the clerical ranks of the United Methodist Church but also unveiled a deeper understanding of structural racism. Seminary classes, racial reconciliation workshops, and key friendships with black and Latina clergywomen prompted new reflection on white privilege. Her education revolutionized how she lived justice principles through a lens of religious faith and led her to proclaim racial equality from the pulpits in which she preached. While her BLM activism predated Bonner's work in Waller County, on-site participation in a prayer vigil at Waller County Jail, a commitment to Bland's family, and what she described as a divine call from God energized her civil rights groundwork in the Sandra Bland movement. Reverend Bonner's embodied solidarity with people of color was also, as she put it, a ministry of "sustained discomfort" that assaulted white privilege in sermons, writings, and everyday conversation.[17]

For Bonner, harnessing religion in the Sandra Bland movement has involved keeping front and center the voice of Sandra Bland through Sandy Speaks videos. She called this a ministry of amplification, where she put the voices and experiences of black women front and center. Moreover, a shared denominational heritage between the two women led Bonner to refer to Bland as "a great evangelist in the Methodist movement." However, a particular Sandy Speaks video spoke more clearly to Bonner than the others because of Bland's proclamation that God inspired her own justice work, and that religion was a foundational inspiration for her support of black dignity. "That is why when I saw Sandra pause and then continue forward—saying that God is the one who called her to work to end injustice—I felt convicted," wrote Bonner of the Sandy Speaks video. "She was a woman who was as unapologetic about her faith as she was about her love for herself and others. She chose to intertwine the articulation of her faith into her pursuit of justice, because it was her faith that had led her into action."[18]

On the ground in Waller County, religion shaped the Sandra Bland movement in other ways through the construction of an Ebenezer behind Waller County Jail. In August 2015, Bonner started the Ebenezer on her daily prayer walks around the jail, and supporters and allies contributed to the Ebenezer as they joined the eighty-day vigil. In the Christian tradition, the practice of stacking stones into an Ebenezer, which symbolizes hope and dependence upon God, comes from the Old Testament account in 1 Samuel where the Hebrew prophet built a stone monument to memorialize faith and hope. In addition to constructing the Ebenezer, vigil-keepers daily recited Psalm 23. The "The LORD is my shepherd" verse, which also includes "I will fear no evil, for you are with me," is a well-known Bible passage invoked to conjure feelings of peace and poise. For Bonner and other activists, the symbolism of building an Ebenezer in a carceral space invested protest actions with Christian meaning. Reciting Psalm 23 as a prayer to conclude daily vigil vocalized Christian scriptures, verbalized comfort in the midst of distress, and displayed a politics of hope as an expression of struggle.[19]

A few days into the Waller County Jail vigil, a Houstonian named Carie Cauley arrived to proclaim solidarity with Sandra Bland. A divinity student studying at Southern Methodist University's Perkins School of Theology in Dallas and a millennial, Cauley commented that her actions on behalf of the Sandra Bland movement stemmed from her own parallels with Bland as a "young, black, educated, and Christian woman." The visibility of Bland's case in the digital universe, Cauley explained, coupled with the "antecedents" of Michael Brown's death in Ferguson and Freddie Gray's death in Baltimore, prompted her decision to participate in the vigil. Moreover, since the Bland events took place within forty-five minutes of her home, Cauley felt she could involve herself in localized social justice groundwork. Her actions on behalf of Sandra Bland mirrored her parents' political work in mid-century civil rights struggles. Barbara Jordan inspired Cauley's mother to engage in social justice politics while her father participated in protests with Martin Luther King. In addition to her parents' example, Cauley cited King's nonviolent concept of the

Figure 8.5. Ebenezer behind Waller County Jail, August 2015. Photo courtesy of Hannah Bonner.

beloved community as well as Malcolm X's bold confrontation with white supremacy as inspiration. Cauley's religious convictions also justified vigil participation because she saw Bland as a human being and connected to her religious faith.[20]

Cauley observed that the "lack of care" American society displays toward black bodies through chokeholds, systematic injustice, and microaggressions rooted her determination to remain present in Waller County for Sandra Bland. It provided an opportunity to put her religious faith into action. "God touched me and compelled me to move," Cauley stated. "And I believe that God allowed me to come out [to Waller County Jail] . . . to continue to pray and stand watch and be present . . . and alert to what was going on in [Bland's] situation. . . . God compelled me to move beyond being fearful." Cauley admitted that her fears stemmed from the reality that in Waller County she sensed a feeling of hostility to her presence as a black woman, most especially in her oppositional presence sitting vigil outside of the jail in which Sandra Bland died. Other sources of tension in Cauley's experience that blunted the possibility of organizing around the "common cause of the Sandra Bland movement" included divergent interests of other activists. At the same time, creating spontaneous community with a range of vigil participants—Christians, atheists, LGBTQ activists, teachers, and religious leaders, among others—fueled Cauley's commitment to justice work. Ultimately, she explained that faith in the midst of fright and anxiety brought her into a place of constant prayer for strength and tenacity, which included "asking the question and joining in unity to ask the question what happened to Sandra Bland. . . . We're standing in the gap" for justice.[21]

Another black woman, Karisha Shaw, joined the vigil at Waller County Jail as a sister comrade. She noted that her presence signaled "standing up for justice for the life of Sandra Bland, and all the other black lives that have been lost this year alone due to police brutality." As a lifelong resident in the American South and a member of Generation X, Shaw has had a long tenure with antiblack racism and over-policing in the region that has positioned her to understand some of the issues connected to the case of Sandra Bland. As a resident of Houston, Shaw felt like she could "say something" about violence against black bodies, and specifically black female bodies. With roots in rural Northwest Florida, in a town like Hempstead, where black Americans suffered countless racist indignities, Shaw's work prior to the Sandra Bland movement covered homelessness and LGBTQ activism.[22]

In her early twenties and an ardent atheist, Shaw experienced a spiritual change and resolved to "follow a path of Christlikeness" because "Jesus was a humanitarian." Although Shaw was a Christian, she said that the Christian church has more often sided with power and privilege rather than embraced the marginalized and destitute. As a result, her inspiration for social justice action emanated from a wide variety of sources: the writings of Leo Tolstoy, Lao Tzu, Martin Luther King's *Letter from Birmingham Jail*, and the autobiography of Assata Shakur. Her commitment as a Christian drew on New Testament passages along with the Hebrew prophets Isaiah and Jeremiah. Proclamations about strength, vigilance, wisdom, and hope—most notably Isaiah 54:17—"no weapon that is formed against you will prosper"—became meaningful as Shaw reflected and prayed while sitting vigil in Waller County. She felt that this action on behalf of Sandra Bland not only embodied her individual faith

Figure 8.6. *L to R*: The author, Karisha Shaw, Carie Cauley, and the Reverend Hannah Bonner, August 11, 2015, Waller County Jail. Photo from author's collection.

commitment but also expressed an enduring belief in "black self-love," an integral dimension in any social movement. Existential sustenance also came when Shaw met Geneva Reed-Veal. Shaw recalled that as the two embraced, Bland's mother provided "nuggets of wisdom" and counsel to continue the quest for justice. "Her daughter is my sister," Shaw said, "because she's a black woman." In this regard, Shaw spoke about the power of solidarity in local, civil rights groundwork: "With every movement that's ever had any great momentum, it started with people sitting, just to learn what they were actually dealing with. As long as there's injustice in the world, I think that people need to be sitting somewhere. And for me, it's in Waller County."[23]

While accounts of sister comrades present some aspects of the story, clergy solidarity was another way that religion inhabited the politics of the Sandra Bland movement. For example, Michael Rinehart, a white bishop in the Evangelical Lutheran Church in America, published a letter in support of the Sandra Bland vigil. Based in Montgomery, a small town northeast of Hempstead, Rinehart stated, "Rev. Bonner and those with her are a living witness to what it means to be the church. They are working to tear down the walls of classism, sexism, and racism while building bridges of unconditional love. Their presence in these vigils embodies what it means to be Christ in the world," he wrote. "Their peaceful actions demonstrate how Christians respond to injustice with love," he continued. "We join with them in committing ourselves and our prayers to the important work of building bridges to those divided from us by reasons of hatred, fear, racism, injustice, and oppression. Finally, and most importantly, we remember and proclaim that Sandra Bland was a beloved child of God."[24]

In addition to local clergy, from across the nation pastors traveled to Waller County to support and hold vigil with activists. Erin Hawkins, a black woman from the United Methodist Church who worked as the general secretary for the General Commission on Religion and Race, was one such clergywoman who expressed her solidarity. Hawkins's article for the *United Methodist Reporter* "Enough Is Enough" not only described her travels to Texas, but it also presented the weariness of facing daily the reality of police brutality and state-sanctioned violence. "For the last few months, I've been caught in what seems like a perpetual struggle, trying to decide whether or not to write a statement after each incidence of violence toward black people at the hands of law enforcement or racist hatemongers," she wrote in mid-August 2015. "It seems that just as I find the words to respond to one act of terror, another one becomes the headline story of the day. I can't form the words fast enough. Truth be told, I can't process the emotions fast enough to make a statement that fits within the timeline of the 'talking heads cycle of commentary.'" At the same time, Hawkins expressed the resolve necessary to name injustice in efforts for freedom and dignity. Invoking the faith tradition that she represents, Hawkins vowed to continue the struggle. She stated, "There simply aren't enough words, enough statements to do justice to the truth that all people of good will—all people who proclaim to follow Jesus who said, 'in as much as you did it unto the least of these you did it to me'—must join hands, say 'enough is enough,' and take action if we are to break through the physical and spiritual forces of violence and hatred that plague us." As a practical step to counter fatigue from a protracted fight for equality, Hawkins sounded a pastoral and prophetic tone, "I believe that prayer is powerful, and I encourage leaders at every level in the Church to continue praying and calling for prayer." Hawkins drew a connection between prayerful meditation and action: "I believe that declarations of solidarity and support are an important first step in building relationships with the harmed and hurting. I also believe that if those are the only two things that you are doing in the face of the staggering realities of racism, sexism, and classism—which are being made more and more visible every day, all around the world—then you are a part of the problem."²⁵

While clergy and activist allies defined the role of religion in the Sandra Bland movement, opposition to local black freedom work also expressed itself in religious terms. On Monday, August 10, less than twenty-four hours after the Day of Remembrance and Response concluded, and on the same day activists delivered petitions to the Department of Justice for a federal investigation into Sandra Bland's death, protesters returned to Waller County Jail mid-day to continue holding vigil. The hundred-plus-degree temperatures served as a metaphor as things heated up in the afternoon outside of the jail. Waller County sheriff R. Glenn Smith confronted Pastor Bonner and other activists, reminding the group of four not to block the entrance. Bonner respectfully replied that none of those holding vigil had ever blocked the front doors in twenty-plus days sitting outside of the jail. In a series of heated exchanges that followed, Smith acidly criticized activities of the Day of Remembrance and Response. He then levied threats against those holding vigil by photographing the license plates of activists' cars, including my own. Then, as the Waller County sheriff walked back toward the jail's entrance he turned directly to Bonner and told her, "Why don't you go back to the Church of Satan you run." By this point Bonner had begun recording the sheriff's combative rhetoric. Later that afternoon once she posted the video of Smith's confrontational comments on social media the story went viral. National and international news outlets reported on this development. On behalf of the United Methodist Church, Cynthia B. Astle composed an open letter to Sherriff R. Glenn Smith. A sheriff's abusive comments and threats caught on camera, like the racist rhetoric of southern police commissioners half a century ago that appeared on television, had the double effect of displaying brash arrogance while garnering support for black freedom.[26]

Smith's provocation, while it reeked of patriarchal aggression against a female pastor, deployed religious rhetoric by associating a universal symbol of evil, "Satan," with the protest work of Christian clergy on behalf of a black woman who made known her solidarity with BLM. Smith was not the only law enforcement officer to associate blackness with evil in the era of BLM. Ferguson police officer Darren Wilson used the word "demon" to describe Michael Brown in the infamous confrontation on Canfield Drive that resulted in the eighteen-year-old's death. While activists have used religion to justify insurgent actions in support of black dignity, law enforcement officials have in turn dismissed black humanity through categories of moral evil.[27]

The individual stories of Sandra Bland's sister comrades and the abusive rhetoric of law enforcement officers illuminates how both religion and social media figured into the movement's first days and weeks. A brief look at commemorative events surrounding the one-year anniversary of Bland's death also shows the ways that digital work, protest actions, and religion factored into the Sandra Bland movement's freedom struggles.

The "She Speaks" event that marked the anniversary of Bland's arrest drew on a variety of religious resources. The program's emcee, Houston spoken-word poet Kayenne Nebula, offered a traditional African prayer and called on Olodumare, a deity in the Yoruba West African tradition. She also poured out several libations to summon the memory of black people recently killed by state-sanctioned violence. Nebula commented, "Sandra Bland is an ancestor now. . . . We want her essence to be present," after which those assembled replied, "Ashe," or amen, in agreement. A Houston artist of Mexican-American culture, Blanca A. Alanis, read a poem on multicultural identity and sang "I Just Ask God" in Spanish. Willy Showtime, a spoken-word poet from Houston, started his performance with a proclamation, "I got a dream inside of me to be happy and free," and concluded with invocations that connected a Christian notion of God and Black Power politics by describing a "voice [that] shook the ground" and "a fist clenched over our prayer." Finally, PVAMU student Mirissa Joy Tucker called on participants to contribute to the Sandra Bland movement based on their own abilities and fields of expertise, a hallmark of civil rights groundwork. As an actor and singer, Tucker sang "Lord, I need your direction. . . . Let your Spirit lead me," as part of the "She Speaks" program. The conclusion of the "She Speaks" event inaugurated the beginning of a sixty-four-hour sit-in at Waller County Jail.[28]

The one-year memorial sit-in at Waller County Jail wrapped Christian rituals into daily rhythms. Prayer walks promoted meditation and contemplation to fortify spiritual perspectives in preparation for political protest. Communion services, held in the morning and evening at the jail, provided participants with a reminder of Christianity's central story of Jesus's death even as it promoted existential fortitude to carry out a witness for justice. A makeshift altar—a wooden TV dinner tray—held the bread and wine that participants consumed. Reverend Bonner used Facebook

Figure 8.7. "She Speaks" event emcee Kayenne Nebula pours a libation for black lives ended by police brutality, July 10, 2016. Photo by author.

Live to broadcast the communion services; archived videos of the services document how students and activists helped in the distribution of bread and wine, prayed, sang, and preached. Prayers, sermons, and songs are part of organized political activity documented the religious character of the Sandra Bland movement and call to mind images of kneel-ins, protest anthems, and public prayers captured on film during the civil rights battles in Montgomery and Selma during the 1950s and 1960s.[29]

Creatively subversive uses of digital technology also defined the Waller County Jail sit-in. Activists played Sandy Speaks video during the day,

Figure 8.8. Sandra Bland arrest site memorial in front of Good Hope AME Church, Prairie View, Texas. Photo by author.

broadcasting through a large amplifier. As sheriffs walked by, and as people walked in and out of the jail's front entrance, they heard Bland's voice. At night, activists used a projector to plaster images of Bland on the stucco walls of the jail. Bland's image literally lit up the evening, and her picture radiated out to the community as if she were a living icon. Not only did sit-in participants project her images, but they also played Sandy

Speaks videos so that her voice reinhabited the carceral space in which she breathed her last breath. Finally, in the closing hours of the sit-in on July 13, 2016, activists played a Sandy Speaks video as black female PVAMU students raised a black fist in beautiful defiance against Bland's unjust arrest and death, a wonderfully provocative symbol of Black Power that inaugurated year two in the Sandra Bland revolution.

The case of Sandra Bland has been one of the most visible of the racial tragedies in the BLM era, while it has inspired some of the most creative and persistent activist responses to state violence against black people. Reasons for its visibility include the stunning digital record of her arrest, along with innovative use of social media by participants in the Sandra Bland movement. The role of religion in shaping Sandra Bland movement activism is another reason for the enduring attention it has received, and observing this offers one vantage point from which to observe contemporary BLM activism. The centrality of digital resistance deployed by Sandra Bland movement activists built a living black history and documented how the mobilization of religious resources offered tangible energies for existential strength. Furthermore, Bland's own Christian convictions displayed in the digital resurrection of her archived Sandy Speaks videos influenced the political actions of those who drove the movement that bears her name. While the case of Sandra Bland remains in progress, the first year of the Sandra Bland revolution tapped deep historical precedent and displayed tenacious ingenuity and insurgent resolve in the long and enduring struggle for black freedom and liberation.

Acknowledgments

This chapter began as a post on *Black Perspectives*, the blog of the African American Intellectual History Society (AAIHS). I thank AAIHS president Chris Cameron for providing an online forum in which I first shared some of these ideas. I thank Keisha Blain, Eddie Carson, and Lerone Martin for helpful questions and suggestions on an early version of this research. I presented parts of this paper at the 2017 "#SayHerName: The Sandra Bland Movement" forum at Sam Houston State University and at the 2017 Texas State Historical Association annual meeting; for probing questions and insightful feedback I salute Malachi Crawford and Bernadette Pruitt. Thanks go to the Reverend Hannah Bonner for use of the Ebenezer image, and to Carie Cauley and Karisha Shaw for sharing their stories.

Notes

1. Hebah H. Farrag, "The Role of Spirit in the #BlackLivesMatter Movement: A Conversation with Activist and Artist Patrisse Cullors," *Religion Dispatches,* June 24, 2015, http://religiondispatches.org/the-role-of-spirit-in-the-blacklivesmatter-movement-a-conversation-with-activist-and-artist-patrisse-cullors/.

2. The scholarship on religion and the civil rights movement is expansive and growing, and it includes attention to Christian and Jewish groups, along with participants from the Nation of Islam, for example. A sampling of books that reflects the range of important subjects that this essay addresses includes James F. Findlay, *Church People in the Struggle: The National Council of Churches and the Black Freedom Movement, 1950–1970* (New York: Oxford University Press, 1997); Andrew M. Manis, *Southern Civil Religions in Conflict: Civil Rights and the Culture Wars* (Macon, GA: Mercer University Press, 2002); David L. Chappell, *A Stone of Hope: Prophetic Religion and the Death of Jim Crow* (Chapel Hill: University of North Carolina Press, 2004); Paul Harvey, *Freedom's Coming: Religious Culture and the Shaping of the South from the Civil War through the Civil Rights Era* (Chapel Hill: University of North Carolina Press, 2005); Charles Marsh, *The Beloved Community: How Faith Shapes Social Justice, from the Civil Rights Movement to Today* (New York: Basic Books, 2005); Charles Marsh, *God's Long Summer: Stories of Faith and Civil Rights* (Princeton: Princeton University Press, 2008); Peter Slade, *Open Friendship in a Closed Society: Mission Mississippi and a Theology of Friendship* (New York: Oxford University Press, 2009); Peter Slade, Charles Marsh, and Peter Goodwin Heltzel, eds., *Mobilizing for the Common Good: The Lived Theology of John M. Perkins* (Jackson: University Press of Mississippi, 2013); and Carolyn Renée Dupont, *Mississippi Praying: Southern White Evangelicals and the Civil Rights Movement, 1945–1975* (New York: New York University Press, 2013).

Scholarship on BLM is in its earliest stages, as is work on BLM and religion, with which this essay converses. Helpful studies include Stephen C. Finley and Biko Mandela Gray, "God Is a White Racist: Imminent Atheism as a Religious Response to Black Lives Matter and State-Sanctioned Anti-Black Violence," *Journal of Africana Religions* 3/4 (2015): 443–53; and Shannen Dee Williams, "The Global Catholic Church and the Radical Possibilities of #BlackLivesMatter," *Journal of Africana Religions* 3/4 (2015): 503–15. See also the digital forum "Religion, Secularism, and Black Lives Matter," *Immanent Frame,* Sept. 22, 2016, http://blogs.ssrc.org/tif/2016/09/22/religion-secularism-and-black-lives-matter/?disp=print, along with the essays by Anthony Pinn, Joseph Winters, and Terrence L. Johnson in the "Religion and Black Lives Matter" forum at Georgetown's Berkley Center for Religion, Peace, and World Affairs (Oct. 24, 2016), https://berkleycenter.georgetown.edu/forum/religion-and-black-lives-matter.

While advocacy-oriented confessional scholarship is written primarily for religious communities, the following studies are nevertheless vital for understanding how BLM and Christianity have intersected so far: Leah Gunning Francis, *Ferguson & Faith: Sparking Leadership & Awakening Community* (St. Louis: Chalice, 2015); Kelly Brown Douglas, *Stand Your Ground: Black Bodies and the Justice of God* (New York: Orbis, 2015); and Jim

Wallis, *America's Original Sin: Racism, White Privilege, and the Bridge to a New America* (Grand Rapids: Brazos, 2016).

3. Representative work on local civil rights history useful for this chapter includes John Dittmer, *Local People: The Struggle for Civil Rights in Mississippi* (Urbana: University of Illinois Press, 1994); Jeanne Theoharis and Komozi Woodard, eds., *Groundwork: Local Black Freedom Movements in America* (New York: New York University Press, 2005); Charles Payne, *I've Got the Light of Freedom: The Organizing Tradition and the Mississippi Freedom Struggle*, 2nd ed. (Berkeley: University of California Press, 2007); and Emilye Crosby, ed., *Civil Rights History from the Ground Up: Local Struggles, a National Movement* (Athens: University of Georgia Press, 2011).

4. Brian Ward, *Radio and the Struggle for Civil Rights in the South* (Gainesville: University Press of Florida, 2004); Maurice Berger, *For All the World to See: Visual Culture and the Struggle for Civil Rights* (New Haven: Yale University Press, 2010); Martin A. Berger, *Seeing through Race: A Reinterpretation of Civil Rights Photography* (Berkeley: University of California Press, 2011); Leigh Raiford, *Imprisoned in a Luminous Glare: Photography and the African American Freedom Struggle* (University of North Carolina Press, 2013); Aniko Bodroghkozy, *Equal Time: Television and the Civil Rights Movement* (Urbana: University of Illinois Press, 2013).

5. For the blog post that gave birth to this chapter, see Phillip Luke Sinitiere, "What Is Happening in Waller County?: Sandra Bland and the Sister Comrades Who #Sayhername," *Black Perspectives*, Aug. 12, 2015, http://aaihs.org/what-is-happening-in-waller-county-sandra-bland-and-the-sister-comrades-who-sayhername/. In this essay, the following work informs my reference to history in the present tense: Manning Marable, *Living Black History: How Reimagining the African-American Past Can Remake America's Racial Future* (New York: Basic Books, 2005), xx; Claire Bond Potter and Renee C. Romano, eds., *Doing Recent History: On Privacy, Copyright, Video Games, Institutional Review Boards, Activist Scholarship, and History That Talks Back* (Athens: University of Georgia Press, 2012), 1–22. Also helpful on history in the present tense is Renee C. Romano's comment from *Doing Recent History* in her chapter "Not Dead Yet: My Identity Crisis as a Historian of the Recent Past" (23–44). She writes, "By being careful to position ourselves in relation to our work, and being articulate about that without being defensive, historians of the recent past can reject the charge that we lack 'sufficient detachment' to undertake our studies" (39).

6. Hannah Bonner, "What Happened to Sandra Bland?" *Soulunbound.com*, July 17, 2015, https://soulunbound.com/2015/07/17/what-happened-to-sandra-bland/. All Soulunbound.com articles cited in this chapter are also available at www.archive.org and https://thatshowthelightgetsin.wordpress.com/.

7. Sinitiere, "What Is Happening in Waller County?"; Hannah Bonner, "How Sandra Bland Changed my Life," *Soulunbound.com*, Sept. 1, 2015, https://soulunbound.com/2015/09/01/three-lessons-from-sandra-bland/; Hannah Bonner, "50 Days Later: Still Grieving, Called, Woke," *Soulunbound.com*, Sept. 2, 2015, https://soulunbound.com/2015/09/02/50-days-later-still-grieving-called-woke/.

8. Sinitiere, "What Is Happening in Waller County?"

9. Sinitiere, "What Is Happening in Waller County?"; Hannah Bonner, "Sandra Bland in a Sea of Red: Remembering the Names We Forget," *Soulunbound.com,* Oct. 13, 2015, https://soulunbound.com/2015/10/13/sandra-bland-in-a-sea-of-red-remembering-the-names-we-forget/; Hannah Bonner, "When Bernie Promised to #SayHerName #Sandra Bland," *Soulunbound.com,* Oct. 14, 2015, https://soulunbound.com/2015/10/14/when-bernie-promised-to-sayhername-sandrabland/.

10. Phillip Luke Sinitiere, "#SandyStillSpeaks: 'Living Black History' and Resources on Sandra Bland," *Black Perspectives,* Jan. 28, 2016, http://www.aaihs.org/sandystillspeaks/. See also Shelia Jackson Lee, "Press Statement: CBC Members Seek Justice for Sandra Bland," Jan. 15, 2016, http://jacksonlee.house.gov/media-center/press-releases/congresswoman-sheila-jackson-lee-and-cbc-members-seek-justice-for-sandra.

11. Bryan Smith, "Sandra Bland: An American Tragedy," *Chicago Magazine,* Dec. 14, 2015, http://www.chicagomag.com/Chicago-Magazine/January-2016/Sandra-Bland/.

12. Sinitiere, "#SandyStillSpeaks"; Debbie Nathan, "The Real Reason Sandra Bland Got Locked Up," *Nation,* Dec. 18, 2015, https://www.thenation.com/article/the-real-reason-sandra-bland-got-locked-up/, and "What Happened to Sandra Bland?" *Nation,* Apr. 21, 2016, https://www.thenation.com/article/what-happened-to-sandra-bland/.

13. On January 25, 2016, activist Hannah Bonner posted a picture of Needham's testimony on Instagram (https://www.instagram.com/p/BA_a-oZqgss/). On the UN Working Group of Experts on People of African Descent, see "Statement to the Media by the United Nations' Working Group of Experts on People of African Descent, on the conclusion of its official visit to USA, 19–29 January 2016," http://ohchr.org/EN/NewsEvents/Pages/DisplayNews.aspx?NewsID=17000&LangID=E.

14. Reed-Veal quoted in Fauzeya Raham, "Ceremony Marks Name Change to Sandra Bland Parkway," *Houston Chronicle,* Apr. 15, 2016, http://www.houstonchronicle.com/news/houston-texas/houston/article/Ceremony-marks-name-change-to-Sandra-Bland-Parkway-7252056.php.

15. Using Facebook Live, activist Hannah Bonner brought the "She Speaks" ceremony to a global audience. The event is archived on Bonner's Facebook page (https://www.facebook.com/hannah.a.bonner/videos/vb.100001231239403/1193549680696062/). For a summary of the event and the sit-in at Waller County Jail, see Phillip Luke Sinitiere, "Sandra Bland (1987–2015): Art, Remembrance, Commemoration," *Black Perspectives*, July 13, 2016, http://www.aaihs.org/sandra-bland-1987-2015-art-remembrance-commemoration/.

16. See "From Michael Brown to Assata Shakur, the Racist State of America Persists," and "The Truth Telling Project: Violence in America," in Angela Y. Davis, *Freedom Is a Constant Struggle: Ferguson, Palestine, and the Foundations of a Movement* (Chicago: Haymarket Books, 2016), 77–90. Additional reference points for the contemporary historical context of Black Lives Matter include, among others, Keeanga-Yamahtta Taylor, *From #BlackLivesMatter to Black Liberation* (Chicago: Haymarket Books, 2016); Marc Lamont Hill, *Nobody: Casualties of America's War on the Vulnerable, from Ferguson to Flint* (New York: Atria, 2016); Eddie S. Glaude, *Democracy in Black: How Race Still Enslaves the American Soul* (New York: Crown, 2016); Wesley Lowery, *"They Can't Kill Us All": Ferguson, Baltimore, and a New Era in America's Racial Justice Movement* (New York: Little,

Brown, 2016); and Jelani Cobb, "The Matter of Black Lives," *New Yorker*, Mar. 14, 2016, http://www.newyorker.com/magazine/2016/03/14/where-is-black-lives-matter-headed.

17. Bonner's biography here is based on Reverend Hannah Bonner, interview by the author, Houston, Texas, Sept. 25, 2015; and Christian Holder, "Her Voice Like a Trumpet," *Duke Magazine* 102, no. 2 (Summer 2016): 34–43. On her BLM activism in Ferguson, see Hannah Bonner, "Take Off Your Shoes," *Soulunbound.com*, Sept. 24, 2014, https://soulunbound.com/2014/09/24/take-off-your-shoes/, and "My Feet Are Planted," *Soulunbound.com*, Apr. 28, 2015, https://soulunbound.com/2015/04/28/my-feet-are-planted/. On her preaching ministry of "sustained discomfort" see Hannah Bonner, "A Time to Listen, A Time to Speak," *Soulunbound.com*, Jan. 12, 2015, https://soulunbound.com/2015/01/12/a-time-to-listen-a-time-to-speak/, and "Dear Fellow White People: An Appeal for Sustained Discomfort," *Soulunbound.com*, Feb. 10, 2015, https://soulunbound.com/2016/02/10/dear-fellow-white-people-an-appeal-for-sustained-discomfort/. On Bonner's sense of religious commitment in social justice work related specifically to Sandra Bland, see "100 Days with Sandra Bland . . . and Counting," *Soulunbound.com*, Oct. 22, 2015, https://soulunbound.com/2015/10/22/100-days-with-sandra-bland-and-counting/. For Bonner's theological rationale behind organizing, art, and political protest, see Hannah Adair Bonner, *The Shout: Finding the Prophetic Voice in Unexpected Places* (Nashville: Abingdon, 2016).

18. On Bland as a Methodist evangelist see Sam Hodges, "United Methodist Pastors Respond to Texas Jail Death," *United Methodist News Service*, Aug. 11, 2015, http://www.umc.org/news-and-media/united-methodist-pastors-respond-to-texas-jail-death. On Bonner and Sandy Speaks videos see Hannah Adair Bonner, "The Prophetic Preaching of Sandra Bland," *Sojourners*, Sept. 16, 2015, https://sojo.net/articles/faith-action/prophetic-preaching-sandra-bland.

19. During the eighty-day vigil, Bonner posted several photos of the Ebenezer on Instagram and included a video of protesters reciting Psalm 23: Aug. 10, 2015 (https://www.instagram.com/p/6OjGHrqglI/); Aug. 5, 2015 (https://www.instagram.com/p/6BM04RKgmq/); Aug. 7, 2015 (https://www.instagram.com/p/6GXny8qgkc/); Aug. 11, 2015 (https://www.instagram.com/p/6QtYUpKgqV/).

20. Carie Cauley, telephone interview by the author, Oct. 2, 2015. For Cauley's work, see also Joe Holley, "Waller County's Past, Present Merge along Hempstead Roads," *Houston Chronicle*, July 31, 2015, http://www.houstonchronicle.com/news/houston-texas/houston/article/Waller-County-s-past-present-merge-along-6417392.php#photo-8395292; and Instagram comments made by Cauley that were posted by Hannah Bonner, Aug. 5, 2015 (https://www.instagram.com/p/6BIQlYqgtu/).

21. Carie Cauley, telephone interview by the author, Oct. 2, 2015; Holley, "Waller County's Past"; Cauley comments on Instagram, Aug. 5, 2015 (https://www.instagram.com/p/6BIQlYqgtu/).

22. Karisha Shaw, telephone interview by the author, Sept. 23, 2015. For Shaw's work, see also Dan Solomon, "Scenes from the Waller County Jail," *Texas Monthly*, Aug. 7, 2015, http://www.texasmonthly.com/the-daily-post/scenes-from-the-waller-county-jail/; along with Instagram commentary posted by Hannah Bonner, Aug. 5, 2015 (https://www.instagram.com/p/6BKLiNqghW/).

23. Karisha Shaw, telephone interview by the author, Sept. 23, 2015; Solomon, "Scenes from the Waller County Jail"; Bonner commentary on Instagram, Aug. 5, 2015 (https://www.instagram.com/p/6BKLiNqghW/).

24. Bishop Michael Rinehart, "A Letter in Solidarity with the Sandra Bland Vigil Participants in Waller County," BishopMike.com, Aug. 17, 2015, https://bishopmike.com/2015/08/17/a-letter-in-solidarity-with-the-sandra-bland-vigil-participants-in-waller-county/.

25. Erin Hawkins, "Enough Is Enough," *United Methodist Reporter,* Aug. 15, 2015, http://unitedmethodistreporter.com/2015/08/05/commentary-enough-is-enough/.

26. I was present with those holding vigil the morning of Monday, August 10, and witnessed Smith's provocation firsthand. For reporting on Smith's "church of Satan" comment see Dylan Baddour, "Waller County Sheriff: 'Go Back to the Church of Satan,'" *Houston Chronicle,* Aug. 11, 2015, http://www.chron.com/news/houston-texas/texas/sandra-bland/article/Waller-County-Sheriff-go-back-to-the-Church-of-6436136.php; Abby Ohlheiser, "Sheriff to Pastor Protesting for Sandra Bland: 'Go Back to the Church of Satan,'" *Washington Post,* Aug. 12, 2015, https://www.washingtonpost.com/news/acts-of-faith/wp/2015/08/11/sheriff-in-the-county-where-sandra-bland-died-tells-protesting-methodist-pastor-to-go-back-to-the-church-of-satan/; Rachelle Blidner, "Texas Sheriff Tells Pastor Keeping Vigil for Sandra Bland She 'Runs Church of Satan,'" *New York Daily News,* Aug. 11, 2015, http://www.nydailynews.com/news/national/sandra-bland-sheriff-tells-pastor-runs-church-satan-article-1.2321433; and Andrew Buncombe, "Sandra Bland: Sheriff at Jail Where Black Woman Died Tells Pastor She Belongs to 'Church of Satan,'" *Independent,* Aug. 11, 2015, http://www.independent.co.uk/news/world/americas/sandra-bland-sheriff-at-jail-where-black-woman-died-tells-pastor-she-belongs-to-church-of-satan-10450672.html. See also Cynthia B. Astle, "An Open Letter to the Waller County Sheriff," *United Methodist Insight,* Aug. 11, 2015, http://um-insight.net/perspectives/views-from-a-ridge/an-open-letter-to-the-waller-county-sheriff/.

27. Two recent books reference Wilson's description of Michael Brown as "demonic" and "subhuman" although the authors do not comment on the religious nature of this dehumanizing rhetoric. See Taylor, *From #BlackLivesMatter to Black Liberation,* 3–4; Hill, *Nobody: Casualties of America's War on the Vulnerable, from Ferguson to Flint,* 8–13.

28. The "She Speaks" program is available at https://www.facebook.com/hannah.a.bonner/videos/vb.100001231239403/1193549680696062/.

29. Reverend Hannah Bonner archived communion ceremonies during the sit-in on her Facebook page. The first ceremony is available at https://www.facebook.com/hannah.a.bonner/videos/vb.100001231239403/1193611587356538/; the service that included a prayer from W.E.B. DuBois, the third of six Eucharist celebrations, is available at https://www.facebook.com/hannah.a.bonner/videos/vb.100001231239403/1194710450579985/; and the fourth communion service, at which a Prairie View student preached, is available at https://www.facebook.com/hannah.a.bonner/videos/vb.100001231239403/1195168190534211/.

AFTERWORD

Bearing Witness

How the Movement Changed My World

WALDO MARTIN

On February 1, 1960, when Ezell A. Blair Jr. (Jibreel Khazan), Franklin E. McCain, Joseph A. McNeil, and David L. Richmond sat down at the Woolworth lunch counter in Greensboro, North Carolina, they rocked the world. They sparked the sit-in phase of the Modern Black Freedom Struggle, leading directly to the founding of the Student Nonviolent Coordinating Committee (SNCC).[1] At the time, I was a precocious nine-year-old black boy, born and bred in Greensboro with no direct connection to the Movement. I recall being aware that something big was happening all around me, especially downtown at the local Woolworth's, but exactly what was unclear. I did understand, however, that the student activists and their allies were fighting to desegregate the lunch counter.

But, as Ella Baker always reminded us, the Movement was much bigger than a hamburger.[2] In fact, as I would come to understand, it was both a black rights movement and a human rights movement. A lot of folks in both Morningside Homes, the all-black housing projects where we lived at the time, and United Institutional Baptist, the all-black church that helped raise me, intensely discussed and eagerly participated in the protests. I don't remember any family members' direct involvement, though.

These escalating nonviolent civil disobedience protests in my hometown aimed at integrating public facilities locally, regionally, and nationally radically transformed the rapidly intensifying civil rights movement.

Only in time, however, as I came of age socially, politically, and intellectually, would I come to understand and appreciate this critical fact. Simply put, only in time would I come to realize the historical importance of the connection between my hometown and the Movement. Nevertheless, that connection would profoundly shape not just my world—that of a young black boy coming of age in late Jim Crow America—and the rapidly accelerating Movement. But, it would also help remake America and the world, becoming integral to global history as well as our national history.

Black Power entered my life like a thunderbolt during my senior year (1968–69), when militant student protests erupted at the all-black James B. Dudley Senior High School, where I was student council president. The immediate cause of the protests was the refusal of the repressive school administration, on orders from the even more repressive downtown administration, to allow junior Claude Barnes, the clear student choice, to run to succeed me as student council president. The alleged reason was that he was a communist, or worse. We vigorously rejected the official reasoning as a vicious, anti-progressive smear campaign. The underlying causes of the ensuing student uprising were of course complex, including an authoritarian school administration that neither listened to nor heard student voices. Students were not allowed to leave campus for lunch (a common practice in the other largely white city high schools). A backward dress code disallowed sporting Afros and wearing jeans. Eventually the student protests at Dudley spilled into the streets and into the student movement at the local historically black A&T State University. The National Guard was summoned, and a shootout at A&T led to the death of Willie Grimes, an A&T student, at the hands of the National Guard. By the time the dust cleared, the repressive Dudley regime had dramatically loosened its grip on students.

Personally, the civil rights–Black Power movement, notably affirmative action programs, helped enable my family's ascent, and the ascent of many family members and friends, from working class to lower middle class.[3] Subsequently, it enabled my own personal ascent, again like so many family and friends, from the lower middle class into the much-vaunted middle class.

The Movement also contributed to my becoming a historian and ultimately doing civil rights–Black Power history, a life journey that only came into view when I was an undergraduate at Duke from 1969 to 1973. Growing up, I never really knew what a historian was and what one did. I certainly never envisioned becoming one. Nevertheless, becoming a civil rights–Black Power historian ultimately affirmed the all-black world that nurtured me, enabling me to go forth into a wider, desegregating, diverse world.

Both enduring and being a part of, even in small ways, the related affirmation of blackness and all-out assault against Jim Crow that helped constitute the Movement have profoundly shaped my consciousness and understanding. That transformative experience has also crucially shaped my day-to-day reality. First and perhaps most important, being a part of, even if only in small ways, the awesome assertion of blackness and the related hugely successful destruction of Jim Crow incalculably enhanced my self-respect, race pride, and growing commitment to my people's liberation struggle. Second, it helped me understand that people organized and committed to social change can make a powerful difference in the world. Third, it showed me, over time, that not only does history matter, but who writes history matters equally as much. Hence, I write history out of deep-seated progressive commitments to democracy, justice, and equality, as well as to freedom.

Those who were there who helped make and who remain a part of the Movement have continually affirmed not just black humanity but our common humanity. They must always tell their instructive and inspiring stories, no matter how large or small. As Jesse Jackson has consistently reminded us, precisely because the struggle continues, "We must keep hope alive!"[4] We must always center the empowering reality that African Americans, the unsung and the heralded, and their allies, white and nonwhite, affirmed our common humanity, defeated Jim Crow, and bequeathed to America and the world the Black Power and civil rights revolutions.

As a result, I must acknowledge the inextricable connection between the Movement and historical scholarship, including my own. Like our very world, recent and contemporary scholarship owes an immeasurable debt to the Movement.

It bears reiteration: I bear personal witness to that debt.

Notes

1. The classic local study is William H. Chafe, *Civilities and Civil Rights: Greensboro, North Carolina, and the Black Struggle for Freedom* (New York: Oxford University Press, 1980).

2. Barbara Ransby, *Ella Baker and the Black Freedom Movement: A Radical Democratic Vision* (Chapel Hill: UNC Press, 2003); Joanne Grant, *Ella Baker: Freedom Bound* (New York: Wiley, 1998).

3. Stephen L. Carter, *Reflections of an Affirmative Action Baby* (New York: Basic, 1991).

4. Marshall Frady, *Jesse: The Life and Pilgrimage of Jesse Jackson* (New York: Simon and Schuster, 2006).

Contributors

Stefan M. Bradley is associate professor and chair of the Department of African American Studies at Loyola Marymount University in Los Angeles. He is the author of *Upending the Ivory Tower: Civil Rights, Black Power, and the Ivy League* and *Harlem vs. Columbia University: Black Student Power in the Late 1960s*. He is the coeditor of *Alpha Phi Alpha: A Legacy of Greatness, the Demands of Transcendence*.

Reginald K. Ellis is associate professor of history at Florida A&M University in Tallahassee, Florida. He is the author of *Between Washington and Du Bois: The Racial Politics of James Edward Shepard*.

Charles H. Ford is professor of history at Norfolk State University in Norfolk, Virginia. He and his coauthor Jeffrey L. Littlejohn have published a number of important works in twentieth-century Virginian history—most notably *Elusive Equality: Desegregation and Resegregation in Norfolk's Public Schools*.

Teresa Blue Holden is dean of the College of Arts and Sciences and a faculty member in the history/political science department at Greenville University in Greenville, Illinois.

Peter B. Levy is professor in the Department of History and Political Science at York College in York, Pennsylvania. He is the author of numerous books and articles, including *The Great Uprising: Race Riots in Urban America during the 1960s* and *Civil War on Race Street: The Civil Rights Movement in Cambridge, Maryland*.

Jeffrey L. Littlejohn is professor in the Department of History at Sam Houston State University in Huntsville, Texas. He has published numerous articles and books with his coauthor Charles H. Ford, including "Booker T. Washington High School: History, Identity, and Educational Equity in Norfolk, Virginia" (*Virginia Magazine of History and Biography*).

Waldo Martin is Alexander F. & May T. Morrison Professor of American History & Citizenship at the University of California, Berkeley. He is the author or editor of numerous articles and books, including *No Coward Soldiers: Black Cultural Politics in Postwar America* and *Freedom on My Mind: A History of African Americans with Documents*, which he coauthored with Deborah Gray White and Mia Bay.

Mary Potorti is affiliated faculty at the Institute of Liberal Arts and Interdisciplinary Studies at Emerson College. Recent publications include "'Feeding the Revolution': The Black Panther Party, Hunger, and Community Survival" in the *Journal of African American Studies* and "Eat to Live: Culinary Nationalism and Black Capitalism in Elijah Muhammad's Nation of Islam" in *New Perspectives on the Nation of Islam* edited by Dawn-Marie Gibson and Herbert Berg.

Phillip Luke Sinitiere is professor of history at the College of Biblical Studies, a predominantly African American school located in Houston's Mahatma Gandhi District. His books include *Protest and Propaganda: W.E.B. Du Bois, the* Crisis, *and American History*, with Amy Helene Kirschke, and *Salvation with a Smile: Joel Osteen, Lakewood Church, and American Christianity*. In 2018, Sinitiere co-organized the online forum "Remembering Sandra Bland" on *Black Perspectives* and published "The Aesthetic Insurgency of Sandra Bland's Afterlife" in *Souls: A Critical Journal of Black Politics, Culture, and Society*.

Rosie Jayde Uyola is an independent scholar, K–12 teacher, documentary filmmaker, and researcher of memory, commemoration, and Black American life and culture. She is an alumna of the W.E.B. Du Bois Institute at Harvard University and an NEH fellow. She currently develops digital humanities projects with Columbia University. Her publications include "The Digital City: Memory, History, and Public Commemoration" in *Ácoma: International Journal of North-American Studies* and "Home Sweet Home: Race, Housing, and the Foreclosure Crisis" in *The War on Poverty: A Retrospective* edited by Kyle Farmbry.

Index

Page numbers in *italics* refer to illustrations.

Abu-Jamal, Mumia, 197
Advancing Democracy (Shabazz), 11
AFL-CIO Industrial Union Council of Cook County, 153n123
African American Intellectual History Society (AAIHS), 201, 221
African American Male Scholars (AAMS) Initiative, 191, 195
Agnew, Spiro, 96, 97
Agriculture, 121, 123–24
Aiken County, SC, 84, 87–88
Alabama, 30, 40, 145
Alachua County, FL, 24
Al-Amin, Jamil Abdullah, 131, 185
Alamo, 177
Alanis, Blanca A., 218
Alberta, Canada, 85
Alcazar Ballroom, 99
Aldinger, Stewart, 104
Alexander, Michelle, 3
Allen, Lillie Belle: accused killers of, 85–86, 98–99, 105, 113n48; family of, 84–85, 88; investigation into murder of, 112n31; murder of, 84–85, 91, 102, 103, 104, 105
All God's Children's Church, 76–77
Allied Chemical Corporation, 72
Almond, J. Lindsay, 55, 65
American Chain and Cable, 88
American Civil Liberties Union, 155
American Journal of Nursing, 36
American Missionary Association (AMA), 11–14, 15
American Missionary Association Annual Report, 13
"American Tragedy, An" (Smith), 206
AmeriCorps, 158
Anderson, James D., 21
Anglicanism, 202
Ann Arbor, MI, 126, 130
Anti-Tuberculosis Association, 46
Anti-Tuberculosis League, 46
Aqua Dynamics, Ltd., 74
Aquilla Howard Elementary School, 93
Armstrong, Neil, 84
Armstrong, Samuel C., 10
Arrow (poet), 208
Artis, Elizabeth, 174
Ashe, Victor, 67
Askew, James A., 67
Association for the Advancement of Black-Owned Businesses, 100
Astle, Cynthia B., 217
Atheists, 214
Atlanta, GA: black education in, 47; black health care in, 28, 30, 31, 43, 46; black neighborhoods in, 28, 31, 44–45, 46, 47; Neighborhood Union in, 30, 31, 43, 44, 45, 46; race riot in, 5; segregation in, 28, 43, 45, 47; SNCC headquarters in, 142, 153n126
Atlanta Constitution, 45–46
Atlanta Cotton State Exposition, 23
Atlanta University, 28, 31, 45
Atlantic City, NJ, 96
A&T State University, 228
At the Dark End of the Street: Black Women, Rape, and Resistance (McGuire), 3

Auburn, GA, 24
Ausby, Clarence, 103

Bailey, Lionel, 99, 103
Baker, Ella, 227
Baltimore, MD: 2015 riots in, 154; Charity Tucker in, 25; death of Freddie Gray in, 154, 212; history conferences in, 157, 178n3; immigrants in, 157; population of, 89; race in, 3; scholarship on, 157; segregation in, 162; Thomas DeSaille Tucker in, 25
Baltimore, MD, 1968 riots in: 40th anniversary of, 157–60, 169–70, 176, 177, 181n27; and Baltimore '68 Mosaic Monument, 160–70; causes of, 162, 165, 167; details of, 157, 160, 161, 162; legacy of, 158, 159–60, 161; oral histories of, 155–56, 158, 161–62, 178n2; scholarship on, 181n27
Baltimore '68: Riots and Rebirth, 155, 156, 158–59
Baltimore City Paper, 159
Baltimore Community Relations Commission, 167
Baltimore County, MD, 97
Bamberg County, SC, 87, 89
Bank of Commerce, 125
Bank Street Baptist, 59
Baptists, 38
Baraka, Amiri, 181n27
Barfield, Sam T., 70
Barley, Nevin, 95
Barnes, Claude, 228
Barry, Marion, 60
Bateman, Fred, 81n34
Beecher, A. N., 12
Bell, Aubrey, 125–26
Bell, Derrick, 183, 196
Belzoni, MS, 123
Benton, James, Jr., 69
"'Be Real for Me': Representation, Authenticity, and the Cultural Politics of Black Power" (Martin), 9n8
Bevel, James, 60
Bible, 164, 178n10, 212, 214
Big Bad Committee, 172, 173, 176
Birmingham, AL, 93–94
Birt, Robert, 162
Bishop, Gardner, 189

Black Freedom Struggle. *See* Civil rights movement, historic; Civil rights movement, modern
Black history, living, 201
Black History Month, 2
Black Lives Matter (BLM), 155, 186, 193, 198, 206. *See also* Civil rights movement, modern
Blackmon, Traci, 195
Black Panther Party, 3, 100, 145
Black Perspectives, 201, 221
Black Power: and gender, 112n35; inclusion of, in *Eyes on the Prize*, 2; Malcolm X and, 5; and religion, 218; and riots, 86, 169, 170, 174; Sandra Bland movement and, 221; scholarship on, 2; Waldo Martin and, 228
Black Power (Carmichael and Hamilton), 5
Blacks: 21st-century treatment of, 213; and affirmative action, 228; as candidates for office and elected officials, 4, 20; and car ownership, 87; as civil war veterans, 20; and confrontation, 96; and convict leasing, 40; and economic oppression, 146n8; and GI Bill, 181n25; goals of, 5, 10; and government, 93, 94; and health care, 34, 47–48; and home ownership, 89; killings of, 207; and law enforcement, 93–94, 207–8, 216, 217–18, 219; and media, 32–33, 186, 189; middle-class, 11, 17, 19, 228; and migration, 87, 105, 147n21; and nutrition, 40–41; and political participation, 18; and poverty, 118; as public officials, 174; and riots, 156; scholarship on, 116; and Social Security, 181n25; standard of living of, 40–41; in suburbs, 178n11; and voting rights, 87; white perceptions of, 19, 34, 45–46, 48, 58–59; as World War II veterans, 87. *See also* Education, for blacks; Women, black
Blacks, occupations of: activists, 188; artists, 188; attorneys, 53, 68, 188; barbers, 54; business leaders, 188; college professors, 188; custodians, 54, 89; day laborers, 89; diversity trainers, 188; doctors, 22, 28, 34, 39, 45, 46, 47, 48; domestics, 54; educational administrators, 188; farmers, 40, 87, 118, 119, 123; farm laborers, 124; laundresses, 46; municipal employees, 188; nonprofit leaders, 188; nurses, 30, 32, 35–36, 45, 46,

48; pastors, 211; pharmacists, 129, 145n1; police officers, 106; porters, 89; psychologists, 188; sharecroppers, 40, 116, 117–18, 120, 124, 141, 147n12, 147n13, 150n61; teachers, 47, 48, 93
Black's Law Dictionary, 175
Black Unity Movement (BUM), 100
Blain, Keisha, 221
Blair, Ezell A., Jr., 227
Bland, Sandra: arrest and death of, 6, 197–98, 202, 205, 206, 208, 209, 214; characteristics of, 212, 221; family of, 203, 204, 205, 206, 207, 208, 211, 215; media coverage about, 206–7, 209; and religion, 211–12; YouTube videos by, 197, 203, 206, 208, 209, 211–12, 219–21. *See also* Sandra Bland movement
"Blinding of Isaac Woodard, The" (Guthrie), 88
Block, Sam: arrests of, 135–36, 137; background of, 128, 136; characteristics of, 128, 150n66; early experiences of, in Greenwood, 136; and food aid, 128, 133, 135; on situation in Mississippi Delta, 128, 153n121
Blogs, 200, 202
Bloxham, William D., 20, 24
Bonner, Hannah: background of, 211; and commemoration of Charleston Nine, 202; description of, 202; and "Justice or Else" anniversary, 205; and Sandra Bland movement, 202, 211–12, 215, 217, 218; and "She Speaks" ceremony, 224n15; use of social media by, 224n13, 224n15, 225n19, 226n29
Bonney, Hal, Jr., 54, 58–59
Booker, Cory A., 155, 171, 173, *174*, 176, 177
Booker T. Washington High School, 47, 55–56, 70, 72
Book of Common Prayer, 202
Boston, MA, 30, 32, 35, 49, 126
Boston Massacre, 89
Bowman, Madelyn, 102
Brachman, Lavea, 177n1
Bradley, Alphonso, 184–85, 187
Bradley, Stefan M., 6, 183–91, 196
Breeden, Edward, Jr., 65
Breihan, John R., 178n3
Brewbaker, J. J., 56
Brewster, Kingman, 190

Brooklyn, NY, 84
Brooks-Higginbotham, Evelyn, 29
Brown, G.W.C., 71
Brown, H. Rap, 86, 131, 185
Brown, James, 172
Brown, Michael, Jr.: Angela Davis on, 210; commemoration of death of, 203; family of, 190–91; funeral of, 188; killing of, 6, 154, 170, 183, 191, 192, 212, 217, 226n27
Brown v. Board of Education: commemoration of, 189; enforcement of, 55; inclusion of, in *Eyes on the Prize*, 1; quality of black education after, 147n17; Stefan Bradley on, 189; as turning point, 49n5, 92, 93, 120
Buffalo, NY, 172
Burfoot, Anthony, 54
Burgess, Marie Louise, 35–36
Burnham, Dorothy, 2
Burroughs, Nannie, 38
Butts, Evelyn T., 66, 70, 74

Cairo, IL, 40
California, 125, 143
California Western Law, 189
Cambridge, MA, 2
Cameron, Chris, 221
Camp Hill, PA, 95
Canton, MS, 153n125
Carlin, Leo P., 171
Carmichael, Stokely: and black power, 145; and food aid, 131, 146n6, 146n7; and Mississippi Delta, 120, 144; scholarship on, 3, 185; and SNCC, 120, 131, 144, 145, 146n7; and voting rights, 131; works by, 5
Carson, Eddie, 221
Carter, Bennie, 103
Carter, Gregg Lee, 109n3
Cauley, Carie, 212–14, *215*, 221
Cedar Cliff High, 95
Central High School, 100
Chalk, Ocania, 100
Chantiles, Peter, 97
Charity Hospital, 39, 51n33
Charleston, MS, 133
Charleston, SC, 4, 202
Charleston Nine, 202
Charlottesville, VA, 71
Cheney, Ednah Dowe, 35

Chesapeake Bay, 157
Chicago, IL: 1968 Democratic National Convention in, 96; and black migration, 125, 147n21; churches in, 197; Congress of Racial Equality in, 153n123; Dick Gregory in, 131; food donations from, 126, 130, 131, 134, 153n123; Hull House in, 44; and media coverage, 144; Sandra Bland in, 197, 206; SNCC in, 131; Southern perceptions of, 132
Chicago Magazine, 206, 207
Childress, Calvin, 58, 59
Chinese, 49n8
Christ Church, 57
Christians and Christianity, 168–69, 211, 214, 222n2
Churchill, C. H., 13
Cisgender persons, 202
Citizens Advisory Committee (CAC), 69–70
Citizen's Board of Inquiry on Hunger and Malnutrition in the United States, 149n40
Citizens' Council (Mississippi), 120
Citizen's Council of York, 97
Civil Rights Act of 1964, 72, 86, 92, 96
Civil rights movement, historic: Angela Davis on, 210; black women and, 29, 210; and Cold War, 3; cultural impact of, 6; goals of, 5, 6; internationalization of, 208; Kennedy and Johnson administrations and, 121; legacy of, 196; during Progressive era, 29–30; in public memory, 1–2, 169; and religion, 200, 201, 211, 219, 222n2; scholarship on, 2–7, 49n5, 179n14, 183, 199–200, 222n2; stages of, 5, 170; strategies and tactics of, 4, 86, 115, 116, 209, 219, 227; teaching of, 185; and technology, 200, 217; terms for, 183; UN Working Group on, 207; white resistance to, 65, 115, 120, 122–23, 124, 125, 127, 128, 137, 142, 153n123
Civil rights movement, modern: Angela Davis on, 210; in Ferguson, MO, 191; and religion, 198–200, 201, 210, 216, 222n2; scholarship on, 200, 222n2; and technology, 200–201. *See also* Sandra Bland movement
Clark, Kenneth, 189
Clark, Laura, 21
Clarke, Cecelia, 56
Clarke, J. Calvitt, Jr., 75
Clarksdale, MS: Aaron "Doc" Henry in, 131, 145n1; as agricultural depot, 150n59; and black migration, 147n21, 150n59; Dick Gregory in, 131; as food and clothing drive headquarters, 127, 128, 129–30, 131, 151n82; as home to blues musicians, 150n59; law enforcement in, 130; leaders from, 149n45; location of, 129
Clarksdale Press Register, 134, 151n82
Clark University, 189
Clayton, W. J., 22–23
Cleveland, MS, 128, 149n45
Cleveland, OH, 55, 172
Clock Tower Accords, 190, 193, 194, 195
CNN, 206
Coahoma County, MS, 129
Coalition for Public Safety, 155
Coastal Pharmaceuticals, 72–74
Cobb, Charlie, 128, 129, 135, 136
Coffman, Dean, 102
Cold War, 3
Cole, Rebecca, 34
Collins, Herbert M., 74
Colored State Teachers Association, 22
Colored Teachers Association of Florida, 22
Colored Women's Hospital Aid Society, 40
Columbia University, 183, 184, 190, 196
Colvin, Bunny, 154
Commission on Civil Rights, 88
Commission on Interracial Cooperation, 5
Communist Party, 64
Company D, Second United States Colored Infantry, 20
Congressional Black Caucus, 205
Congress of Racial Equality (CORE), 60–61, 99, 100, 145n1, 153n123, 153n125
Cook, James W., 9n8
Cooper, Esther, 2
Costopoulos, William, 113n48
Council of Federated Organizations (COFO): on disenfranchisement and poverty, 150n57; establishment and reestablishment of, 145n1; and food aid, 128, 129; and hunger, 126; leaders of, 129, 145n1; in Mississippi Delta, 130; scholarship on, 145n1; and SNCC, 115, 116, 145n1; and voting rights, 115, 143, 144
Craly, Nathaniel, 96
Crawford, Malachi, 221
Crespino, Joseph, 7

Crispus Attucks, 89, 100
"Crossroads: A Neighborhood's View of Despair, Riot and Recovery in Newark" (Parks), 178n2
"Crying Indian" ad, 168, 180n15
Cullors, Patrisse, 198–99
Cultural pride, 5
Cultural turn, 9n8
Cultural Turn in U.S. History, The: Past, Present, and Future (Cook, Glickman, and O'Malley), 9n8

Dailey, Janet, 18
Dallas, TX, 212
Danville, VA, 60
Danville Massacre, 17–18
Daughters of Zion of Avery Chapel, 39
David T. Howard Elementary School, 47
Davis, Angela, 185, 210
Dawley, Edward, 68
Day, Charles P., 15
Day, L. L., 61
Defenders of State Sovereignty and Individual Liberties, 58
Delk, Marcus, 69
"Democracy Experiment, The: Black Youth in America" (Bradley), 189
Democracy Now!, 181n27
Democrats and Democratic Party, 59, 96, 143, 144, 153n128
Dennis, Dave, 145n1
Department of Public Safety (DPS), 197, 203, 204, 205
Detroit, MI, 4, 86, 125, 130, 172, 176
Digital technology, 201, 209, 212, 219–21
Dillard University, 17
Diseases and medical conditions: in Atlanta, 45; diphtheria, 28; malnutrition, 116, 122, 129; pulmonary, 48; tuberculosis, 34, 42, 46, 48; typhoid fever, 14, 42
District of Columbia, 14, 205
Dittmer, John, 145n1
Dixie Hospital and Hampton Training School for Nurses, 35
Doddsville, MS, 120
Doing Recent History . . . (Potter and Romano), 223n5
"Domestic Science," 37, 38

Donaldson, Ivanhoe, 130, 151n74
Donovan, Carolyn Albert, 205
Dorrough, C. M., 128
Downing, Jim, 76
DuBois, Burghardt, 28, 37, 48
DuBois, Nina, 28–29, 37, 48
DuBois, W.E.B.: and Booker T. Washington, 4, 24; and education, 4, 10; family of, 28, 48; on hospitals, 51n33, 205; scholarship on, 6; on seed time, work, harvest, and playtime, 1; works by, 39, 48, 226n29
Duke Divinity School, 211
Duke University, 228
DuPage AME Church, 197

Eastland, James O., 120
East Lansing, MI, 130
Ebenezer Baptist Church, 47, 155
Eckford, Elizabeth, 100
Economic Opportunity Act, 148n37
Edmund Pettus Bridge, 2
Edmunds, Alfred, 66
Education, for blacks: Booker T. Washington and, 4, 10–11; curriculum for, 21; and desegregation, 55–59, 65; in Florida, 18, 19; freedmen and, 13, 14–15, 17, 40; and health and health care, 39, 48; liberal arts, 10, 11, 23, 24, 25; middle class and, 11, 41; in Mississippi, 147n14; in North, 35; nursing, 39; and poverty, 118; quality of, 147n14, 147n17; at Russell Plantation Settlement, 42; scholarship on, 11, 21; and segregation, 11, 24, 45, 47, 118; and sharecropping, 118; in South, 35; vocational, 10–11, 22–23, 24, 25; W.E.B. DuBois and, 4, 10; whites and, 10–11, 19, 25, 87; women and, 41. *See also* Florida State Normal and Industrial School for Coloreds (FSNIS)
Edwards, Mitchell, 103
Eighth Amendment, 170, 180n20
Eisenhower, Dwight, 55, 64
Eissler, Mark, 98
Elder, Eugene B., 34
Elfenbein, Jessica, 157, 158, 178n3
Elliot, R. B., 17
Ellis, Reginald, 4
Ellison, Ralph, 99
Elmore, Charles J., 51n33

Emanuel AME Church, 202
Emergency Relief Committee, CORE, 153n123
Emory College, 24
Encampment for Citizenship Program, 79n11
Encinia, Brian, 197, 205
"Enough Is Enough" (Hawkins), 216–17
Epps, Linda, 175, 182n28
Equal Suffrage Address, 54
Evangelical Lutheran Church in America, 215
Experiment in International Living project, 79n11
Eyes on the Prize, 1–2, 8n3

Facebook, 200, 202, 218–19, 224n15
Fairchild, E. H., 12–13, 14
Fallis, Melvin, Jr., 60, 69
Farmer, James, 99
Farrelly brothers, 180n15
Fayette County, TN, 153n123
Federal Housing Administration, 181n25
Feminism, 96
Ferguson, MO: Angela Davis in, 210; Barack Obama on, 155; city council of, 195; killing of Michael Brown Jr. in, 6, 154, 183, 184, 191, 192, 212, 217; police in, 183, 185, 187, 188, 190, 191, 192, 193, 195; protests in, 154, 170, 183–87, 191–93; race in, 3; Stefan M. Bradley and, 183–91, 196; St. Louis University students in, 191, 195; traffic enforcement in area surrounding, 206
"Ferguson: A Report from Occupied Territory," 206
Ferguson Commission, 188
Ferguson & Faith (Francis), 200
Fieldston School, 79n11
Fifteenth Amendment, 119
"Fifty Years of Negro Public Health" (Jones), 48
First Amendment, 170, 180n20
First Baptist Bute Street, 59
First Church of Christ (Holiness), 54
First Congress of Colored Women, 32
First National Conference of Colored Women, 39
First Unitarian Church, 189
Fleming, Francis, 22
Florida, 17, 18, 19–20, 22, 24
Florida A&M, 2–3, 4, 11, 17, 25, 26n15. *See also* Florida State Normal and Industrial School for Coloreds (FSNIS)
Florida State Normal and Industrial School for Coloreds (FSNIS): admission to, 21; as black state-supported school, 11; black support for, 22; curriculum at, 11, 21, 22–23; expenses at, 22; location of, 20–21; Nathan Benjamin Young as president of, 25; opening of, 21; as predecessor to Florida A&M, 11; scholarship on, 21; staff of, 21, 22–23; third commencement at, 22; Thomas DeSaille Tucker as president of, 4, 11, 19–21, 22–23, 24–25; whites and, 22, 23–24
Florida Times-Union, 18
Food aid, 121–22, 131–32, 133, 134–35. *See also* Student Nonviolent Coordinating Committee (SNCC): and food aid
Food for Freedom campaign, 117, 129, 140, 142, 143. *See also* Student Nonviolent Coordinating Committee (SNCC): and food aid
Foods and beverages: blacks and, 5; bread, 147n13; canned goods, 131, 133; cereal, 133; chicken bones, 126; cornbread and cornmeal, 118, 122, 147n13; cultivation of, 123; dairy products, 122; flour, 122, 133; fruits, 131; meats, 122; milk, 122, 147n13; molasses, 118; nutritional value of, 121–22; onions, 147n13; pork, 118; potatoes, 127; rice, 122, 133; stew, 126, 127; storage and transportation of, 122; vegetables, 131
Ford, Charles H., 4
Forman, James: background of, 146n4; on Fannie Lou Hamer, 149n43; and food aid, 140, 150n56, 153n123; on hunger in Mississippi, 139–40; on SNCC goals and tactics, 139, 144–45; and SNCC workers, 120, 128, 150n66
Fort Bragg, 157
Fort Monroe, 13, 14–17
Foster, John, 75
Fourteenth Amendment, 187
Fourth Circuit Court, 75
Francis, Leah Gunning, 200
Frankhouse, Roy, 98
Franklin, John Hope, 183, 189, 196
Freedom, Orville, 149n54
"Freedom Press," 60
Freedom Schools, 147n14

Freedom Summer, 144, 153n126
Freedom Vote, 142, 144, 152n113
Freeland, Stephen, 84, 103
Friendly Temple Missionary Baptist Church, 188
"From Michael Brown to Assata Shakur, the Racist State of America Persists" (Davis), 210
From Mobtown to Charm City: New Perspectives on Baltimore's Past (Elfenbein, Breihan, and Hollowak), 157, 178n3
Fruitvale Station, Oakland, CA, 4

Gainesville, FL, 17
Galveston, TX, 40
Gandhi, Mahatma, 71
Gary, IN, 134
Gaston, Wyoma, 60
Gay, James F.: and 1963 March on Washington, 69, 70; and Allied Chemical Corporation, 72; arrest of, 66; as attorney, 76, *77*; background of, 54; and boycotts, 4; business practices of, 72–74; as candidate for office, 74; and Central YMCA, *71*; characteristics of, 72; and Coastal Pharmaceuticals, 72–74; and desegregation of public accommodations, 69–70; disbarment of, 53, 76; education of, 53, 61, 70, 71, 72, 73; final years and death of, 53, 76–77; and *Herbert M. Collins Sr. v. City of Norfolk*, 74–76, 77; legacy of, 77–78; as local leader, 53; and marches, 4; and Mayor Roy Martin, 70, 72; and miscegenation laws, 72; and Moral Rearmament program, 71; and NAACP, 55, 56, *57*, 58, 59, 60, 61, 66, *69*, 76, *77*, 79n11; and National Business League, 72; and politics, 71–72; and school desegregation, 69; and sit-ins, 4, 61, 63, 64, 68; and Student Committee against Discrimination, 68; and Student Cooperative Association, 55–56; and Student Relations Association, 63; and Thurgood Marshall, 56; and Tidewater Area Business League, 72; and US Supreme Court, 53, 75; *Virginia Weekly* article on, *73*; and voter registration, 4, 71; and Young Democrats, 71–72, 73
Gay, Marvin (friend of James Gay), 70
Gay, Milton, Jr.: background of, 54, 55; civil rights activities of, 4, 53; death of, 76; departure of, from Norfolk, 68; education of, 60, 68; and Encampment for Citizenship program, 79n11; at Grace Episcopal Church, 72; marriage of, 76; and NAACP, 55, 56, *57*, 58, 59, 60, *69*, 79n11; and sit-ins, 61, 62, 63, 64, 67–68; and Student Cooperative Association, 55–56; and Student Relations Association, 63; and Thurgood Marshall, 56
Gay, Milton, Sr., 54, 74
Gay, Thelma, 54, 74
Gaye, Marvin (singer), 98
General Commission on Religion and Race, 216
Ghana, 79n11
Ghent Arms Nursing Home, 74
Gibbs, Jonathan, 19
Gibbs, Thomas Van Renssaler, 19, 20, 21, 22
GI Bill, 181n25
Giddens, Donald M., 81n44
Giddens, William, *57*
Gilbert, Stanford, 102
Girarders, 98, 99, 101
Glickman, Lawrence B., 9n8
Godbolt, Patricia, 56–58, 60
GoFundMe, 204
Good Hope AME Church, 197, 198, *199*, 220
Goodling, George, 96–97, 101
Goodling, William, 97
Goodman, Amy, 181n27
Google, 175
Grace Episcopal Church, 59, 72, 77
Graham, Randy, 98
Grant's. *See* W.T. Grant's
Gray, Freddie, 212
Great Depression, 89, 171
Great Migration, 87, 88, 107, 147n21, 150n59
Green, Clifford, 101
Green, Joseph N., Jr., 74, 75
Greensboro, NC, 60, 227–28
Greenwood, MS: churches in, 133; cities near, 149n45; civil rights activists in, 120, 131, 135, 136; demonstrations in, 132, 135–36, 137–38; food aid in, 117, 126, 128, 129, 130, 131, 132–33, 136, 138, 140, 143; law enforcement in, 132; leadership in, 149n45; March Against Fear in, 145; Negro Elk's Club in, 132; segregation in, 135; SNCC in, 138–39,

Greenwood, MS—*continued*
  140, 142, 151n90, 153n126; violence in, 132, 135; voting rights in, 117, 124–25, 126, 127, 129, 132, 136
Greenwood Commonwealth, 131, 132, 133, 138, 150n59
Gregory, Dick, 130–31, 132, 133–34
Griffin, Daisy, 123
Grimes, Willie, 228
Guardian, 210
Gunn, William John, 22
Guthrie, Woody, 88
Guyot, Lawrence, 125

Hall, Jacquelyn Dowd, 2, 6, 8n3, 49n5
Hamer, Fannie Lou: and hunger, 147n13; organization of farm cooperative by, 143, 153n127; on politics, 145; on sharecropping, 147n13; and SNCC, 139; as Sunflower Co., MS, resident, 120; and voter registration, 124, 149n43
Hamilton, Charles, 5, 149n51
Hamilton, W. L., 59
Hamm, Larry, 181n27
Hampton, VA, 13–14, 20, 35
Hampton Institute, 56, 57
Hanna Penn Junior High School, 93
Harding, Vincent, 6, 183, 196
Harlem, NY, 134, 196
Harlem Renaissance, 36
Harlem vs. Columbia University (Bradley), 184
Harris, Fred R., 178n11
Harrisburg, PA, 95
Harris County, TX, 201
Harris-Stowe State University, 189
Harry and Jeanette Weinberg Family Center Y, 163
Harvard University, 2–3, 8n4, 71
Hawaiians, 49n8
Hawkins, Erin, 216–17
Hawkins, John, 5
Hayakawa, S. I., 190
Hayes, Chris, 183, 186
"Health and Beauty from Exercise," 37
Health care: blacks and, 5; segregation of, 28, 30, 33–34, 40. *See also* Women, black: and health care

"Heaven" (Reverend Sekou and the Holy Ghost), 197
Hebrew Bible, 164
Hempstead, TX, 197, 201, 202, 215
Henderson, J. B., 59
Henry, Aaron "Doc," 129, 130, 145n1
Herman, Max, 106, 181n27
Higginbotham, Evelyn Brooks, 179n14
Highlander Folk School, 32
Hittner, David, 205
Hoffman's Meat Market, 95
Hold, Leonard, 68
Holden, Theresa, 5
Holder, Eric, 155
Hollowak, Tom, 157, 178n3
Holmes, Theodore, 99
Hood, G. H., 123, 148n39
Hoover, J. Edgar, 169
Hope, Lugenia Burns, 30, 43–44
Hopewell, VA, 75
Hose, Jacob, 97, 107
Houser, George, 98
Houston, Charles Hamilton, 189
Houston, TX: artists from, 218; Black Lives Matter activists from, 212; federal court in, 205; Phillip Luke Sinitiere in, 201; poets from, 208, 218; Sandra Bland movement in, 200, 205, 208; Sandra Bland movement participants from, 202, *203*, *204*
Howell, Henry, 58, 59
Hull House Maps and Papers (Kelley), 44
Hull House settlement, 44
Human Rights Division, United Nations, 207–8
Humphreys County, MS, 123
Hunger. *See* Food aid; Student Nonviolent Coordinating Committee (SNCC): and food aid
Hunger USA, 149n40
Hunt, A. P., 64
Hyannis Port, MA, 134

Ifá, 198
"I Just Ask God," 218
Ilgenfritz, Craig, 98
Immigrants, 42, 44, 157
Independent Party, 18

Indianola, MS, 139
Instagram, 200, 224n13, 225n19
Institute on Ethnicity, Culture, and the Modern Experience (IECME), Rutgers University, 172
Internet, 200, 202
Interracial Ministers Fellowship, 55
Invisible Man, The (Ellison), 99
Irish, 157
Isaiah (Hebrew prophet), 214
Israel, 79n11
Ithaca, NY, 64

Jackson, David H., Jr., 24
Jackson, Jesse, 188, 229
Jackson, MS, 128, 153n125
Jakes, T. D., 188
James, Ellis, 65
James B. Dudley Senior High School, 228
James Smallwood Elementary School, 93
James v. Almond, 65
Jennings, William Sherman, 24
Jeremiah (Hebrew prophet), 214
Jeter, Carl, 74
Jews, 49n8, 156, 157
Jim Crow: George Wallace as symbol of, 96; impact of, 43, 87, 118; opposition to, 2, 5, 53, 54, 60–61, 63, 70, 89, 135, 229; UN Working Group on, 207; Waldo Martin and, 228
Jocelyn, Simeon, 12
John A. Anderson Memorial Hospital, 36
John Hope Franklin Series in African American History and Culture, 8n4
Johns, Barbara, 189
Johns, Ethel, 37
John Sealy Hospital, 40
Johnson, Dorian, 188
Johnson, Lyndon B., 1, 96, 108, 178n11
Jones, Charles, 16
Jones, Clarence B., 140
Jones, Eric, 61, 66
Jones, Hilary, 70
Jones, Joshua, 191–95
Jones, S. B., 47, 48
Jordan, Barbara, 212
Jordan, Joseph, Jr., 59, 66, 68, 75
Joseph, Peniel, 2, 3

Journal and Guide, 59, 66, 68, 69, 70
Judeo-Christian tradition, 164
Judiasm, 222n2
Justice or Else event, 205

Kansas City, MO, 70
"Keep America Beautiful," 168
Kelley, Florence, 44
Kelly, Blair, 8n4
Kenney, John A., 36, 42
Kentucky, 17
Kerner Commission report, 105, 165, 178n11, 189
Khazan, Jibreel, 227
Kimbrough, O. L., 136
King, Martin Luther, Jr.: and 1960 march in Richmond, VA, 60; advisors to, 140; Angela Davis on, 210; assassination of, 93, 94, 96, 97, 157, 162, 167, 178n11, 179n13; awards received by, 167; and beloved community, 200, 212–13; birthday holiday honoring, 2; characteristics of, 168; depictions of, 2, 163, 164, 167, 168, 169; education of, 47; family of, 47; as figurehead, 5; followers of, 212; and J. Edgar Hoover, 169; and Montgomery bus boycott, 60; and nonviolence, 181n22; and poor people's march, 96; quoted by Eric Holder, 155; on riots, 86, 170, 181n22; and Southern Christian Leadership Convention, 60; in St. Louis, 185; vision of, 167; writings of, 214
King, Rodney, 170
Kingpin, 180n15
Kirk, Grayson, 190
Kirkland, Eric, 89
Kittrell, Adam, 95
Knouse, Rick, 98–99
Koch brothers, 155
Kohler, Clifton, 103
Kresge's. *See* S.S. Kresge's
Ku Klux Klan, 18, 87–88, 98, 120

Lake, Marvin, 69
Landis, Chief, 94
Langsdale Library, 157
Larsen, Nella, 36, 37
Lassiter, Mathew D., 7

Latinas and Latinos, 174, 181n25, 189, 211
Law enforcement: in Aiken, SC, 87, 88; Angela Davis on, 210; in Atlanta, 5; in Baltimore, 169; Bunny Colvin on, 154; in Ferguson, MO/St. Louis Metropolitan Area, 170, 184, 185, 186, 187, 188, 190, 191, 192, 193, 195, 206, 217; and minorities, 155, 189; in Mississippi, 120, 130, 132, 135; in Newark, NJ, 173, 174, 175, 177; in Norfolk, VA, 65, 66, 67; and race, 206; and religion, 217–18; and riots, 154, 156, 170; and Sandra Bland movement, 198, 203–4, 205, 206, 207–8, 209, 214, 216, 217, *219*, 220; in Texas, 206; UN Working Group on, 207–8. *See also* Brown, Michael, Jr.: killing of; Schaad, Henry; York, PA: law enforcement in
Lee, Barbara, *57*
Lee, Shelia Jackson, 205
Leflore County, MS: demonstrations in, 137–38; Dick Gregory and, 131; food aid in, 117, 125–26, 128, 131–32, 138, 141, 149n51, 150n56; population of, 126; voting rights in, 117, 125, 150n57
Legacy Cities, 155, 169, 177n1
Legislation: anti-trespass, 65, 81n34; Civil Rights Act of 1964, 72, 86, 92, 96; Economic Opportunity Act, 148n37; Federal Highway Act of 1956, 181n25; on miscegenation, 72; National Housing Act of 1934, 181n25; REDEEM Act, 155; Sheats Law, 24; Voting Rights Act of 1965, 1, 74, 86, 144
Lehmann, Nicholas, 147n21
Lentz, Albert, 98
Leon County, FL, 20
Letters from Birmingham Jail (King), 214
Levy, Peter, 4
Lewis, Earl, 54
Lewis, John, 60, 144
LGBTQ persons, 202, 214
Life magazine, 63
Literary activism, 32–33
Littlejohn, Jeffrey L., 4
Little Rock, AR, 100
Litwack, Leon, 2
Living black history, 201
Living Black History . . . (Marable), 223n5
Lockwood, Lewis, 15
London, England, 85

Los Angeles, CA, 86, 153n123, 170
Louisiana, 17
Louisville, KY, 70, 130
Lowman, Bertha, 87–88
Lowman, Clarence, 87–88
Lowman, Damon, 87–88
Lowman, Sam, 87–88
Lutherans, 202, 205, 215
Lynch, Loretta, 205
Lynchburg, VA, 65
Lynchings, 87–88, 115, 207
Lynne, Kimberley, 160

Macon, GA, 34
Macon Hospital, 34
Madison, J. Hugo, 67
Madison County, MS, 153n125
Magida, Arthur, 95
Malcolm X, 5, 100, 210, 213
Mallach, Alan, 177n1
Manson, Sam, 93
Mantz, Francis M., 68
Marable, Manning, 6, 201, 223n5
March Against Fear, 145
Marches, 4, 209
March on Washington, 179n14
Marlowe, B. D., 124
Married . . . with Children, 180n15
Marseilles, France, 11
Marshall, Thurgood, 56, 189
Martin, James G., IV, 54
Martin, Lerone, 221
Martin, Richard, 59
Martin, Roy, 68, 69, 70, 72
Martin, Trayvon, 3
Martin, Waldo E., 2, 3, 8n4, 9n8, 227–29
Maryland Historical Society, 178n3
Maryland Institute College of Art, 161
Mary S. Peak School, 20
Mason, Vivian Carter, 59
Massachusetts, 189
Massive Resistance, 54, 59, 65
Mattes, Bari, 176
Matthews, Victoria Earle, 32–33
McCaig, Albert, 205
McCain, Franklin E., 227
McComb, MS, 116, 124, 149n45
McCoy, Ronald, 103

McCulloch, Robert, 183, 190
McGuire, Danielle, 3
McHenry, Elizabeth, 32
McInnis, Obadiah, 54–55
McKane, Alice Woodby, 51n33
McKane, Cornelius, 51n33
McKane Hospital, 51n33
McKendree, W. I., 58
McKinley Elementary School, 93
McLaurin, Charles, 128, 139, 140, 141
McNeil, Joseph A., 227
"Mediated Memory . . ." (Simonetti), 181n27
Memory, 156, 158, 165, 170, 177
Memphis, TN, 39, 128, 131
Menard, John Willis, 18, 19
Mendi Mission, 13, 16
Meredith, James, 145
Messersmith, Robert, 102, 105
Methodism and Methodists, 198, 202, 211, 216, 217
Metro Baptist Ministers Conference, 67
Meyers, Frank, 103
Meyers, Mrs. Frank, 103
Meyers, VonDerrit, Jr., 190, 193
Michigan, 130
Michigan State University, 130
Miller, Walt Party, 95–96
Million Man March, 205
Milwaukee, WI, 172, 181n27
Miss America pageant, 96
Mississippi: 1890 constitutional convention in, 119; 1963 Freedom Vote in, 142, 144, 152n113; 1964 Freedom Summer in, 144, 153n126; agriculture in, 123–24, 127; black education in, 119, 125, 139, 147n14, 147n17; black employment in, 127; black family size in, 125; and black migration, 119, 125, 147n21; black mobility in, 124; as civil rights symbol, 121; civil rights tactics in, 115–17, 120; Council of Federated Organizations in, 115; Delta region of, 119–20, 123, 124–25, 126, 127, 128, 129, 130, 137, 139, 142–43, 144, 147n21, 153n121; Dick Gregory in, 133–34; federal government and, 120, 121; food aid in, 117, 122, 123, 125–26, 128, 134, 135, 137, 142–43, 145, 149n54; food and clothing drives in, 127; health in, 116, 125; hunger and food insecurity in, 116, 117, 121, 122–23, 124, 125–27, 135, 145, 146n4, 149n40, 153n121; national interest in, 144; population of, 119–20, 123; poverty and wealth in, 115–16, 117, 120, 121, 124; power structure in, 119, 121, 123, 125, 142, 147n14, 148n31; race in, 126; segregation in, 135; sharecropping in, 117–18; SNCC in, 120, 124–25, 140, 144, 145n1; standard of living in, 128; towns in, 145n1; violence in, 120; voting rights in, 115–16, 117, 119, 123, 124, 125, 127, 137, 142, 144, 145, 147n14, 147n16, 147n17, 148n39, 152n113; wages in, 124; welfare in, 121, 122, 125, 134, 138, 148n37; white resistance to civil rights in, 115, 120, 122–23, 124, 125, 142; winter of 1962–63 in, 127
Mississippi Freedom Democratic Party, 143, 144, 153n128
Mississippi River, 119
Missouri, 187, 200
Montgomery, AL, 219
Montgomery, TX, 215
Montgomery bus boycott, 60, 210
Moody, Anne, 153n125
Moral Rearmament program, 71
Morehouse, Henry L., 10
Morehouse College, 31, 43, 44, 45
Morningside Homes, 227
Moses, Bob: on black education and voting rights, 147n17; characteristics of, 126; and Council of Federated Organizations, 145n1; disillusionment of, 144; on Greenwood, MS, 138–39, 149n45; and hunger and food aid, 126–27, 132, 136–37, 146n6; on McComb, MS, 149n45; on Mississippi power structure, 148n31; and reaction to Sam Block's arrest, 135–36; and voter registration, 120, 124–25, 127, 136–37
MSNBC, 183, 186
Muhammad, Deric, *204*
Multry, Louis, 103
Mutual Benefit Life, 171

Nash, Diane, 60
Nashville, TN, 60
Nathan, Debbie, 206–7
Nation, 206, 207
National Advisory Commission on Civil Disorders, 165

National Association for the Advancement of Colored People (NAACP): 1958 national convention of, 55; and Atlanta schools, 47; attorneys for, 67; on civil rights goals, 5; and Council of Federated Organizations, 145n1; leaders of, 145n1; Legal Defense Fund of, 130, 148n37; local and state leaders of, 53, 54, 55, *57*, 60, 66–67, *69*, 71, 76, 77; national leaders of, 55, 60, *69*, 87; and Norfolk, VA, teacher pay parity cases, 54; state conventions of, 56, *57*, 60; tactics of, 4, 68; Virginia State Youth Conference of, *69*; and voter registration, 56–57, 79n11; in York, PA, 89, 106; Youth Council of, 55, 56, *57*, 58, 59–60, 66, 79n11

National Association of Colored Women, 32
National Biscuit, 102
National Black United Front, 202, 203, *204*
National Business League, 72
National Convention, 38
National Council of Churches, 131
National Guard, 104, 156, 184, 228
National September 11 Memorial, 164
National Training School for Women and Girls, 38
Nation of Islam, 134, 202, 222n2
Nealon, William, 102, 106–7
Nebula, Kayenne, 218, *219*
Needham, Shante, 207, 208, 224n13
Neff, Greg, 105
"Negroes of Virginia, The—Have They Earned Equal Rights?," 58
NEH Seminar, 6
Neighborhood Union: and Anti-Tuberculosis Association, 46; and churches, 47; and educational institutions, 44, 45, 47; establishment of, 31, 43; goals of, 43, 47; impact of, 30, 46; men and, 47; strategies of, 30, 43, 44, 45, 46–47, 49; and whites, 45–46, 47; Women's Civil and Social Improvement Committee of, 47; and women's clubs, 47
Newark, NJ: Black Power in, 174; decline of, 171, 181n25; diversity of leadership of, 174; inequality in, 175; as large city, 4, 86; mayors of, 171, 173, 174, 176, 177; nonprofits in, 182n28; as older city, 171; and plans to demolish Fourth District Precinct Building, 177; police in, 175; population of, 4; and urban renewal, 171

Newark, NJ, 1967 riots in: commemorations of, 155–56, 171–77, 178n2, 181n27; details of, 171, 173, 174, 176; scholarship on, 86, 181n27
Newberry Street Boys, 91, 98, 99, 102, 104
New Black Panther Party, 202
New Deal, 121, 181n25
New England, 14
New England Hospital for Women and Children, 35
New Jersey Historical Society (NJHS), 172, 173, 175
New Jersey National Guard, 174, 175
New Jersey State Troopers, 175
New Jim Crow, The (Alexander), 3
New Orleans, LA, 17
"New South and Civil Rights, The," 158
Newsweek, 85
New Testament, 214
New York, NY, 72, 79n11, 126, 164, 183
New York Freeman, 19
New York Globe, 18–19
New York State, 14
New York Times Sunday Book Review, 3
Neyland, Leedell, 21, 26n15
Nightingale, Florence, 38
Nineteenth Amendment, 47
Nix, Elizabeth M., 158
Nixon, Richard M., 96, 106
Noah (Biblical character), 164, 178n10
Noel, Debbie, 111n19
Norfolk, VA: black leaders in, 59; black protests in, 54; black publications in, 59; blacks in, during Civil War, 54; boycotts in, 66–67; churches in, 59, 72, 76–77; city council of, 74–76; civil rights movement in, 53; desegregation of public accommodations in, 69–70; desegregation of restaurants in, 61–68, 81n34; distribution of NAACP literature in, 66–67, 81n44; and diversity in city government, 53; elites in, 53–54; mayors of, 68, 75; NAACP in, 4, 53, 54, 55, *57*, 59–60, 66, 74, 77; population of, 75; school desegregation in, 55–59; segregation in, 53, 54; state representatives from, 58–59, 65; teacher pay parity cases in, 54; wealthy

neighborhoods in, 75–76; white moderates in, 59; YMCAs in, 71
Norfolk 17, 58
Norfolk Alliance of Political Action Committees (NAPAC), 59
Norfolk Democratic Party Committee, 74
Norfolk Public Library, 55
Norfolk State College/University, 72
Norfolk Teachers Association, 54
North, 87, 88, 89, 105, 132
North Carolina, 47
North Carolina A&T, 60
North County, MO, 186, 188
Norview High School, 58, 59
Notes on Nursing: What It Is and What It Is Not (Nightingale), 38
"Nursing of Sick Children, The," 37

Oakwood Civic League, 70
Obama, Barack, 107, 155, 210
Oberlin College, 12, 13, 16, 17, 25
#OccupySLU, 190, 193–94, 196
"Of the Passing of the First-Born" (DuBois), 28
Ohio, 12, 14, 15
Oklahoma City National Memorial, 164
Old Testament, 212
O'Malley, Michael, 9n8
"On 40th Anniversary of Newark Rebellion . . ." (Goodman), 181n27
One Particular Saturday, 160
Operation Citizenship, 56–58
Oral history, 161, 201

Parks, Brad, 175, 178n2
Parks, Rosa, 1, 2
Parry, O. Meredith, 97
Paul, Rand, 155
Payne, Charles, 150n57
Peacock, Willie, 133, 151n90
Peebles, J. H., 125
Penn Common Park, 95
Pennsylvania, 87, 92, 98, 107, 211
Pennsylvania Human Relations Commission (PHRC), 92, 93, 101
Pennsylvania Human Rights Commission (PCHR), 97
Pensacola, FL, 17, 20

Pentecostals, 202
People's Organization for Progress, 181n27
Perkins School of Theology, Southern Methodist University, 212
Perrow, Mosby, Jr., 65
Perry, Edward A., 20
Pestello, Fred, 190, 194
Petersburg, VA, 75, 79n11
Philadelphia, PA, 70, 89
Photography, 200
Pilgrimage of Prayer for Public Schools, 60
Plessy v. Ferguson, 11, 18, 33
Poindexter, Lewis, 125
Poison, Jacqueline, 57
Portsmouth, VA, 63, 65
Potorti, Mary, 5
Potter, Claire Bond, 223n5
Poverty, 96–97
Prairie View, TX, 199, 201, 205, 206, *220*
Prairie View A&M University (PVAMU): road to, 205, 208; Sandra Bland and, 6, 197, 202; Sandra Bland movement participants from, 218, 221, 226n29; Sandra Bland Social Justice Scholarship at, 206
Presbyterians, 202
Price, Clement Alexander, 177
Prince George's County, MD, Orphans' Court, 76
Print media, 200
Prisons, 155
Progressive Era, 29, 30–31, 41, 49
Protestant Christianity, 198, 200
Prudential, 171
Pruitt, Bernadette, 221
Psalms, 212
Public Broadcasting System (PBS), 1
Pulphus, Jonathan, 191–95

Quiero, Melvin, 56
Qur'an, 164, 178n10

Race and racism: Angela Davis on, 210; extent of, 84, 86; and inequality, 207; modern discussion of, 155; public perceptions of, 7; scholarship on, 121; structural, 211; UN Working Group assessment of, 207
Racial violence. *See* Violence

Raleigh, NC, 35
Ralls, Christina, 161, 162, 164
Rankin, Ernestine, 103
Rawlings, George, 71
Reading, PA, 100
"Real Reason Sandra Bland Got Locked Up, The" (Nathan), 206
Reconstruction, 17, 39, 40, 119
REDEEM Act, 155
Reed-Veal, Geneva, 205, 208, 215
Reeves, James, 66, 68
Regenerating America's Legacy Cities (Mallach and Brachman), 177n1
Register, Jeannette, 103
Register, Lynn, 103
Reinhart, Michael, 215–16
Religion: 21st-century civil rights movement and, 198–200, 201, 210, 216, 222n2; historic civil rights movement and, 200, 201, 211, 219, 222n2; law enforcement and, 218; Sandra Bland movement and, 210–19; scholarship on, 199–200; white supremacists and, 200
Remembering Newark's Summer of Discontent: Forty Years Later, 155, 156
Republicans, 96
Reverend Sekou and the Holy Ghost, 197
Richardson, Joe, 14
Richardson, Llewelly S., 81n44
Richmond, David L., 227
Richmond, VA, 57, 60, 75, 80n19
Riddick, Paul, 54
Right to Ride: Streetcar Boycotts and African American Citizenship in the Era of Plessy v. Ferguson (Kelly), 8n4
Riots: after Martin Luther King Jr. assassination, 94, 96, 157, 167, 178n11; causes of, 107, 154, 165, 184; characteristics of, 4; commemorations of, 181n27; evidence of, 154; extent of, in 1960s, 86; impact of, on Black Power movement, 86; Kerner Commission on, 105; Martin Luther King Jr. and, 86, 170; media coverage of, 170, 181n27; pre-1960s, 106; scholarship on, 6, 86, 106, 109n3, 109n5, 111n19, 114n51; Student Nonviolent Coordinating Committee and, 86; terms for, 109n3, 162, 169, 175, 176. *See also* York, PA: riots in
Roach, Chester, 94, 95
Robertson, Charlie: as murder defendant, 85–86, 97, 105, 113n48; and white power, 85, 104, 107, 108; as York, PA, mayor, 85
Robertson, Roberta, 55, 57, 60, 69
Robertson, Robert D., 55, 59, 65, 66–67
Robertson, Wibie, 97
Robertson, William P., Jr., 72
Rockefeller Foundation, 37
Rock Hill, SC, 60–61
Rogers, William, 67
Romano, Renee C., 223n5
Roosevelt, Franklin D., 181n25
Rope and Faggot (White), 87
"Rosa Parks, Claudette Colvin and Jo Ann Robinson" (Abu-Jamal), 197
Rosenzweig, Roy, 9n8
Ross, Fred, 134, 138
Ruffin, Josephine St. Pierre, 30, 32, 35, 36
Ruleville, MS: civil rights activists in, 135; Fannie Lou Hamer in, 120; food aid in, 127, 128, 131, 139, 140, 150n61; leaders from, 149n45; SNCC in, 128; voting rights in, 128, 139, 150n61
Rusk, David, 107
Russell, A. J., 22
Russell Plantation Settlement, 40, 41, 42–43
Russians, 49n8
Rutgers University, 172
Rutgers University-Newark, 155

Saint Louis University, 190
Sam Houston State University, 221
Samuel (Hebrew prophet), 212
San Antonio, TX, 70, 177
Sanders, Bernie, 205
Sandra Bland Memorial Parkway, 198, 205, 208, *209*
Sandra Bland movement: and Day of Remembrance and Response, 203, *204*, 217; first year of, 198, 199, 201, 202–8, 210, 221; law enforcement and, 198, 203–4, 205, 206, 207–8, 209, 214, 216, 217, *219*, 220; leaders of, 202; locations of, 197, 198, 200, 201, 202, 203–4, 208–9, 210, 212, 213, *215*, 217, 218–21; media coverage of, 203; participants in, 202, 203, *204*, 205, 214; Phillip Luke Sinitiere and, 201; and religion, 198, 199, 200, 201, 210–19, 221; and "She Speaks" commemoration, 198, 201, 208–9, 218–21, 224n15, 226n29; and

technology, 198, 200–201, 202–3, 212, 217, 218–19, 224n15, 226n29
Sandra Bland Social Justice Scholarship, 206
"Sandy Speaks" (Bland), 197, 203, 206, 208, 209, 211–12, 219–21
SandySpeaksOn.com, 206
San Francisco Bay, 145
San Francisco State College, 190
Savannah, GA, 39
"#SayHerName: The Sandra Bland Movement," 221
"Say It Loud—I'm Black and I'm Proud," 172
Schaad, Henry: accused killers of, 86, 105; blood of, in armored vehicle, 104; shooting and death of, 84, 94, 102–3, 105
Schmidt and Ault Paper, 88
Scott, S. L., Jr., 67
Seawell, Don Costa, 71
Second Reconstruction, 6
Seedtime, the Work, and the Harvest, The . . . (Littlejohn, Ellis, Levy), 2
Selma, AL, 219
Selma to Montgomery, AL, march, 1
Settlements, 41–42, 43, 44
Shabazz, Amilcar, 11
Shafer, Raymond, 104
Shakur, Assata, 210, 214
Shaw, Karisha, 214–15, 221
Sheats, William N., 24–25
Shengay, Sierra Leone, 17
Sherbro, Sierra Leone, 11, 16
"She Speaks," 198, 201, 208, 218–21, 226n29
Shiloh Baptist Church, 59, 75
Shivery, Louie, 31
Showtime, Willy, 218
Shull, Linwood, 88
Sierra Leone, 11, 16–17
Simms, E. Paul, 59
Simonetti, Kristin M., 181n27
Simpson, Bobby, 99, 103
Simpsons, The, 180n15
Sinitiere, Phillip Luke, 6, 201, 215, 217, 226n26
Sit-ins, 4, 60–67, 80n28, 115, 209, 227
Slavery: and community preservation, 29; and corporal punishment, 16; and food politics, 121; legacy of, 40, 207; profitability of, 119; and protest, 29; scholarship on, 121
Slave trade, 16

Smith, Bryan, 206, 207
Smith, Howard, 72
Smith, John, 102
Smith, R. Glenn, 203–4, 217, 226n26
Smith, Roger, 177
SNCC. *See* Student Nonviolent Coordinating Committee (SNCC)
Snyder, John, 93, 94, 101, 103, 104, 105
Social Darwinism, 48
Social media, 200–201, 217, 218, 221
Social Security, 181n25
Sonnier, Alisha, 193
Souls of Black Folks, The (DuBois), 48
South: American Missionary Association in, 13–14; black education in, 11, 21, 23, 35, 40, 118; and black migration, 87, 89, 105, 147n21; black poverty in, 118; Democratic Party in, 143; Dick Gregory in, 131; food aid and food politics in, 121, 140; freedmen in, 13; hunger and food insecurity in, 116, 122, 139; national interest in, 144; power structure in, 121, 122; public perceptions of, 7; rural, 115; scholarship on, 121; segregation in, 60–61, 118; sharecropping and tenant farming in, 118; wages in, 122; white landowners in, 116
South Carolina, 87, 88–89, 139, 202
Southern Christian Leadership Convention, 60
Southern Methodist University, 212
Southern Negro Youth Council, 2
South Park, 180n15
Spellman, Eloise, 174
Spelman College, 31, 45
Spong, William, Jr., 65
Springfield, MA, 128
Springs, Mildred, 69
S.S. Kresge's, 61, 63–64, 67
St. Agnes Hospital, 35–36
Stanton, James, 68
Star-Ledger, 175, 178n2
State Conference of the Colored Men of Florida, 17, 18–19
"State of Cultural History, The . . ." (Rosenzweig), 9n8
Staton, James L., 70
Stellhorn, Paul, 181n25
"Stigmatized City, The" (Herman), 181n27

Still, Douglas M., 131
St. Louis, MO: Angela Davis in, 185; churches in, 185, 189; climate of, 184; Dick Gregory in, 130; and Ferguson uprisings in, 195; killing of VonDerrit Meyers Jr. in, 190, 193; Martin Luther King Jr. in, 185; mayor of, 188; metropolitan area of, 186, 188, 195; #OccupySLU protest in, 190, 193–94, 196; riot commemoration in, 172; Stefan Bradley in, 185, 189; universities in, 189, 190, 191
St. Louis American, 191
St. Louis County, MO, 183
St. Louis University, 6, 191, 193
Stokes, Calvin, 95
Straight University, 17
Strong, Kim, 103
Strong, Mark, 103
Student Committee against Discrimination (SCAD), 68–69
Student Cooperative Association (SCA), 55–56
Student Nonviolent Coordinating Committee (SNCC): and 1963 Freedom Vote, 142, 144, 152n113; and 1964 Freedom Summer, 144, 153n126; Ben Taylor and, 130; and black education, 147n14; Bob Moses and, 120, 124–25, 126, 132, 138–39, 144, 145n1, 151n90, 153n126; Charles McLaurin and, 128, 139, 140; Charlie Cobb and, 128; and clothing drives, 127, 139, 140; and Council of Federated Organizations, 115, 116, 145n1; Dave Dennis and, 145n1; Dick Gregory and, 130, 131, 132; Fannie Lou Hamer and, 139; and food aid, 117, 126, 127, 129–30, 131, 132–33, 136, 137, 138, 139–44, 146n6; formation of, 115, 227; headquarters of, 142, 153n126; on hunger as political issue, 126; Ivanhoe Donaldson and, 130; James Forman and, 120, 128, 139–40, 144–45, 150n66; John Lewis and, 144; Lawrence Guyot and, 125; Mike Thelwell and, 125; practices and tactics of, 116–17, 121, 138–39, 141–42, 145; Sam Block and, 128, 150n66, 153n121; Stokely Carmichael and, 120, 131, 144, 145, 146n7; and urban riots, 86; violence against, 132, 135, 137, 152n113; and voting rights, 126, 131, 136, 138, 139, 140–41, 143, 144
Student Relations Association (SRA), 63, 64
Student Voice, 127, 147n14, 150n61

Sullivan, Patricia, 2, 8n4
Summer Project, 142
Sunflower County, MS, 120, 127–28, 129, 139, 141, 149n51
"Super Bad," 172
Swampers, 98
Sweeney, Taka Nii, 102

Tallahassee, FL, 20–21, 23, 60–61
Tallahatchie, MS, 149n45
Tallahatchie County, MS, 151n90
Taylor, Ben, 130, 151n74
Tea Party, 187
Technology: historic civil rights movement and, 200, 217, 219; Sandra Bland movement and, 200–201, 209, 212, 217, 218–21, 224n15, 226n29
Television, 200, 217
Tennessee, 129
Texas, 206, 209
Texas Department of Public Safety (DPS), 197, 203, 204, 205
Texas Rangers, 205
Texas State Historical Association, 221
Thelwell, Mike, 125
Thompson, Bill, 100
Thompson, George, 12
Thompson, J. D., 17
Thornton, Lucy, 57
Thorton, William E., Jr., 81n44
Tidewater, VA, 53, 70. *See also* Norfolk, VA
Tidewater AIDS Crisis/Community Taskforce, 76
Tidewater Area Business League, 72
Tidewater Educational Foundation, 58
Till, Emmett, 1
Tinsley, Mrs. J. M., *57*
Tobias, Channing, 55
Toles, S. H., 39
Tolstoy, Leo, 214
Toomey, Wayne, 94, 97
Tribe X, 190, 193
Truman, Harry, 64, 88
Tucker, Charity, 20, 21, 25
Tucker, Mirissa Joy, 218
Tucker, Thomas DeSaille: as attorney, 17, 20; in Baltimore, 25; and Booker T. Washington, 25; and Colored State Teachers Association,

22; and corporal punishment, 15–16; death of, 25; education of, 11–13, 15–16, 17; family of, 11, 16–17, 20; at Florida State Normal and Industrial School for Coloreds, 4, 11, 20–21, 22–23, 24–25; at Fort Monroe, 14–17; impact of, 11; in Kentucky, 17; as local leader, 20; in Louisiana, 17; in Pensacola, FL, 17, 20; on role of southern black colleges, 4; as state leader, 21

Ture, Kwame. *See* Carmichael, Stokely

Tuskegee, AL, 23, 40–41

Tuskegee Institute: Booker T. Washington and, 24, 36; graduates of, 25; hygiene at, 41; John A. Anderson Memorial Hospital of, 36; medical director of, 36, 42; nurses' training at, 36–37; whites and, 11

Tuskegee Women's Club, 30, 40, 41, 43, 49

Twain, Mark, 189

Twitter, 155, 200, 202

Tyler, John, 14

"Typhoid Fever," 37

Tzu, Lao, 214

Unitarian Universalists, *203*

United Institutional Baptist, 227

United Methodist Church, 211, 216, 217. *See also* Methodists and Methodism

United Methodist Reporter, 216

United Nations, 188, 207–8, 209

United Packinghouse Workers, 153n123

United Press International, 135, 149n51

University of Baltimore: as anchor institution, 155, 169; and anniversary of 1968 riots, 155, 158–60; and anniversary of Martin Luther King Jr. assassination, 179n13; and definition of *cultural diversity*, 178n7; and *From Mobtown to Charm City* conferences, 157–58

University of North Carolina Press, 8n4

University of Virginia, 76

University of Virginia Law School, 53, 71, 73

UN Working Group of Experts on People of African Descent, 207–8

US Army, 16

US Bureau of Labor Statistics, 44

US Civil Rights Commission, 123, 188, 189

US Commission on Civil Rights, 126, 147n17

US Department of Agriculture, 121, 138, 149n54

US Department of Defense, 175

US Department of Justice, 75, 188, 204–6, 217

US House of Representatives, 120

US secretary of education, 188

US Senate, 148n37, 149n54

US Supreme Court, 11, 33, 56, 75, 120, 189

Uyola, Rosie Jayde, 6

"Value of Race Literature, The" (Matthews), 32

Veterans Administration, 72

Victoria, Sherbro, Sierra Leone, 11

Vietnam veterans, 72

Vietnam War, 96

Violence, 87–88, 115, 132, 207. *See also* Riots

Virginia: anti-trespass laws in, 65, 81n34; Booker T. Washington in, 40; General Assembly of, 58, 65, 81n34; governors of, 55, 65; miscegenation laws in, 72; NAACP in, 69, 79n11, 80n19; post–Civil War, 18; race in, 17; school desegregation in, 58, 65; Thomas DeSaille Tucker in, 14; voter registration in, 79n11

Virginian-Pilot, 53, 63, 64, 65, 80n28

Virginia State Bar Association, 76

Virginia State College, 60, 62, 68, 70, 71

Virginia State College Norfolk, 81n44

Virginia Voters League, 54

Virginia Weekly, 73

Voting rights: black resistance to, 153n125; blacks and, 5; as civil rights tactic, 4; and food aid, 128, 129; NAACP and, 56–58, 79n11; white reactions to, 127, 128, 137, 153n123

Voting Rights Act of 1965, 1, 74, 86, 144

Walker, Henry W. B., 67

Wallace, George, 96, 106

Wallace, John, 20

Wallace, Mike, 181n22

Waller, Oscar, 68

Waller County, TX: Phillip Luke Sinitiere in, 201; police in, 203–4; Sandra Bland in, 6, 197, 198, 206; Sandra Bland movement in, 198, 200, 201, 208, 209, 210, 211, 212, 213, 214, 215, 216; state district court in, 205; tradition of racial injustice in, 6; traffic enforcement in, 206; treatment of black women in, 214; wrongful death suit against, 205

Waller County Jail: Brian Encinia at, 205; death of Sandra Bland in, 197, 214; location of, 197–98; Sandra Bland movement activities at, 198, 201, 202, 203–4, 208–9, 210, 212, 213, 214, *215*, 217, 218–21; wrongful death suit against, 204

Walls, Josiah T., 20

War on Drugs, 189

War on Poverty, 148n37

War on Terrorism, 189

Warren, Robert Penn, 5

Washington, Booker T.: Atlanta Cotton State Exposition address of, 23; and black self-sufficiency, 23, 24; educational approach of, 10–11, 23–24; family of, 30, 41; and first visit to Tuskegee region, 40–41; as former slave, 40; influence of, 4; on nurses and nurses' training, 36; scholarship on, 24; and Thomas DeSaille Tucker, 25; and W.E.B. DuBois, 4, 24; and whites, 23–24

Washington, DC, 14, 205

Washington, George, 177

Washington, John, 102

Washington, Margaret Murray, 30, 41, 42–43

Washington and Lee, 71

Washington Tabernacle Baptist Church, 185

Washington University, 189

Waters, Maxine, 170

Watts, Los Angeles, CA, 86, 172

Wayne's World 2, 180n15

W.E.B. DuBois Center, Harvard University, 2, 8n4

Welfare, 121, 122, 125, 134, 138, 148n37

Welsh, Mary Oliver, 123

Wesley Methodist Church, 133

West, 87

West, Cornell, 190, 193

West Point, VA, *57*

"What Does the Negro Want?" (Commission on Interracial Cooperation), 5

"What Does the Negro Want?" (NAACP), 5

"What Happened to Sandra Bland?" (Nathan), 207

Wheaton College, 3

Whipple, George, 12, 13

White, Deborah Gray, 29

White, Terry, 161

White, Walter, 87

White House Task Force on Policing, 188

Whitehurst, Alfred W., 81n44

Whites: and black education, 10–11, 19, 22, 23–24, 25, 87; and continued ideology of white supremacy, 207; as landowners, 116; and media, 32, 33; moderate, 59; and Neighborhood Union, 45–46, 47; and perceptions of blacks, 19, 34, 36, 37, 41, 45–46, 48, 58–59; and religion, 200; and resistance to civil rights, 65, 115, 120, 122–23, 124, 125, 127, 128, 137, 142, 153n123; as sharecroppers, 118, 147n12; and sit-ins, 65–66; and State Conference of the Colored Men of Florida, 18

Whitten, Jamie, 120

Who Speaks for the Negro? (Warren), 5

Wikipedia, 175–76

Wilberforce College, 21

Wilkins, Roy, 55

William Penn Senior High, 95, 97, 100

Williams, A. D., 47

Williams, Armstead G., *57*

Williams, Ralph, *57*

Williams, Winston, *69*

Williamsburg, VA, *57*

Wilson, Darren, 183, 189, 226n27

Wilson, Woodrow, 5

Wire, The, 154

Woman's Era journal: articles in, 34, 35, 37, 38; contributors to, 32, 34, 35, 38; distribution of, 32, 33; and First National Conference of Colored Women, 39; goals of, 30, 32, 35, 36, 37; on goals of Women's Era Club, 49n8; and nursing, 32, 33, 35, 36, 37

Women, 30–31, 37, 47, 211

Women, black: as activists, 30; Angela Davis on, 210; and churches and religion, 29, 39, 211; and civil rights organizing, 210; as clergy, 216; and clubs, 29, 32, 33, 38, 39–40, 41, 42, 43; communities and networks of, 29, 31–32, 39; elite, 29, 41; employment of, 92; and health care, 28, 29, 30–31, 32, 33, 34, 37–38, 39–40, 48–49; middle-class, 29, 30, 39, 41; occupations of, 30, 35, 36, 46; poor and working-class, 29, 31, 39, 41; and protest, 29, 30; publications for, 30, 32–33; scholarship on, 2, 3, 29–30; strategies of, 48, 112n35; and white media, 32, 33; white perceptions of, 36, 37, 41

Women's Era club, 30, 32, 49
Woodard, Isaac, 87
Woodard, Komozi, 6
Woolworth's: in Greensboro, NC, 60, 227; in Norfolk, VA, 61, 62, 64, 67, 68; US Attorney General and, 67
Wright, Herbert, 60, 69
Wright, Leon "Smickel," 105
Wright, Marian, 148n37
Wright, Michael, 105
W.T. Grant's, 61, 64, 66, 67, 81n44

Yale University, 190
Yates Woman's Club, 39–40
Yazoo-Mississippi Delta, 119–20
Yazoo River, 119
YMCA, 71
York, PA: in 1990s, 85; and black migration, 87, 88, 91, 107–8; blacks in, 88–90, 92–93, 98, 99–100, 101, 105–6, 108; chamber of commerce in, 100, 101; Congress of Racial Equality in, 99; economy of, 88, 91–92, 107; industry in, 88; Ku Klux Klan in, 98; law enforcement in, 93–95, 97, 98, 99, 100, 101, 102–3, 104, 105, 106–7, 108, 111n19; map of, 90; mayors of, 85, 93, 94, 101, 103, 104, 105; NAACP in, 89, 106; neighborhoods and sections of, 96, 97, 98, 103, 104; parks and recreational facilities in, 94, 100, 101, 102; population of, 86, 89, 90–91, 106, 107; poverty in, 92, 107; presidential elections in, 96, 107; race relations in, 108; riots in, 4, 84–85, 86–87, 94–95, 99, 101–7; segregation and discrimination in, 89, 92–93, 106; suburbs of, 90, 107; urban renewal in, 89–90; white gangs in, 85, 91, 98–99, 102, 103–4, 106, 108; white housing in, 91; and white migration, 90–91, 107
York City Youth Organization, 99–100
York College, 98
York Dispatch, 95, 101
York Gazette and Daily, 95–96
Yorklyn Boys, 98, 99
Yorktown Hotel, 97
Yoruba, 198, 218
Young, Faye, 69
Young, Nathan Benjamin, 25
Young, P. B., Jr., 66, 69, 70
Young, Thomas, 59
Young Citizens Council of St. Louis, 188
Young Democrats, 72, 73
Young Republicans, 97

Zimmerman, George, 3

SOUTHERN DISSENT
Edited by Stanley Harrold and Randall M. Miller

The Other South: Southern Dissenters in the Nineteenth Century, by Carl N. Degler, with a new preface (2000)

Crowds and Soldiers in Revolutionary North Carolina: The Culture of Violence in Riot and War, by Wayne E. Lee (2001)

"Lord, We're Just Trying to Save Your Water": Environmental Activism and Dissent in the Appalachian South, by Suzanne Marshall (2002)

The Changing South of Gene Patterson: Journalism and Civil Rights, 1960–1968, edited by Roy Peter Clark and Raymond Arsenault (2002)

Gendered Freedoms: Race, Rights, and the Politics of Household in the Delta, 1861–1875, by Nancy D. Bercaw (2003)

Civil War on Race Street: The Civil Rights Movement in Cambridge, Maryland, by Peter B. Levy (2003)

South of the South: Jewish Activists and the Civil Rights Movement in Miami, 1945–1960, by Raymond A. Mohl, with contributions by Matilda "Bobbi" Graff and Shirley M. Zoloth (2004)

Throwing Off the Cloak of Privilege: White Southern Women Activists in the Civil Rights Era, edited by Gail S. Murray (2004)

The Atlanta Riot: Race, Class, and Violence in a New South City, by Gregory Mixon (2004)

Slavery and the Peculiar Solution: A History of the American Colonization Society, by Eric Burin (2005; first paperback edition, 2008)

"I Tremble for My Country": Thomas Jefferson and the Virginia Gentry, by Ronald L. Hatzenbuehler (2006; first paperback edition, 2009)

From Saint-Domingue to New Orleans: Migration and Influences, by Nathalie Dessens (2007)

Higher Education and the Civil Rights Movement: White Supremacy, Black Southerners, and College Campuses, edited by Peter Wallenstein (2008)

Burning Faith: Church Arson in the American South, by Christopher B. Strain (2008)

Black Power in Dixie: A Political History of African Americans in Atlanta, by Alton Hornsby Jr. (2009; first paperback edition, 2016)

Looking South: Race, Gender, and the Transformation of Labor from Reconstruction to Globalization, by Mary E. Frederickson (2011; first paperback edition, 2012)

Southern Character: Essays in Honor of Bertram Wyatt-Brown, edited by Lisa Tendrich Frank and Daniel Kilbride (2011)

The Challenge of Blackness: The Institute of the Black World and Political Activism in the 1970s, by Derrick E. White (2011; first paperback edition, 2012)

Quakers Living in the Lion's Mouth: The Society of Friends in Northern Virginia, 1730–1865, by A. Glenn Crothers (2012; first paperback edition, 2013)

Unequal Freedoms: Ethnicity, Race, and White Supremacy in Civil War–Era Charleston, by Jeff Strickland (2015)

Show Thyself a Man: Georgia State Troops, Colored, 1865–1905, by Gregory Mixon (2016)

The Denmark Vesey Affair: A Documentary History, edited by Douglas R. Egerton and Robert L. Paquette (2017)

New Directions in the Study of African American Recolonization, edited by Beverly C. Tomek and Matthew J. Hetrick (2017)

Everybody's Problem: The War on Poverty in Eastern North Carolina, by Karen M. Hawkins (2017)

The Seedtime, the Work, and the Harvest: New Perspectives on the Black Freedom Struggle in America, edited by Jeffrey L. Littlejohn, Reginald K. Ellis, and Peter B. Levy (2018; first paperback edition, 2019)

Fugitive Slaves and Spaces of Freedom in North America, edited by Damian Alan Pargas (2018)

www.ingramcontent.com/pod-product-compliance
Lightning Source LLC
Chambersburg PA
CBHW031433160426
43195CB00010BB/716